Publications on the Near East

Publications on the Near East

Poetry's Voice, Society's Song: Ottoman Lyric Poetry
Walter G. Andrews

The Remaking of Istanbul: Portrait of an Ottoman City in the Nineteenth Century
Zeynep Çelik

The Tragedy of Sohráb and Rostám from the Persian National Epic, the Shahname of Abol-Qasem Ferdowsi
Translated by Jerome W. Clinton

The Jews in Modern Egypt, 1914–1952
Gudrun Krämer

Izmir and the Levantine World, 1550–1650
Daniel Goffman

Medieval Agriculture and Islamic Science: The Almanac of a Yemeni Sultan
Daniel Martin Varisco

Rethinking Modernity and National Identity in Turkey
Edited by Sibel Bozdogan and Resat Kasaba

Slavery and Abolition in the Ottoman Middle East
Ehud R. Toledano

Britons in the Ottoman Empire, 1642–1660
Daniel Goffman

The Transformation of Islamic Art during the Sunni Revival
Yasser Tabbaa

Yasser Tabbaa

The Transformation of Islamic Art during the Sunni Revival

University of Washington Press
Seattle and London

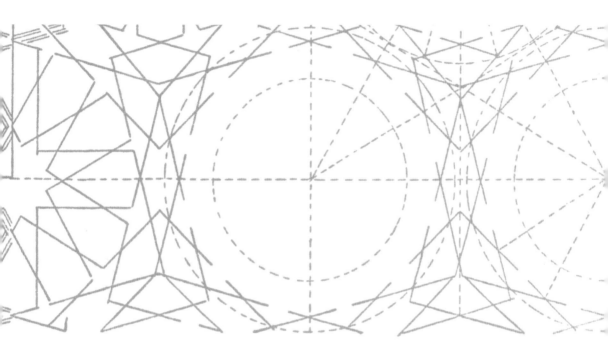

To my family, here and abroad

The publication of this book has been made possible in part by a generous grant from Lina Tewfic Tabbaa.

Printed in China
Designed by Echelon Design

Library of Congress Cataloging-in-Publication Data
Tabbaa, Yasser, 1948–
The transformation of Islamic art during the Sunni revival / Yasser Tabbaa.
p. cm. — (Publications on the Near East)
Includes bibliographical references and index.
ISBN 0-295-98125-3 (cloth : alk. paper) — ISBN 0-295-98133-4 (pbk. : alk. paper)
1. Decoration and ornament, Architectural—Middle East. 2. Architecture, Islamic—Middle East. 3. Architecture, Medieval—Middle East. 4. Decoration and ornament, Islamic—Middle East. 5. Decoration and ornament, Medieval—Middle East. I. Title. II. Publications on the Near East, University of Washington.

NA3573.T33 2001
729'.0917'67109021—dc21 2001027014

The paper used in this publication meets the minimum requirements of American National Standard of Information Sciences–Permanence of Paper for Printed Library Materials, ANSI Z39.48-1984.

Contents

List of Illustrations

All illustrations are by the author unless otherwise noted. Source credits appear in captions.

Preface and Acknowledgments

For those with some knowledge of Islamic art, the title of this book has a familiar ring: it refers to Grabar's *The Formation of Islamic Art* of 1973, still by far the most influential book in its field. At least three reasons stand behind the choice of this title. The first is to demonstrate generational growth and the expansion of knowledge in Islamic art, a field that still suffers from patchy scholarship and thin description. The second is to underline the profound formal changes that Islamic art underwent in the middle period, changes that contributed to the creation of monuments and modes of ornament fundamentally different from those of the early Islamic period covered by Grabar. Finally, the very terms "transformation" and "formation" suggest a process of change and argue, by virtue of their dynamic and developmental implications, against the essentialism and positivism that still permeate the study of Islamic art.

This book grew out of two initially independent pursuits that have occupied me since the beginning of my career in art history: the architecture of Syria and the Jazira between the eleventh and thirteenth centuries, and the question of meaning in medieval Islamic calligraphic, ornamental, and architectural forms. Though it is concerned more with questions of meaning than with specific monuments, this work draws on substantial archaeological resources, including my dissertation on the architecture of Nūr al-Dīn as well as other material published here for the first time. Indeed, the period of Nūr al-Dīn (1146–1174) forms the primary case study in this book and the touchstone for broad exploration of the transformation of medieval Islamic art in the eleventh and twelfth centuries, the epoch of the Sunni revival.

This book's metamorphosis from a focused study of architectural patronage to a wide-ranging work of synthesis was first instigated by a comment made by Frank Peters, who believed that a thesis on the Sunni revival was struggling to emerge from my dissertation. Its full emergence was slow and cumulative, but the publication in 1985 of my article on the *muqarnas* dome convinced me of its feasibility and of the desirability of charting a more comprehensive approach for the interpretation of medieval Islamic architecture. It gradually became clear to me that three fundamental changes were needed to properly understand the transformations that occurred during the epoch of the Sunni revival. First, the temporal and geographical limits of the investigation had to be extended well beyond the limits of the original study on Nūr al-Dīn. Second, some themes deriving from the political and theological concerns of the Sunni revival had to be expanded, while much formal analysis had to be curtailed. And third, the chronological approach of the first project had to be replaced by a typological and thematic approach that specifically focuses on the question of transformations.

In its archaeological stage, this work benefited from the various administrators, archaeologists, and archivists who have facilitated my work in Syria and Iraq. In Syria, I single out the previous Director General of Antiquities and Museums, Afif Bahnasi, for giving me permission to document buildings throughout Syria with complete freedom, and for granting me access to their architectural archives. I was also fortunate to be able to travel throughout Iraq—nearly impossible now and quite difficult even in the 1980s—thanks in large measure to the assistance of Issa Salman and Muayyad Basim Demerji, successive Directors General of Antiquities. The Iraqi calligrapher Yusuf Thannoun was the first to bring to my attention the importance of Ibn al-Bawwāb for both Qur'ānic calligraphy and public inscriptions. His perseverance in tracking down inscriptions and his attention to paleographic details and biographical facts helped me to temper my interpretations and ground them in contemporary history.

I am grateful to the four readers who reviewed this book in its manuscript form, one of whom remains anonymous. Oleg Grabar, the first reader, was involved in this project in its incipient form as a dissertation and subsequently as articles, and now as a book. Despite some intellectual differences and interpretive disagreements, he has been consistently generous with his time and gracefully supportive of the project. Jere Bacharach carefully and insightfully read the entire manuscript, contributing many historical clarifications and suggesting several ways for grounding my interpretations within the contemporary culture. Gülru Necipoğlu, whose recent work on a similar subject cannot be superseded, was extremely supportive of this work and suggested several important exapansions and changes. Finally, the fourth, anonymous reader pointed me to areas of research that I had not adequately considered and directed me toward greater rigor in my interpretations. Although I have not been able to address all the specific queries raised by this reviewer, I have sincerely attempted to do so, and that effort has improved the book.

Wolfhart Heinrichs long ago contributed some valuable advice on the subject of Qur'ānic rescensions and the etymology of the *muqarnas*. Paul Walker was very helpful in the area of Mu'tazilī and Ash'arī theology. Years of discussion with Richard Brotherton sharpened my understanding of medieval Islamic stereotomy, a subject he knows better than any person alive and one on which he will someday publish his own book. I would also like to express my special gratitude to Renata Holod for her support and stimulating discussion and to Julian Raby for encouragement and insightful remarks during a presentation I made in his seminar at the Ashmolean Museum.

Margaret Lourie's careful and intelligent editing of this book removed unnecessary repetition and strengthened the central argument of the chapters. Michael Duckworth of the University of Washington Press took on this book on its own merit and saw it through to its present attractive form. I thank him sincerely for his unfailing support and constant understanding and encouragement.

I began writing this book in 1996 at the house of my mother, Nahla Sabri Tabbaa, in Amman, Jordan, continued it in the winter of 1997 at St. Cross College, Oxford University, and completed it in 1999 at Southern Methodist University in Dallas. I would like to thank my mother for her hospitality and for putting up with a messy corner in her otherwise immaculate house. I thank as well the faculty and staff at the Oriental Institute of Oxford University; and my colleagues at the Division of Art History of Southern Methodist University. Throughout, I have been sustained and nurtured by the love of my wife and children.

A work of synthesis and multidisciplinary approach such as this must by definition summarize long arguments and focus attention to the questions at hand. I hope that I have summarized but not trivialized, and focused without losing sight of the breadth and complexity of important questions in Islamic studies. My forays into fields outside art history have been guided by the scholars mentioned above and others, but I alone am responsible for the conclusions reached in this book.

—Y.T.
January 2001

The Transformation of Islamic Art during the Sunni Revival

Introduction

This book discusses the transformation undergone by Islamic architecture and ornament during the medieval period and investigates the cultural processes by which meaning was produced within the resulting new forms. Focusing on the early developments of these forms in Iran, Iraq, and Syria during the eleventh and twelfth centuries, it argues that this transformation was largely propelled by the religious and political conditions prevailing during the Sunni revival and by the spread of geometric applications to the world of the artisan. Its main case study is the Syrian sovereign Nūr al-Dīn (1146–1174), who was arguably the most important architectural patron of the twelfth century and the motivating force behind the Sunni revival.

The study therefore addresses a number of questions that have long occupied scholars of Islamic art. How and why did such characteristic forms of Islamic art as arabesque, both vegetal and geometric, *muqarnas* vaulting, public inscriptions, and even calligraphy develop? Are these forms meaningful or merely decorative? Are they immanent features of Islamic art with universal meaning, or were they produced under specific historical conditions for a particular purpose or message? Did these forms convey religious messages, embody political propaganda, establish social distinctions, or display technical virtuosity? Did they develop internally through a gradual incremental process, or externally in connection with abrupt changes in patronage, theology, or geometric knowledge, for example? Finally, if a symbolic language did indeed develop, how did it function within the architecture and the urban landscape in general?

Meaning, which is at the foundation of all these questions, has been a hotly contested and highly polarized question among scholars of Islamic art. Archaeologists, Orientalists, aestheticians, and art historians have taken quite contrasting positions on this issue. At the crux of this polarization is the widely held belief that Islam, quite unlike other religions, did not concern itself with architecture and the visual arts as necessary expressions or applications of the dogma, and consequently did not leave a body of texts that dealt with these matters. The lack of such texts and documents led most archaeologists, among them Creswell, Rogers, and Meinecke, to limit interpretation and reject meaning except under very strict conditions.[1] Their main contribution to the interpretation of architectural forms and monuments has been taxonomical and analytical: their work helps us to pinpoint origins, trace developments, analyze forms, and make comparisons. Yet, despite its limited applicability to the question of meaning, the archaeological method sets a standard of clarity and excellence and provides a system of checks and balances against the excesses of interpretation.

For Orientalists and art historians of an earlier generation, meaning abounded in Islamic architectural and decorative forms, but it had a pervasive and immanent nature that could not always be subjected to historical scrutiny. Whether viewing Islamic art through the lens of philology or reflecting upon a lifetime of monographic art historical research,[2] many of these scholars wrote general and often quite perceptive essays on the spirit or aesthetics of Islamic art and architecture. Unhampered by chronology and geographical divisions, these writers combed through more than a millennium of the artistic production in the entire Islamic world to isolate forms and themes that elucidated their idea of Islamic art. Most often these forms—calligraphy, arabesque, geometric patterns, *muqarnas*, symmetrical plan, and of course the absence of figural representation—were engaged to illustrate such themes as the transcendent nature of the word of God, the transience of matter and the natural world, the abstraction of natural forms, the impulse to surface decoration, and the heritage of the past.

Some of these authors refined this paradigm into oppositions of "unity and diversity" or "originality and conformity";[3] Aga-Oglu and others preferred to see the main features of Islamic as "aesthetic trends common to all Orientals" from early times. Yet the myth of these immanent features of the art, these timeless atavisms of the Oriental spirit, remain largely unchallenged on the theoretical level on which they were first proposed.[4] Indeed, even more regionally based scholars have failed to critique this early theorization and to propose acceptable substitutes. Inspired by nationalism and ethnicity, they rejected the pan-Islamic perspective of Orientalism, substituting chauvinistic paradigms in which everything had been "Turkish," "Persian," or "Arabic" practically since the beginning of time.[5] Although this regionalist perspective helped better to link Islamic art with ancient Near Eastern art, it unnecessarily fragmented important issues and made implausible claims regarding the originality and authenticity of the region.

More recently, a group of aestheticians and Muslim fundamentalists, including Burckhardt, Lings, Nasr, the Fārouqīs, Papadopoulo, and others, have attempted to develop a set of theoretical criteria for understanding Islamic art.[6] The writings of these scholars, it should be noted, coalesced around the 1976 World of Islam Festival, whose political agenda was to demonstrate the basic tenets of unity in Islamic culture across time and space. Highlighting their internalist perspective and their close affinity with the culture and the religion, this "curious mixture of Western Orientalists and Islamic fundamentalists"[7] emphasized the aesthetic unity and universalizing symbolic meanings of Islamic art.[8] Rarely addressing specific historical or even theological contexts, and adopting a highly selective attitude toward the available evidence, these writers constructed Islamic art as an exclusively ornamental and calligraphic system that embodied the concepts of *tawḥīd*.[9] In his best-known treatise, Burckhardt, for example, writes:

> Islamic art is at last revealed to be what it really is, namely the earthly crystallization of the spirit of Islamic revelation as well as a reflection of the heavenly realities on earth, a reflection with the help of which the Muslim makes the journey through the terrestrial environment and beyond to the Divine Presence itself, to the Reality which is the Origin and End of Art itself.[10]

Curiously, the aesthetic Islamist approach, though claiming to reject Orientalism, is methodologically very close to it. Both approaches adopt an essentialist perspective that sees the various cultural forms in Islam, including art, as timeless atavisms regardless of their actual temporal or geographical coordinates and their role in society.[11] The difference between the two approaches has perhaps more to do with attitude and selection than with method. The condescension and distance that sometimes tainted Orientalist studies was commonly replaced by an attitude of unqualified reverence that laid particular claim to an internalist view of the culture. Since this view was often based on adherence to one or another facet of Islam, it could not, its proponents insisted, be subjected to externalist criticism and historical verification.[12] Rejecting any possibility of development or change in Islamic art, these writers even insist on the need "to distinguish between Islam and its history," since their aim is "to understand the essence of Islam in terms that pertain exclusively to the Qur'ān and the Sunnah."[13] Thus, even comprehensiveness, possibly the most important legacy of Orientalist scholarship, is rejected by these fundamentalist scholars, who replaced it with a much more restrictive approach that is intended to conform to their theories and remove any possible contradictions.

This theoretical environment still obtains despite the considerable expansion of our knowledge in the last three decades about individual monuments, the patronage of various dynasts, or the art and architecture of specific periods.[14] Although most contemporary writers no longer accept the outdated theories of earlier art historians and the unrigorous methods of the aestheticians, most have chosen to ignore instead of question these publications while pursuing their own specific research agendas. On the whole, their monographic works do not concern themselves with the larger issues of the meaning of forms and the overall significance of architectural styles within an expanded temporal framework.[15] In other words, the increasing refinement and specificity of these investigative works stand in sharp contrast to the crudeness and futility of persisting theoretical models.[16]

Since I first contemplated writing this book, two extremely important works have filled the very gap I have attempted to illustrate above, presenting the first serious and sustained attempts to deal with questions of meaning in Islamic ornament in historical terms. These two books, by Grabar and Necipoğlu, revisit long-untrodden grounds and cast a fresh look at issues long ignored by serious art historians.[17] Equipped with a much broader knowledge of the monuments, a deeper appreciation of the importance of texts—and in the case of Necipoğlu, of treatises and documents as well—for understanding Islamic art, and a variety of theoretical tools that were unavailable a generation earlier, these writers have reformulated many answers and proposed various challenging explanations. Most important, they have in varying degrees rejected the polarities of positivism and essentialism, substituting for them sociological, theological, perceptual, and semiotic modes of interpretation.

There will be other occasions to return to these two books, in particular Necipoğlu's, whose overall vision resembles my own and whose stimulating ideas and engaging discussions have illuminated many passages in this book. But it is equally important to establish differences, which are most clearly apparent in this book's more limited historical and geographic span and in its more focused treatment of the architectural transformations engendered during a specific period of great political and sectarian upheaval. First, by highlighting the Sunni revival and framing its queries from within the dominant discourses of this epoch, the present book acknowledges the distinctiveness of this period while more forcefully rejecting the essentialism and facile continuities of earlier models. It argues, therefore, that Islamic art did not develop smoothly within a predetermined set of religious prescriptions but rather underwent fairly abrupt transformations that were largely prompted by internal or external challenges to the central Islamic polity or system of belief. These political and theological challenges elicited visual or architectural responses and reactions that were intended to buttress the system of belief or power, to embody a new concept, and to establish its difference against the challenging force.

Second, the historical specificity of this project inevitably leads to a forceful rejection of the ahistorical flounderings by essentialist scholars and to a questioning of the multihistorical perspective adopted by Grabar in his attempt to formulate a general perceptual theory for ornamental and calligraphic forms. Contrary to Grabar, I argue, therefore, that Islamic ornament did not always play a mediatory, nonsymbolic role regardless of its historical and geographical parameters, but that it sometimes enjoyed a high and culturally specific symbolic charge that was not equal in all parts of the Islamic world. Without necessarily rejecting their role in mediating the process of perception, I propose that certain calligraphic, ornamental, and architectural forms were engendered within specific discourses and were ultimately intended to mitigate tensions resulting from these discourses. In other words, in addition to being instruments of perceptual mediation, these forms were also carriers and propagators of specific messages, at times even functioning as symbolic forms that bridged the fissures separating a deeply divided Islamic world.

Art, like cultures and even religions, defines itself against its opponents, and the more intense the conflict, the sharper this self-image. In Islamic art this axiom has been successfully applied to conflicts between Byzantium and the early Muslims[18] or between the Umayyads and Christians of Spain,[19] since such interfaith conflicts were perceived as defining moments in Islamic history. Much less has been done, however, with the political upheavals and sectarian schisms that have divided Islam since early times, and the impact of these conflicts on the development of Islamic art has barely been touched. While it is true that some of these inter-Islamic divisions lacked the intensity that often characterized Muslim-Christian conflicts, a few, such as the one dividing the Sunni Seljuq-Zangids and the Ismāʿīlī Fatimids, were especially virulent. Constituting a deep and unbridgeable rupture, this particular conflict was played out on the battlefield as well as in politics, theology, and propaganda. It stands to reason, therefore, that it was also played out in architecture and visual culture and that its dynamic forces of conflict, change, and self-definition, not the prescripts of a static Islam, were behind the transformations in medieval Islamic architecture.

Although this study focuses in particular on the early stages of these transformations, it is not a study of origins and original meanings of decontextualized architectural forms and ornamental patterns. I have taken to heart Gombrich's admonition that, as with linguistics, we would do well to abandon "the search for the original meaning of roots" and focus instead on "how a language actually functions in any one community."[20] This study admits the multivalence of signification and the accretion of meaning as ornamental styles are created, further developed, used by different patrons, or applied to different functions or varying architectural forms. I have, therefore, made a concerted effort to define the new forms and establish their difference from earlier ones, but without rejecting their earlier or later stages of development within the repertory of Islamic art. I have also attempted to read ornamental patterns within the context of specific architectural forms and to investigate the reciprocal process of signification that results from this synthesis; I propose that ornament acquires some of its meaning from these applications while also effecting a change in the meaning of the forms to which it has been applied. All these processes contributed in varying degrees to the production of meaningful forms and to their dispersion within the medieval Islamic world.

The first chapter takes up the political and theological dimensions of the Sunni revival from its populist origins in Baghdad and eastern Iran, through its first systemization under the Great Seljuqs, to its ultimate triumph under Nūr al-Dīn. Envisioned as the primary motivating force behind many of the cultural and artistic changes of the eleventh and twelfth centuries, this movement will be studied politically in connection with the policies of the Abbasid caliphs and the Seljuq sultans and theologically through the dominant religious issues of the time. Controversies regarding the nature of God, the created world, the Qur'ān, and the legitimate state raged in this period and found their ultimate conclusion in the religious politics of Nūr al-Dīn. These issues, therefore, acquired a renewed urgency and purpose as they were used by Nūr al-Dīn and the Berber dynasties of North Africa in their war of propaganda against the Fatimids and other Shī'īs and in support of the revived Abbasid caliphate.

The next two chapters examine what will be shown to have been the first visual manifestation of the Sunni revival, namely the transformation of Qur'ānic writing (Chapter 2) and ultimately, public inscriptions (Chapter 3) from the old angular to the new proportioned cursive scripts. Known previously in chancerial and literary writing, cursive scripts are subjected in tenth-century Baghdad to comprehensive reforms based on precise geometric rules and applied in writing the Qur'ān and, somewhat later, in public incriptions. The use of reformed cursive scripts instead of the earlier Kufic was intended politically to distance the Sunni Seljuq-Zangid state from its Fatimid adversary while manifesting the exoteric tenets of Sunni theology against the esoteric dualism of Ismā'ilism. The role of Nūr al-Dīn in this pan-Islamic transformation is highlighted because he adopted cursive writing in all his public inscriptions and mandated the change in Egypt as well.

Arabesque has been applied variously to two-dimensional Islamic ornament, whether vegetal or geometric, and even to three-dimensional ornament, in the *muqarnas*. Recently, Necipoğlu has proposed using the Persian term *girih* (knot) mode instead of arabesque to designate both two- and three-dimensional Islamic ornament that is characterized by interlaced vegetal elements and interlocked geometric shapes.[21] Although I accept Necipoğlu's definition of this term and use it throughout the book, I have nevertheless chosen to divide the discussion into three chapters. The first (Chapter 4) deals with two-dimensional ornament in its vegetal and geometric varieties, while the next two analyze *muqarnas* vaulting in various media. Chapter 4 argues that despite their ubiquity and gradual development in early Islam, vegetal and especially geometric patterns advanced significantly during the eleventh and twelfth centuries, and that this development took place within the context of the Sunni revival and the increased availability of geometric treatises for use by artisans. Focusing on selected monuments that employ geometric and vegetal ornament in potentially meaningful ways, this chapter proposes a number of interpretations for the early uses of vegetal and geometric arabesque.

Muqarnas, the three-dimensional ornamental system that dominates Islamic architecture between the twelfth and fifteenth centuries, is discussed in Chapter 5. I argue that, though known incipiently in eastern Iran, it was first systematized in Baghdad, where it was first applied to the dome, creating a distinctively Abbasid and highly significant form. I conclude that *muqarnas* vaulting, imported to Syria by Nūr al-Dīn and to North Africa by the Almoravids, reflected a symbolic allegiance to the Abbasid caliphate and embodied some facets of Ash'arī theology regarding the atomistic and occasionalistic nature of the universe. Importing this symbolic form from Baghdad to the revived Sunni world also reflected the renewed allegiance of these dynasties to the center of legitimation and the safeguard of orthodox Islam.

Chapter 6 discusses the assimilation of *muqarnas* and related forms into stone architecture. Related though not identical to stone *muqarnas*, various "gravity-defying" devices, such as foliate arches, pendant vaults, and interlaced spandrels, were developed in the stone architecture of northern Syria sometime in the twelfth century, and subsequently spread to Anatolia, Palestine, and Egypt. These stereotomic forms became one of the defining features of medieval Islamic architecture, and their use in portals, *miḥrābs*, and other significant locations imparts to these forms a sense of luxury and distinction while also highlighting the essential instability of their construction.

Chapter 7 reexamines the impact of the Sunni revival, patronage, and geometric knowledge on medieval Islamic ornamental and calligraphic forms and on the dissemination of these reinvigorated forms throughout the urban landscape and across the Islamic world.[22] Did this new formal language have a metaphorical dimension with a perceptible impact on cities, and what purpose did its dissemination over the Islamic world serve? Was the late Abbasid caliphate engaged in the production of symbolic forms, and why did these forms gain such wide acceptance in the Sunni Islamic world? To what extent did this visual language serve the purpose of a symbolic unity between a center possessing the means of legitimation but lacking power, and a periphery lacking legitimacy but wielding real power?[23]

The central argument of the book—that transformations in medieval Islamic architecture reflected and embodied parallel changes in polity and piety—has two further noteworthy implications. The first is practical and concerns the overriding tendency among artists and architects, particularly those practicing in the Islamic world, to gravitate toward essentialist interpretations of ornament and calligraphy, hoping to find in them components of identity and self-affirmation.[24] I would hope that they can find in the following pages alternatives to such facile explanations and some touchstones that might guide their creative efforts. The second implication is scholarly and raises the possibility of using a similar approach for explaining other, similar periods of change and transformation in Islamic architecture. Did other Islamic dynasties divided by warfare and sectarian affiliation—for example, Ottomans and Safavids—also seek to define their architectural image in contrasting terms? Can we, by problematizing instead of glossing over ruptures, disjunctions, and discontinuities, arrive at a better understanding of the meaning of change in Islamic architecture? And is it not through challenge and controversy that ideas are sharpened, identities reaffirmed, and new concepts created?

The nation of the Egyptians [Fatimids] has gone! This is a new nation and an aimful kingdom. We stand in fear of them, for they would shed our blood for our creed. Our opinion is to pronounce the *khuṭba* in their name, fearing that there would come a time when we would not be saved by either word or action.[1]

1

The Sunni Revival

In 1085 Badr al-Jamālī, the Armenian condotierre of the Fatimid state, began with some urgency to refortify the royal city of al-Qāhira. Dissatisfied with its delapidated brick walls and displeased with local stone manufacture, he called for master masons from his native land in Cilicia and was sent three Armenian brothers to perform the task. The new fortifications, of which two northern gates and one southern gate survive, are widely considered among the strongest and most impressive military works in the medieval world.

What was the urgency? The Crusades were still fifteen years hence, and the danger of Pisan and Genoese maritime raids did not merit such precautions. Rather, the city was refortified to ward off an attack not by a Christian power but by the Great Seljuqs, a Muslim dynasty that had already demonstrated considerable zeal and ability to challenge Fatimid rule.[2] As it turned out, the Fatimids were spared for almost another century, and the Seljuqs themselves lost much of their cohesion and military might shortly after the end of the eleventh century. This was not, however, a false alarm against an imagined enemy but a serious threat to the very existence of the Fatimids from a dynasty that rejected them on political and religious grounds.[3]

The long-term struggle between the Fatimids and the Seljuqs (and then the Zangids and Ayyubids) was only the most extreme manifestation of a deeply rooted conflict that continued to shape political and theological discourse in the Islamic world until the end of the twelfth century. The following discussion outlines the main parties and points of the conflict as it developed from the ninth to the eleventh century, highlighting the theological and political differences separating the opposing groups. The discussion concludes with the period of Nūr al-Dīn, who was the main proponent of the Sunni revival in the twelfth century and the model for Saladin and other dynasts before the Mongol invasion.

The Impact of Rationalism

The peak of Abbasid political power in the ninth century was accompanied by cultural expansiveness and a tendency toward rationalism. The age of translation, which had already begun in the late eighth century, was gradually giving way to an epoch of scientific and medical innovation and a pronounced interest in philosophical speculation. The Abbasid courts at Baghdad and Samarra accommodated the best minds of their times: poets such as Abu Nuwās and Ibn al-Rūmī, critics of the caliber of Ibn al-Muqaffa' and al-Jāḥiẓ, and a succession of physicians from the Christian Bakhtishū' family.[4] Secure under the protection and patronage of Abbasid caliphs or their Persian viziers, these early *udabā'* and philosophers generally embraced a rationalist view of the faith that was occasionally at odds with orthodox religion. Indeed, many of the great thinkers of the early Abbasid period adopted Mu'tazilism, the rationalist theology that had previously used dialectical reasoning in order to defend Islam against attacks from Christian polemicists and other critics.[5] Officially sanctioned and supported by caliph al-Ma'mūn, who even made it "a condition of official service,"[6] Mu'tazilism prospered in the ninth and tenth centuries as the only truly Islamic philosophy and the refuge of free thinkers.

The Mu'tazilīs adhered to an interpretation of Islamic monotheism (*tawḥīd*) that divested God of all human attributes, arguing that such anthropomorphism (*tashbīh*) constituted a form of plurality (*shirk*) that opposed the very essence of Islam. This in turn led them to question the traditionalist view regarding the eternal, uncreated nature of the Qur'ān, for if God is without any human attributes, including speech, then the Qur'ān could not have been "spoken" by him, but must have been created in another way. The Qur'ān was therefore not the eternal uncreated words of God, but was created in history in order to guide Muslims. Since a created Qur'ān that is not coequal with God is more open to interpretation, the Mu'tazilīs stressed the importance of exigesis (*ta'wīl*) but restricted its practice to the elite theologians of the community. In particular, Qur'ānic passages that did not on the surface (*ẓāhir*) fit their logical system were assigned a hidden (*bāṭin*) meaning that coincided with Mu'tazilī theology. *Kalām*, the science of rational argumentation, stood at the foundation of this process, providing a common language for theology, philosophy, and science.[7]

Second, the Mu'tazilīs proposed a view of divine justice (*'adl*) in which humans were held responsible for their actions. God in their view is inclined to justice and wishes for humans to do good, but human actions will be rewarded or punished according to a system of justice that had been created by God but is essentially external to Him.[8] More generally, the Mu'tazilīs believed in a transcendent God, who had created the world but who is not continually involved in its surveillance and administration. These responsibilties and actions radiate from God, the Primary Cause, in a series of Neoplatonic rings that are carried to the world by means of external agents.[9]

Regardless of the intellectual strength of Mu'tazilism and its continuing significance in later Shī'ī theology, it was almost immediately opposed by the traditionalist forces galvanized around the person of Aḥmad ibn Ḥanbal (780–855). Ibn Ḥanbal argued for an all-powerful God possessed of all the literal anthropomorphic attributes as stated in the Qur'ān. Since these attributes included above all the power of speech, the Qur'ān was viewed quite literally as God's speech, as uncreated and eternal as God Himself. Ibn Ḥanbal was imprisoned and tortured for his combative opposition to Abbasid official doctrine, and for some time his doctrine and all traditionalist forces were held in check by the so-called Abbasid inquisition (*miḥna*) of the Ḥanbalis and perhaps also by the expansiveness of the time.[10]

Mu'tazilism continued as a state doctrine through the reigns of al-Mahdī and al-Mu'taṣim but was decisively rejected during the reign of the caliph al-Mutawakkil (847–861). The Abbasids' earlier fascination with Mu'tazilism turned into aversion, instigated no doubt by the increasing influence of Ḥanbalism on al-Mutawakkil and later Abbasid caliphs, who, with few exceptions, remained true to this strictest of all Sunni sects nearly until their end in the thirteenth century. More generally, the Abbasids' disavowal of rationalism suggests a kind of intellectual retrenchment, possibly brought about by their decreasing power and shrinking territory.

The political decline of the Abbasids began at the turn of the tenth century and was greatly accelerated by the secession of various provinces. Beginning in the ninth century when local governorships developed under the Abbasid umbrella (e.g., Tulunids and Tahirids), this schismatic movement culminated in the tenth century when various dynasties seceded from the caliphate and, in the case of the Andalusian Umayyads and the Fatimids, even proclaimed counter-caliphates. With the exception of the Umayyads, nearly all these dynasties were Shī'īs, a complete reversal of the first three centuries. As Momen wrote: "To Shī'īs in the mid 4th/10th century it must have seemed that everything was going their way. Almost the whole of the Muslim world was under the control of Shī'īs of one sect or another."[11] The Hamdanids (904–991) took over northern Syria and the Jazīra but were too preoccupied with fighting the Byzantines to pose any threat to the Abbasids. The Persian Buyids first proclaimed their independence in western Iran, then in 955 actually subjugated the Abbasid caliphate, which they controlled until the Seljuq takeover in 1050. The Zaydis took Yemen, and the Idrisids claimed the Maghreb before they were themselves ousted by the more extreme Fatimids.

With the exception of the Fatimids, the Abbasids were never directly threatened by any of these dynasties, including their Buyid overlords, all of whom were moderate Twelver Shīʿīs who had no intention of bringing them down and ruling in their place.[12] The Fatimids were an entirely different story: they not only professed the extreme Ismāʿīlī Shīʿism, but they also proclaimed themselves caliphs. Almost immediately after they rose to power in Tunisia (Ifriqiyya) in the early tenth century, they called for an end to the usurping and ineffectual Abbasid state and the reestablishment of a new caliphate based on their alleged genealogical legitimacy and adherence to what they considered to be true Islam. Their uncompromising creed and messianic zeal, spread by their advanced system of propaganda (*daʿwa*), put them at irreconcilable odds with the Abbasids.[13]

Abbasid domain, which had once extended from Central Asia to North Africa, was now reduced to little more than Iraq, and the caliph was a mere figurehead under the control of the Buyids. Despite their Shīʿism, the Buyids never once allied themselves with the Fatimids and generally refrained from forcing their creed upon the population of Baghdad. They did, however, continue to promote Muʿtazilī thought, thereby contributing to the transformation of Twelver Shīʿism from a rather naive theology of extremism (*ghuluww*) and opposition to one of enlightened accommodation.[14] More generally, the enlightened policy of the Buyids and their opposition to Ḥanbalism held at bay the rising tide of orthodoxy and religious conservatism until the following century.[15]

The Traditionalist Reaction

In the event, neither rationalist Muʿtazilism nor antirationalist Ḥanbalism would claim center stage in the succeeding centuries. Instead, a third theological movement, Ashʿarism, rose to prominence by claiming to mediate between the two extremes. Abu'l-Ḥasan al-Ashʿarī (d. 935) was in most respects a traditionalist Sunni theologian, but his previous affiliation with Muʿtazilīs equipped him to use *kalām* to support his views. Ashʿarism, which al-Ghazzālī later brought into accord with Shāfiʿism, argued for an omnipotent God possessed of human attributes that were themselves not God, but not other than God. The Qur'ān was therefore the eternal and uncreated word of God, cotemporal with God and part of His essence without being God Himself. Humans were supposed to believe without speculation (*bilā kayf*), since some aspects of the divine would always remain unknown and unknowable to them.[16] Finally, the Ashʿaris adopted the Muʿtazilī view of an atomistic universe but insisted on its occasionalistic nature in terms that vindicated the absolute power of God (a point to which I return in chapter 5).

Ashʿarism prospered in Khurasan (eastern Iran) from the second half of the tenth century, when it began an affiliation with the Shāfiʿī legal school that was subsequently formalized by al-Ghazzālī. In eleventh-century Khurasan, specifically Nishapur, this new coalition directly confronted the oldest Sunni *madhhab*, Ḥanafism, whose adherents were at the time drawn to Mu'tazilī theology.[17] The nature of these legal affiliations and the terms of the century-long controversy between Shāfi'īs and Ḥanafīs does not concern us here. But this struggle gave birth to two important and pan-Islamic phenomena: the rise of Sufism and the incipient beginnings of Sunni ecumenicism, or Jamā'ī Sunnism.

Mystical practices in Islam are noted as early as the eighth century, but only around the middle of the fourth/tenth century did these practices become identified specifically with the Sufis. Standing at first outside the boundaries of Sunnism, Sufism gradually became associated with the Shāfi'ī party, which found in it the means to rise above Ḥanafī rationalist inclinations and to compete with Shī'ī populism and esotericism. But it was none other than al-Ghazzālī, the foremost Shāfi'ī theologian of all time, who "forged a bond between Ash'arī theology and Sufism on the one hand and the broad middle road of Islamic thinking on the other, which was to dominate Muslim religious development for centuries to come."[18] Since al-Ghazzālī, especially in his later years, had accepted the temporal authority of the Great Seljuqs over Islam, Sufism was quickly taken over by the Seljuqs and their successors and actively promoted through various acts of patronage.

Sunni ecumenicism, or at least the ultimate rapprochement between Shāfi'īs and Ḥanafīs, perhaps began, albeit negatively, in the opposition of both parties to the disruptive presence of the populist Karrāmiyya party. The Karrāmiyya, founded in Nishapur in the mid-ninth century by Muhammad b. Karam al-Nīshabūrī (d. 869), stood apart theologically from other Sunni sects in its moderate view of Shī'ism, and socially in its direct appeal to the oppressed masses. Karrāmīs, first supported by the Ghaznavid dynasty, proved useful in the struggle of Maḥmūd of Ghazna (998–1030) against the Ismā'īlis. But the growing animosity between them and the Shāfi'ī-Ash'arīs, and especially the increasingly strident Ḥanbalism of Caliph al-Qādir (991–1031), led Maḥmūd to turn against them in the early eleventh century, and from around 1035 the Karrāmīs were openly persecuted and their buildings looted.[19] Overall, the Karrāmīs' most important legacy may have been their patronage of institutions with a distinctly traditionalist and initially populist bias, in particular the *khānqāh* and the *madrasa*.[20]

Like the Abbasids, the Ghaznavids were staunch Sunnis at a time when it might have been more advantageous to accept some form of Shī'ism. The two dynasties were joined religiously in their traditionalism and politically in their desire to destroy the Ismā'īlī Fatimids and end Buyid hegemony over the Abbasid caliphate. In the second decade of the eleventh century, Caliph al-Qādir began a series of public condemnations of the Fatimids, their Ismā'īlī sympathizers, and all other parties and dynasties that did not support the

Abbasids and their traditionalist beliefs. Embraced and amplified by Ash'arī theologians, in particular al-Bāqillānī (d. A.H. 404/A.D. 1013), these declarations were collated to form the famous *al-Risāla al-Qādiriyya* (The Epistle of al-Qādir).[21] The Qādiri Creed, equal in magnitude to the *miḥna* of al-Ma'mūn but opposite in effect, became the cornerstone of the new Abbasid orthodoxy and the official dogma of the caliphate. This traditionalist creed rejected Shī'ism and rationalism in all its forms but saved its severest condemnation for the Fatimids and their Mu'tazilī theologians. Drawn heavily from Ḥanbalī theology but benefiting from the dialectical reasoning of the Ash'arīs, Qādirism reaffirmed its belief in an all-powerful God with human attributes, an eternal uncreated Qur'ān with an explicit message and meaning, and an occasionalistic universe that was continually under the manipulation and mercy of God.[22]

I shall return to this pivotal epistle and examine its impact on the artistic production of the eleventh century. But it is important at this point to note that whereas the theologies of the Sunni revival prospered mainly in the central and eastern Islamic world, they also resonated early in the emergent Sunni dynasties of North Africa. Although in the tenth and first half of the eleventh centuries, central North Africa was ruled first by the Fatimids and next by their vassal states, the situation changed drastically in the second half of the eleventh century. It was then that the first Berber dynasty, the Almoravids (1056–1147), conquered Morocco, parts of Algeria, and much of southern Spain, recognizing the Abbasid caliphs as their spiritual overlords and declaring their opposition to the Fatimids. Adopting the conservative Mālikī law school, which remained dominant in North Africa, they were nevertheless greatly influenced by the theological changes brewing in the east, which had culminated in al-Ghazzālī.[23] We shall see below the extent to which these political and theological linkages between the Almoravids and the Abbasids facilitated the transmission of artistic ideas across a vast geographic distance.

The struggle between traditionalism and its opponents was played out not only on the level of rulers and theologians; it also had a popular dimension in which ceremonies and commemorations fleshed out legalistic divisions and arcane discourses. In this arena, the Shī'īs had a clear advantage over their Sunni rivals, for Shī'ī commemorations had long played a central role in fostering the popular appeal of the sect, though it was the Buyids who first sanctioned and gave institutional form to the great Shī'ī commemorative festivals. In 962, Baghdad saw two great Shī'ī public commemorations: *'Ashūra*, the martyrdom of al-Ḥusayn on the tenth day of Muḥarram; and Ghādir Khumm, the festival commemorating the Prophet's nomination of 'Ali as his successor. These commemorations were often accompanied by the erection of temporary shrines (*qubāb*), some of which eventually assumed a more permanent form as places of visitation and pilgrimage.[24]

Shī'ī festivals "provoked an extraordinary state of unrest among the Sunni population of Iraq and there was more than one request to the Buyid *amir* to reconsider."[25] Unable to curb these fervent manifestations, the Sunnis of Baghdad and Khurasan reacted by staging festivals of their own, including a commemoration of the day Abu Bakr stayed with the Prophet in the cave, and the death of Muṣ'ab ibn al-Zubayr, who had defeated Mukhtār.[26] Furthermore, according to Ibn al-Jawzī, the Sunnis of Khurasan erected commemorative shrines specifically as a countermeasure against Shī'ī commemorations.[27]

The controversy between Sunnis and Shī'īs was also echoed in the populist practice of tomb inscriptions. A large group of Egyptian tombstones from the ninth and tenth centuries and a smaller group of Iraqi tombstones, possibly dating to the tenth or eleventh century, address some of the central issues of the Sunni revival, such as the uncreated nature of the Qur'ān, the verity of the Day of Judgment, and allegiance to the four Companion caliphs, whose succession was passionately contested by Shī'īs.[28] Undoubtedly commissioned by Sunnis—whether Shāfi'is or Ḥanbalīs we cannot say—these tombstones were intended to identify the deceased with orthodox belief and to distinguish them from those with different beliefs, in this case the Ismā'īlis. An especially interesting specimen is a *miḥrāb*-shaped tombstone discovered by Herzfeld in the mosque al-'Umariyya in Mosul.[29] Datable on paleographic grounds to the first half of the eleventh century, it cedes the Sunni caliphal succession to the Umayyads, asserts the eternity of the Qur'ān, proclaims God's omnipotence in actions good and evil, and declares the verity of a vision of God on the Day of Judgment. Each of these proclamations serves the dual purpose of reaffirming Sunni belief and disputing the basic tenets of Mu'tazilism, including the createdness of the Qur'ān, humans as the ultimate source of all evil actions, and the possibility of actually seeing an anthropomorphic God:

> (1) God the Lord (2) I bear witness that there is no God but God (3) Muhammad is the prophet of God, Abu Bakr and (4) 'Umar and 'Uthmān and 'Ali and 'Ā'isha (5) and Mu'āwiya, peace been upon them (6) the Qur'ān is God's speech (7) revealed, not created; from Him is creation (8) and to Him we return. All good (9) and evil are from God. (10) Death is truth, resurrection is (11) truth, judgment is truth, (12) heaven is truth, hell is truth, (13) Munkar and Nakīr are truth. (14) And verily God Almighty (15) will be seen on the Day of Judgment (16) and the afterlife is everlasting (17) [1 word] In God we trust (18) and he is the best trustee.

Competition with Shī'ism also took an institutional form, specifically calculated to undermine the Fatimid institutions of Ismā'īlī propaganda by offering Sunni alternatives to them. Fatimid propaganda was centered in the royal capital al-Qahira, specifically in al-Azhar mosque, founded by Caliph al-Mu'izz in A.H. 359/D.H. 970, and the *Dār al-Ḥikma* founded by Caliph al-Ḥākim in A.H. 395/D.H. 1005.[30] But it was also disseminated by means of the various *dār al-da'wa*s that the Fatimids established throughout the Islamic world, including Syria and Iran.[31] Although the first *madrasas* perhaps "had no special mission to serve against Shī'ism or Mu'tazilism,"[32] they soon proved an effective weapon in this ideological battle. Associated from the beginning with the resurgence of Islamic traditionalism (*salafiyya*), they served as intellectual meeting grounds for various sects opposed to Mu'tazilism. Nishapur, for example, had *madrasas* founded for Shāfi'īs, Ḥanbalīs and Karrāmīs; and Bayhaq (modern Sabzawar) had *madrasas* for Ḥanafīs, Shāfi'īs, Karrāmīs, and even 'Alids.[33] Thus, the Sunni revival in its early pre-Seljuq form was not dominated by a single *madhhab* or a uniform theological orientation but was, despite internal controversy, united by its traditionalist inclinations and opposition to Shī'ī doctrines, which at the time were variously influenced by rationalism.[34]

The Great Seljuqs

This traditionalist revival "occurred early in the [eleventh] century, at a time when the Tughril-Nizām-Ghazzālī triad could not possibly have come into being."[35] While it is true that the Seljuqs were not the innovators of this revival and that they themselves may have "played little or no role in the rise of the *madrasas*,"[36] the fact remains that they were the patrons of the vizier Niẓām al-Mulk, who was certainly behind these developments in the second half of the eleventh century. Furthermore, as staunch Sunnis the Seljuqs supported and drew their legitimacy from the Abbasid state and opposed all its enemies, particularly the Fatimids and their Ismā'īlī sympathizers. And as a warrior dynasty not rooted in the newly conquered lands, they seem to have valued the permanence and tangibility of buildings and institutions more than the transience of ideas.

Ironically, the very leaders who were called to restore Sunnism were thus reluctant to adopt the caliphal Ḥanbalī doctrine precisely because it was deemed too orthodox. Shunning Abbasid Ḥanbalism, Seljuq policy, as it was formulated by Niẓām al-Mulk, favored diversity and a measure of tolerance. The sultan and his family were Ḥanafīs; Niẓām al-Mulk and other state officials were Shāfi'īs; while the caliph remained true to his Ḥanbalism. Clearly, some of the population in Baghdad and the Iraqi countryside held on to Imami Shī'ism, a situation that still obtains today.

The *madrasa* perfectly suited the political agenda of the Seljuqs and their vizier Niẓām al-Mulk, who saw in it the ideal means for providing the new empire with a moral framework while countering the power and influence of the Fatimid caliphate. According to Bosworth, "Niẓām al-Mulk desired to speed up the provision of educational institutions within the eastern Sunni world and to make them comparable with those still flourishing in Umayyad Spain and Fatimid Egypt."[37] In addition to their anti-Shī'ite charter, the Niẓāmiyyas served the equally important if somewhat more mundane function of training a loyal body of state officials, including notaries, judges, and other *madrasa* professors. Such systemization of education seems perfectly congruent with Niẓām al-Mulk's political ideas as explicated in his treatise, the *Siyāsat-Nama*, whose central theme is the use of trained individuals to maintain order and enforce control and power. Thus, rather than originating the *madrasa*, Niẓām al-Mulk laid out its institutional framework and made it a necessary instrument of Sunni rulership.

The Sunni revival suffered a great setback in 1092, when both Sultan Malikshāh and his great vizier Niẓām al-Mulk died under mysterious circumstances. The ensuing internecine struggle among the contenders for the Seljuq throne and other rival Turkish princes ended the centralized rule of the Great Seljuqs and considerably slowed the traditionalist trend of the preceding century. By the end of the eleventh century, both Seljuqs and Fatimids had become mere shadows of their former selves and, as such, completely unprepared to defend against the totally unexpected attack of the Crusades. Although the Crusaders stand outside the scope of this book, their takeover of the Levant at the end of the eleventh century focused attention on Syria, which thenceforth became once again a confrontation state and the line of defense between Christians and Muslims.

The geographic shift from Iraq/Iran and Egypt to Syria greatly contributed to the revival and repopulation of its main cities, which began in the twelfth century to reverse several centuries of demographic and cultural stagnation. Located just east of the newly established Frankish principalities, Aleppo and Damascus became the fiefs and military entrepots for a succession of petty Turkish dynasties. Aleppo had a faulty start: with its volatile mix of sects and ethnic groups and its location exposed to Crusader attacks, it remained in a state of sectarian turmoil and political chaos for most of the first half of the twelfth century. The mutual distrust between Turks and Arabs was fostered by sectarian differences: the Turks were Sunnis, whereas the Muslims of Aleppo were generally Shī'īs. Shī'ism became entrenched in Aleppo from the time of the Hamdanids and developed under the Mirdasids and the Fatimids, remaining a substantial, perhaps dominant, minority until the middle of the century.[38] Indeed, the numerical and political strength of Shī'īs in Aleppo was sufficient to modify or even reverse the general trend of Sunnism throughout the first half of the twelfth century. Its last Seljuq prince, Riḍwān, even went so far as to pronounce the *khuṭba* in the name of the Fatimid caliph, but had to recant under pressure from Damascus.[39]

Damascus, on the other hand, enjoyed a half-century of relative stability and uninterrupted Sunni dominion under its Burid rulers. Successors to the short-lived Seljuq rule, the Burids continued their Sunni policy and began the large-scale foundation of *madrasas* and other Sunni institutions, a movement that persisted for the next two centuries. By the middle of the twelfth century Damascus possessed nine *madrasas*, primarily for Ḥanafīs and Shāfi'īs, whereas

Aleppo had only one, a discrepancy that can only be attributed to their differing sectarian composition and dynastic experience. Indeed, for all practical purposes the center of the Sunni revival shifted from Baghdad to Damascus during the twelfth century, particularly its second half.[40]

The Zangids

In 1127, the Seljuq sultan Maḥmūd appointed ʿImād al-Dīn Zangi b. Aqsunqur to Mosul, and a year later he took Aleppo. Zangi, a transitional figure between a Turkish conquistador and a post-Seljuq sovereign, was a redoubtable warrior against the Crusaders, from whom he took Edessa in 1144. But he had little inclination for the politics of the Sunni revival or for the patronage of pious institutions, adopting instead a tolerant attitude toward Twelver Shīʿism and local shrine cults.[41]

Zangi's vast domain, which stretched from Mosul to Aleppo and from Edessa to Baʿalbak, was split immediately after his death in 1146 between his two eldest sons. Sayf al-Dīn Ghāzī, the elder, took Mosul, while Nūr al-Dīn took Aleppo. With his eastern flank safe under his brother's dynasty, Nūr al-Dīn was able to turn southward to Damascus and to his ultimate dreams of taking Jerusalem from the Crusaders and Egypt from the Fatimids. After several failed attempts, Nūr al-Dīn finally captured Damascus in 1154, ending a half-century of benign Burid rule. For the first time in centuries, the two main cities of Syria stood united under one ruler, presenting a unified front against the Crusaders.

Although during the first half of his career Nūr al-Dīn was primarily concerned with *jihād* against the Crusaders, he turned in his later years to the even more troublesome problem of the Fatimids. Indeed, the stabilization of his borders with the Crusaders after 1154 created a militarily familiar and theologically acceptable stalemate between Muslim and Christian forces. But the Fatimids were entirely unacceptable on any ground; their elimination was sanctioned by law and actively encouraged by the Abbasids. The Abbasid caliph al-Muqtafī ordered his renowned vizier and Ḥanbalī theologian Ibn Hubayra to write Nūr al-Dīn about this untenable situation, urging him to rid the Islamic world of Ismāʿīlī heresy. In fact, al-Muqtafī, as early as 1154, went so far as to grant Nūr al-Dīn a charter for Egypt and its Palestinian provinces at a time when the Fatimids were still very much in control.[42]

Motivated by imperial ambitions, Sunni zeal, and the blessing and encouragement of the caliphate, Nūr al-Dīn sent several military expeditions to Egypt in 1163, 1167, and finally in 1169. Under the military expertise of his Kurdish commanders Shīrkuh and his nephew Salāḥ al-Dīn (Saladin), these campaigns finally produced the desired result: in 1171 Saladin denounced the Fatimids and proclaimed the suzerainty of Nūr al-Dīn and the Abbasid caliphate over Egypt.[43] Thus, although the fall of the Ismāʿīlī Fatimid state is generally associated with Saladin—who was, of course, the one to reap its benefits—it was in fact the culmination of a nearly two-century struggle that had reached its peak under Nūr al-Dīn.

Nūr al-Dīn ruled over Syria, parts of the Jazira, and Egypt until his death in 1174, at which time Saladin began his ultimate northward expansion into Syria and the Levant.[44] Saladin completed Nūr al-Dīn's planned conquests by taking Jerusalem in 1187, thereby earning a place of unparalleled honor in the eyes of Muslims, particularly in later periods. Despite this grandiose image, Saladin was in most respects a follower of Nūr al-Dīn and a faithful heir to his former master's religious adherence to the Sunni revival and political allegiance to the Abbasid caliphate. As Lyons and Jackson observe, "It is difficult to over-stress the influence of Nūr al-Dīn on Saladin's political education and on his career."[45] It is therefore Nūr al-Dīn, rather than Saladin, who marks the political and religious turning point in the history of the central Islamic world.

The Religious Policy of Nūr al-Dīn

Although in his first two years of rule Nūr al-Dīn continued his father's complacent policy with regard to Shī'ism, in 1148 he began systematically to practice a more strident Sunni doctrine and to undermine local Shī'ī power. He put an end to all Shī'ī manifestations, including their divergent form of *adhān* (call to prayer), and began a campaign of *madrasa* and *khānqāh* construction that was also emulated by state officials and various Sunni notables.[46] His policies were at first strongly opposed by the local Shī'ī community, which, in 1157, even went so far as to destroy some of the *madrasas* and *khānqāhs* that he had just built in Aleppo.[47] But their resistance was of little avail in the face of the ecumenical Jamā'ī Sunnism favored by Nūr al-Dīn.[48]

The religious politics of Nūr al-Dīn were largely inspired by Ibn Hubayra (d. 1165), an important jurist and vizier under the two Abbasid caliphs al-Muqtafi and al-Mustanjid.[49] Ibn Hubayra's theology, which is fully explicated in his book *Kitāb al-Ifṣāḥ*, is a form of enlightened Ḥanbalism that draws on Nizām al-Mulk's toleration of the four Sunni sects. Indeed, Ibn Hubayra preached an ecumenical view toward the four Sunni sects and even moderate Shī'ism, proposing that they should form a united front in the face of the Ismā'īlī Fatimids. He further wrote that *madrasas*, just like mosques, should not be restricted to a single *madhhab* to the exclusion of the other three sects, but should be open to all Sunni Muslims.[50] Finally, Ibn Hubayra stood for a united Sunni Muslim state under the temporal and spiritual authority of the Abbasid caliphate. He was, therefore, opposed not only to the Fatimids but also to the last Seljuqs, who still exerted a feeble hold on the caliphate.

It is said that Nūr al-Dīn owned a copy of Ibn Hubayra's book and to have corresponded with him. An anecdote in Abū Shāma vividly illustrates Nūr al-Dīn's adoption of the ecumenicism of Ibn Hubayra. A *madrasa* professor had died, and his colleagues were deliberating on who was to replace him.

> We, the jurists, were divided into two groups: Arabs and Kurds. Some of us leaned toward a literal reading of the law and wanted to summon the shaykh Sharaf al-Dīn ibn abi 'Aṣrūn, who was in Mosul. The others leaned toward the discipline of observation and controversy and wanted to summon al-Quṭb al-Nīsābūrī. ... The ensuing discussion led to discord and division among the jurists. Nūr al-Dīn heard of the matter and summoned us to the citadel in Aleppo. Majd al-Dīn ibn al-Dāya then addressed us on behalf of Nūr al-Dīn, saying: "We only built *madrasas* in order to spread Sunni knowledge and obliterate heresy from this city. ... What has occurred among you is unsuitable and incorrect. ... We shall therefore satisfy both groups and summon both Sharaf al-Dīn ibn abī 'Aṣrūn and Quṭb al-Dīn al-Nīsābūrī, each to preside on his own *madrasa*."[51]

Of course, Nūr al-Dīn's decision does not perfectly accord with Ibn Hubayra's views that *madrasas* should not be restricted to one *madhhab* but open to all four. It does, however, show the sovereign's even-handedness toward the Sunni sects (in this case Ḥanafīs and Shāfi'īs), a policy designed to foster unity and eliminate unnecessary controversy. This policy stands at the very foundation of Jamā'ī, or ecumenical, Sunnism, whose ultimate aim was the unification of all Muslims under an exoteric Islam that favors obedient observance and ritual practice over rational speculation and the intercession of saintly figures and Shī'ī imams.

Another manifestation of the ecumenicism of Nūr al-Dīn is evident in the formula of the *khuṭba* (Friday sermon), which was developed during his reign. Ibn Jubayr, who traveled in the central Islamic world about two decades after the death of Nur al-Din, described two Friday sermons, one in the mosque al-Azhar in Cairo and the other in the Ḥaram of Makka. In both sermons the *khaṭīb* evoked at great length and with uncommon passion the special merits of Muhammad, the four Companion Caliphs, the uncles of the Prophet, the wives of the Prophet, and even the sons of 'Ali, al-Ḥasan and al-Ḥusayn.[52] Beginning and ending with lavish praise and oaths of homage to the Abbasid caliph, these sermons were intended to drive home the two main themes of the Sunni revival, *salafiyya* (traditionalism) and allegiance to the Abbasid caliphate, while also appealing to moderate Shī'ites.

Ibn Jubayr describes the *khuṭba* during the time of Saladin, but a similar Sunni formula was already known, and may have originated, under Nūr al-Dīn. One mosaic inscription of Nūr al-Dīn and two others attributable to him in the Umayyad mosque in Damascus use abbreviated versions of this formula. Datable to A.H. 554/A.D. 1159,[53] each inscription mentions in the same order the Prophet and the Companion Caliphs: Abu Bakr, 'Umar, 'Uthmān, and 'Ali. One mentions the name Nūr al-Dīn at the end, and another completes the list with al-Ḥasan, al-Ḥusayn, 'Ā'isha, and Fāṭima.

Whether inscribed or spoken, this Sunni formula was intended to counteract the common Twelver Shīʿī *taṣliya* that gave the names and attributes of the twelve descendants of al-Husayn and totally ignored the Companion Caliphs. Their main purpose was not to gloat over the victory of Sunnism, but rather to present a formula that united the Sunni sects and might be found acceptable to some Shīʿīs.[54]

In addition to his pivotal importance during his lifetime, Nūr al-Dīn eventually achieved a nearly legendary status, becoming a model of ideal rulership for later medieval dynasts. Overstating the point, but reflecting the consensus of many Muslim historians,[55] the contemporary writer Ṭāha Wāli proclaims that "the engineer of victory against Crusader occupation and the true hero of the movement to correct the faith [i.e., the Sunni revival] is none other than the sultan Nūr al-Dīn Maḥmūd b. Zanki. All those who succeeded him of the Ayyubid and Mamluk dynasties simply followed his steps and traced his actions."[56] Indeed, rulers from Saladin to Baybars to Qaytbay followed Nūr al-Dīn's policy of *jihād*, inclusive traditionalism, and dedication to public welfare. More specifically, there is little question that Nūr al-Dīn's architectural patronage set a precedent and offered an incentive for these rulers to build pious foundations in their respective cities.

I have outlined above some of the main tenets and lines of development in the movement of the Sunni revival, from its origins in Baghdad and Khurasan to its culmination in Syria under Nūr al-Dīn. Beginning in mutually opposed grassroot sects and legal schools, this movement gradually attained considerable unity by calling for a return to traditionalism and opposing the rationalism of the Muʿtazilīs and the Ismāʿīlīs. Politically, the Sunni revival was promulgated by the Abbasids and a succession of Sunni dynasties (Ghaznavids, Seljuqs, Zangids, and Ayyubids) achieving in the process an institutional framework and a measure of unity. The earlier state of opposition and confrontation among Ḥanafis, Shāfiʿīs, Ashʿarīs, and Ḥanbalīs was resolved in the second half of the twelfth century in an ecumenical Sunnism that accommodated all four *madhhabs* and even made overtures to Twelver or Imāmī Shīʿism. The downfall of the Fatimids at the behest of Nūr al-Dīn marked the decline of political Shīʿism and brought about some tolerance of its pietistic aspects, allowing a state of rapprochement between unified Sunnism and Imami Shīʿism, a situation that continued until the Mongol invasion.[57]

I have also proposed in this chapter three ways that the ideology of the Sunni revival may have penetrated architecture and art. The first and most direct was the creation of specifically Sunni institutions, such as *madrasas* and *khānqāhs*, whose traditionalist purpose and anti-Shīʿite message were understood equally by their founders and by their opponents among the Shīʿites. The second level of analysis is oratorial and textual; it concerns the *khuṭbas* and pious inscriptions that emphasized the inclusive *Jamāʿī* nature of the Sunni revival. Often uttered or inscribed within the very institutions that had been founded by Sunni patrons, these two discourses emphasized each other, contributing a populist dimension to what had been previously a privileged and arcane discourse. The third level, which concerns the very architectural and epigraphic forms that may have been inspired or mandated by the forces of the Sunni revival, will be discussed in the following chapters. It is these new forms that fleshed out the textual and verbal discourses of the new ideology, producing a symbolic language that was intended to mediate between the myth of Sunni ecumenical unity and the reality of political fragmentation.

Ibn Muqla is a prophet in the field of handwriting; it was poured upon his hand, even as it was revealed to the bees to make their honey cells hexagonal.[1]

2

The Transformation of Qur'ānic Writing

Several factors conjoin to give writing in Islam a sacred aura and a spiritual dimension. First, according to the Qur'ān, the act of writing is nearly synonymous with revelation, for it was the means by which the divine scriptures were transmitted to humanity. Second, the transcribed Qur'ān was, from early on, the object of considerable calligraphic attention, a precedent that in itself seems to have elevated the status of beautiful writing in Islam above other means of expression. Indeed, writing, if not calligraphy, begins with the first Muslim century—thus predating all other specifically Islamic art forms—and continues uninterrupted across time and space. Finally, in a largely aniconic and nonsymbolic artistic tradition, calligraphic writing often occupied the physical and iconographic space usually taken up by sculpture or painting.

For these reasons and others, the case for an essentialist interpretation of calligraphy in Islamic art has been relatively easy to make and quite difficult to dislodge. Writers espousing such an approach valorize calligraphy above all other aspects of Islamic art, considering it the truest manifestation of the revelation and the most essential embodiment of the dogma. But these very writers are disinclined to deal with variation and transformation in Islamic calligraphy in any kind of historical or sociological sense, labeling these changes instead as merely other symptoms of "variety within unity." Calligraphy is therefore presented as an ahistorical phenomenon, a disembodied form deprived of all its rich associations with culture, politics, patronage, and even theology.

More scientific approaches to calligraphic writing, as practiced by epigraphers, palaeographers, or even art historians, stand clearly at odds with such essentialist and ahistorical interpretations. Overall, however, the positivist approach adopted by many of these scholars has hindered exploration of the underlying causes of calligraphic developments and the particular meanings associated with certain calligraphic styles. Rejecting the essentialism of the aesthetic-fundamentalist approach, these writers have themselves failed to provide alternative interpretations for the often quite drastic changes in calligraphic styles, whether in Qur'ān manuscripts or in monumental inscriptions. The static and pervasive associations attributed to calligraphy by essentialist scholars have either been dismissed or replaced by a case-by-case interpretation of outstanding examples.

Indeed, a deeply rooted bias against exploring the iconographic, or more broadly semiotic, dimension of writing has long permeated the specialized methods and inflexible agendas prevailing in epigraphy and palaeography. Research in Islamic epigraphy has generally been restricted to the recording and translation of inscriptions on monuments, and somewhat later to their interpretation.[2] Little attention has been given to calligraphic form, whose relevance to the very specialized endeavor of the first epigraphists has gone largely unnoticed. While this is understandable given the enormous scope of epigraphic documentation projects, the dismissal of the formal qualities of the script is far more problematic in the recent works of art historians who have used epigraphy as an interpretive tool.[3] By simply perpetuating the restrictive methodology of the epigraphists, they have reduced calligraphy to mere information and diminished the meaning and impact of inscriptions instead of enriching them.[4]

As for palaeographers, despite their many important contributions to the classification and insights into the historical development of Arabic calligraphy, they have generally failed to consider the reasons for changes in calligraphic form.[5] Instead of searching for underlying cultural causes, most palaeographers have tended to explain developments in Arabic and Persian scripts in terms of regional variation, autonomous chronological change, or, at best, artisanal improvements determined primarily by the innovations of a few well-known calligraphers and the lesser contributions of minor calligraphers.[6]

This overly specialized approach is problematic in at least two respects. First, in its emphasis on authenticating the works of the most important calligraphers and its dismissal of all "questionable" specimens, it has tended to lose sight of the broad artistic trends of the period and even of the legacy of the calligrapher under consideration. This tendency is especially troublesome in the case of Ibn Muqla, of whose calligraphy no specimens have survived but whose method is known to have influenced several generations of calligraphers. Second, traditional palaeography has not concerned itself with the impact of external factors, such as politics and religion, on the world of the calligrapher, factors that may have directly or indirectly contributed to palaeographic changes.[7] Primarily concerned with problems of dating, provenance, and authorship, palaeographers have left unexamined the question of the transformation of Arabic writing from angular to cursive and have generally dismissed the question of meaning in calligraphic forms.

But the limited attention paid to the transformation of Arabic writing should not in any way detract from its centrality and importance. Indeed, before the large-scale introduction of modern printing techniques in the early nineteenth century, this was perhaps the most drastic transformation to which official Arabic writing had been subjected. Occurring first in Qur'ān manuscripts in the tenth century and later in monumental inscriptions, this transformation had a deep and long-lasting impact, shaping the subsequent evolution of Islamic calligraphy for several centuries. It was also a geographically widespread change, and although it began in the central Islamic world—most likely in Baghdad—no Muslim country from India to Spain was left unaffected by it.

A development of this magnitude cries out for an explanation. Furthermore, since calligraphy was the most visible and prevalent medium for conveying political and pietistic messages, this explanation can no longer be restricted to the formal changes in the script but must reach into the cultural factors that required, facilitated, and implemented this transformation. A new course of analysis is required, one that taps into the findings of both epigraphers and palaeographers but that ultimately investigates the historical and ontological questions neglected by both. To what extent was the transformation of Arabic writing, which has been singularly attributed to the creative genius of Ibn Muqla and Ibn al-Bawwāb, linked to the political and theological views of the Abbasid and Buyid states? What was the significance of this transformation and the meaning of the new calligraphic modes? Finally, how was the role of calligraphy changed after this transformation? Since the change in monumental epigraphy lagged by about one century behind the Qur'ānic transformation and was contingent upon it, it seems logical to proceed chronologically from Qur'ān manuscripts to public texts, which are discussed in the following chapter.

What sort of evidence can be brought to bear on these questions, which are not just palaeographic and aesthetic but also historical and sociological? The primary cache of evidence remains the palaeographic specimens themselves (Qur'ānic manuscripts in this chapter and public inscriptions in the next), which exist in sufficient numbers to permit their classification and dating. These specimens are then juxtaposed against a variety of textual sources, including biographical dictionaries, chancerial and secretarial manuals, and treatises on calligraphy and calligraphers. Many of these sources have been examined by Nabia Abbott in her attempt to identify the myriad of early calligraphic pens among extant specimens of calligraphic writing. But despite the apparent soundness of this method, it has been recently questioned by Whelan and Déroche, who have critiqued its reliance on secretarial manuals for the identification of Qur'ānic scripts.[8] Whereas Whelan opts for a comprehensive approach that includes "textual, palaeographic and codicological evidence," Déroche completely rejects these sources, opting for a purely positivist method that relies exclusively on the close examination of large collections of Qur'ān manuscripts.[9]

These reactions to the unrigorous methods of an earlier generation are clearly warranted, and Déroche's single-minded emphasis on palaeographic and codicological questions has brought to light subtle differences and minute variations that had gone unnoticed by earlier scholars. But the very emphasis on small changes and rejection of the "official history" of Islamic calligraphy have produced classes and implied developments that appear suspended in a historical vacuum. What seems needed, therefore, is not to silence the literary sources but to utilize them comprehensively and more critically than they had been in previous studies. Despite their often ambiguous statements, impressionistic ideas, and lack of originality, these texts can nevertheless provide a point of departure and a framework for investigating the remaining specimens.[10]

Before Ibn Muqla

The present study of the transformation of Arabic writing in the tenth and eleventh centuries is greatly facilitated by the substantial palaeographic research on the three first centuries of Islam. This scholarship demonstrated that cursive Arabic writing did not originate from an older angular script; but rather, that the two forms coexisted from the earliest days of Islam.[11] Second, early cursive scripts were used exclusively for secular purposes, never for the Qur'ān, which was written in the angular Kufic script (fig. 1).[12] Third, secular and Qur'ānic scripts were subject to totally different calligraphic rules, those applied to the Qur'ān being far more exacting.[13] And finally, most treatises on calligraphy dealt with secular, not Qur'ānic scripts, since their authors tended to be scribes and officials of the administration.[14]

With few exceptions, Qur'ānic script from the first two-and-a-half centuries of Islam is extremely uniform, a fact that Arthur Arberry attributed to "the tenacious conservatism of many Koranic scribes."[15] There is in fact so little variation in the Kufic script of these Qur'āns that palaeographers have had to depend on diacritical and orthographic marks and decorations for their dating and classification.[16] The great uniformity of Qur'ānic writing from the first three centuries of Islam bespeaks a highly conservative and restrictive attitude toward the transcription of the Qur'ān (fig. 2). With ambiguous and often undifferentiated letter forms and a scattered disposition on the page, early Kufic Qur'āns were practically illegible except to those who had already memorized the text (i.e., *ḥuffaẓ*).[17] In other words, these Qur'āns were created less to be

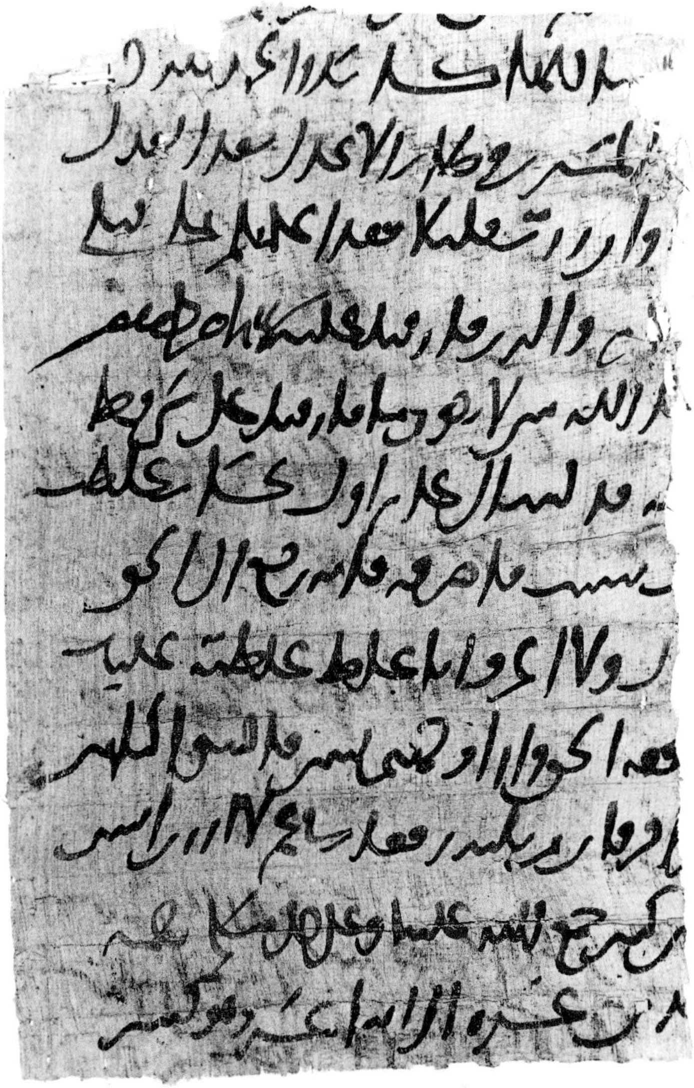

1 Egypt, papyrus fragment, A.H. 3rd/A.D. 9th century. Ann Arbor, Kelsey Museum of Archaeology, 67.1.52.

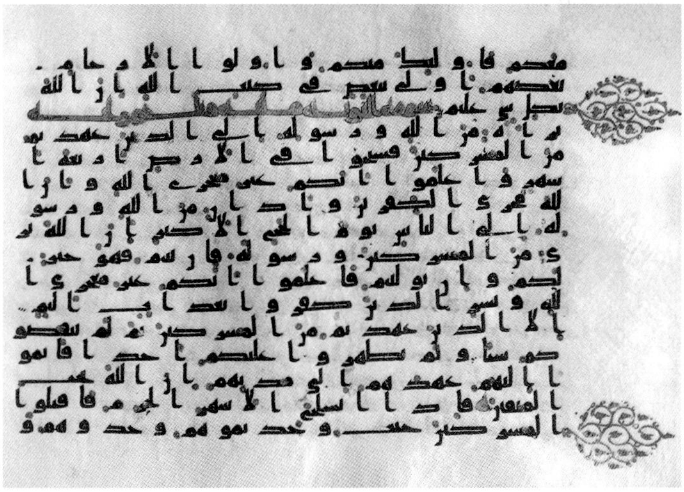

2 Iraq/Iran, page of Qur'ān, A.H. 3rd/A.D. 9th century. Tehran, Iran Bastan Museum, 4251.

read than to validate the act of recitation and to venerate the word of God. Written, according to Ibn Durustūyah and others, by calligraphers (*khaṭṭaṭūn*) with religious training, these manuscripts were intended to restrict the reading of the Qur'ān to those who, like the calligraphers themselves, were already quite well versed in the text.[18] The entire manuscript speaks of privilege: rare materials, exquisite ornament, and a nearly indecipherable script.[19]

By contrast, secular scripts, which can in fact be subdivided into scribal scripts and book scripts, were quite legible, despite their considerable variation.[20] By the end of the ninth century, Ibn al-Nadīm had listed twenty-six styles, ranging from large and angular to small and cursive (fig. 3).[21] So large a number of scripts existed by the end of the ninth century that Ibn Wahb al-Kātib, a contemporary of Ibn al-Nadīm, complained that "the scribes were no longer aware of all the different styles of the olden days."[22] Nabia Abbott, who had tried with limited success to identify some of the chancerial script,[23] concluded that they mostly represented subtle variations on the major scripts, but the sheer number of scripts and the subsequent need for reform seem to suggest a loss of standard and a general decline in scribal writing.[24]

Book scripts, on the other hand, were quite commonly used in literary and scientific manuscripts of the ninth and tenth centuries (fig. 4). Ranging from semi-angular in the ninth century to fully cursive by the late tenth century, these scripts precede their cognates in Qur'ānic calligraphy by nearly one century. Although little palaeographic work has been done on these book scripts, they seem to display considerable formal and qualitative variation, especially when compared to Qur'ānic scripts. This may have to do with the fact that some literary and scientific treatises were copied by the authors themselves, while others, perhaps the majority, were written by professional copyists (*warrāqūn*).[25]

Interestingly, these "transitional" book scripts were also commonly used in a variety of eastern Christian texts, including Gospels, psalters, and monastic anthologies (fig. 5). A cursory survey of this little-known phenomenon suggests that Christian manuscripts were written in semi-Kufic scripts as early as the last quarter of the ninth century, whereas those written in cursive scripts generally date to the second half of the tenth century.[26] In other words, the use of book scripts in Christian manuscripts long predates the transformation in Qur'ānic writing but is generally contemporary with their use in Arabic secular manuscripts. The use of these scripts for Christian texts attests to their popularity and strengthens the case for their "secular" background, from an Islamic perspective, that is. It is highly unlikely that they would have been used for writing the Qur'ān before the reform of Ibn Muqla.

It seems clear, therefore, that a wide range of semi-angular and cursive scripts had been in use in the chancery and for copying books since the first or second Islamic century. This realization invalidates the earlier view that cursive writing totally replaced angular writing sometime in the tenth century.

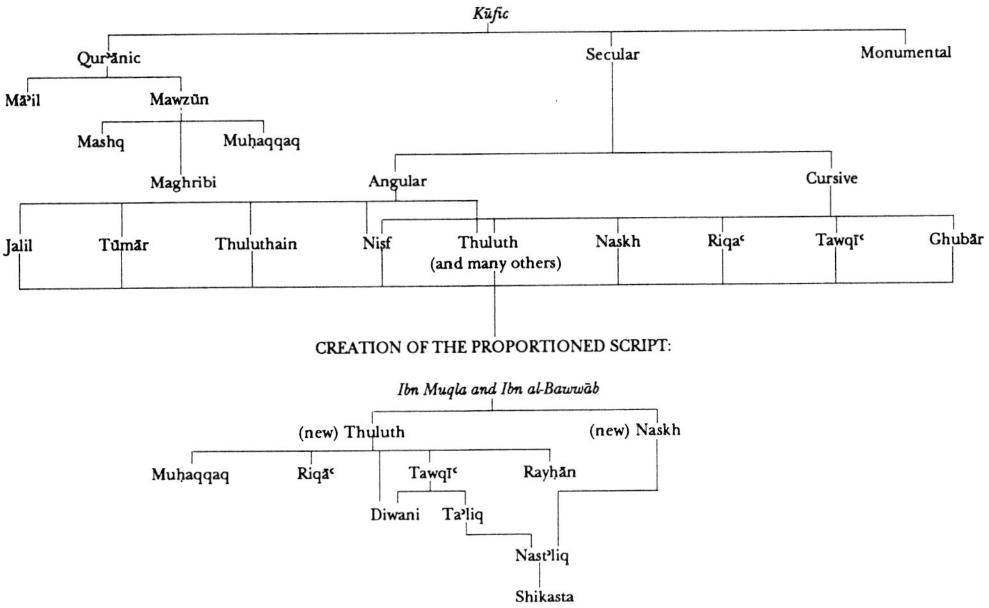

3 Table showing the development of Arabic calligraphic scripts. The term *Kūfic* refers to the mother Arabic script, not just to its well-known angular variety.

4 Al-Aṣma'ī, *Ta'rīkh mulūk al-'Arab*, A.H. 243/A.D. 957. Paris, Bibliothèque Nationale, Arabe 6726, fol. 2v.

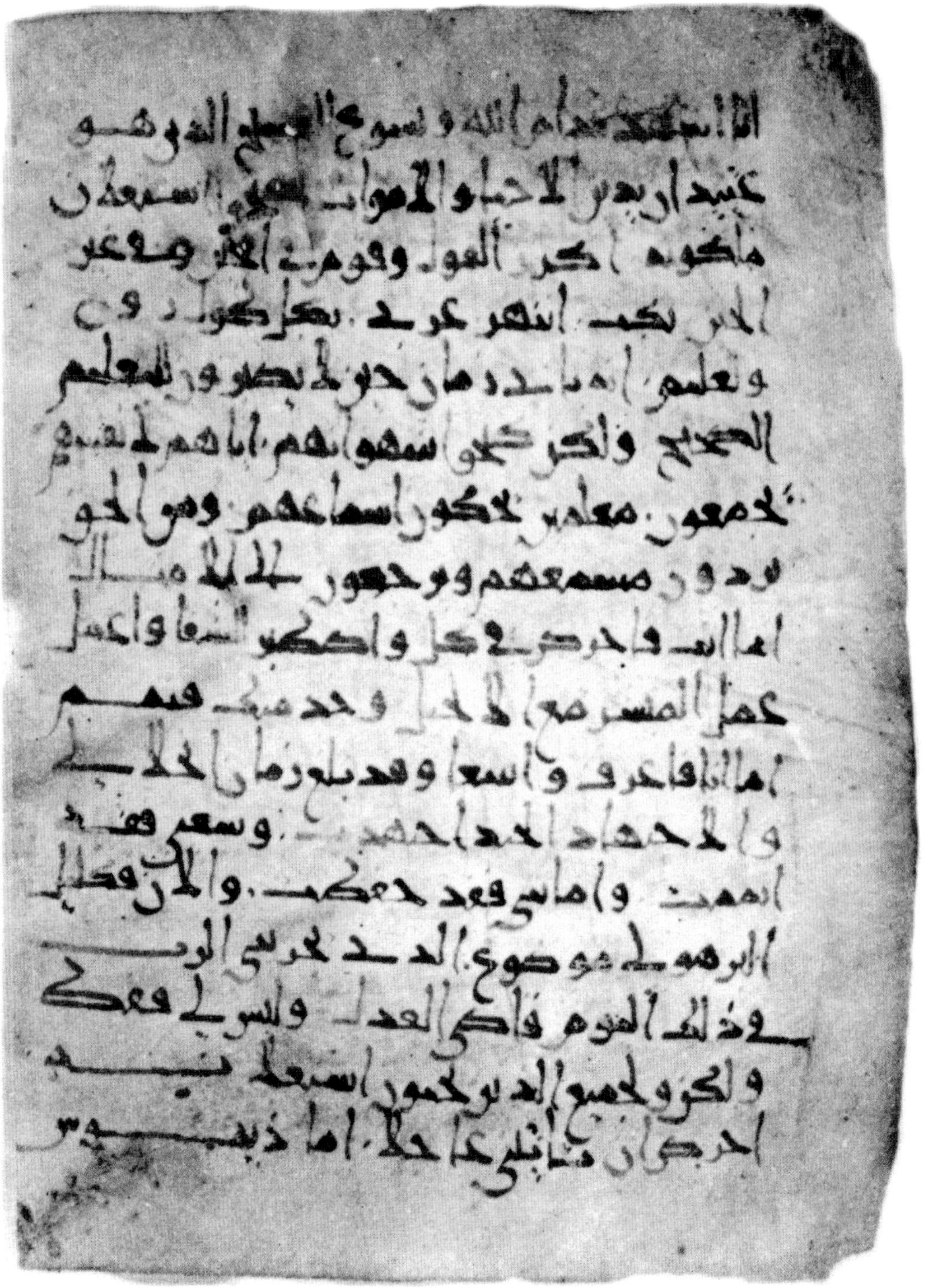

5 New Testament, Timothy IV, 1f, Jerusalem, 902. Paris, Bibliothèque Nationale, Arabe 6725, fol. 5v

But it also has had the unfortunate effect of trivializing the palaeographic transformation that did take place, by assuming that it was a slow and incremental process rather than an abrupt and highly significant rupture.[27] This view inevitably undermines the narrative as told in the contemporary literary sources, reducing it from a version of history to a kind of apocryphal tale that was invented to validate previously established changes.[28] This reductionist attitude to Arabic sources is especially troubling in the case of calligraphy, whose elevated status and quasi-religious nature have guaranteed it ample, if somewhat repetitive, discussion in Arabic literature.

What, therefore, can we learn from these canonical texts about the early actors and their actions in the field of official Arabic writing? Interestingly, nearly every historical treatise on Arabic calligraphy presents an almost identical list of calligraphers and the various innovations for which they were responsible. The origin of writing is invariably attributed to legendary pre-Islamic figures such as Enoch, Solomon , or Tahmuras Divband—an honor that is then passed on to the early caliphs 'Ali and 'Uthmān and other pious persons, who were the first to perfect Arabic calligraphy.[29] In the early Abbasid period, calligraphic writing tended to be in the hands of high officials, such as al-Faḍl b. Sahl, al-Aḥwal and the vizier Ibn Muqla.[30] Finally, under the Buyids and later Abbasids, calligraphy was practiced primarily by scribes who had demonstrated a special talent for this art, including Ibn al-Bawwāb and Yāqūt al-Musta'ṣimī.

This canonical narrative raises a number of questions regarding the status and independence of early calligraphers. First, the status of calligraphers declined steadily and significantly. The earliest were men of high rank and religious learning—Ibn Muqla was a patrician who became a vizier; Ibn al-Bawwāb (literally, son of the porter) was a man of humble origins who rose to the rank of scribe and librarian; and Yāqūt al-Musta'ṣimī was a slave of the last Abbasid caliph, al-Musta'ṣim. Second, this social decline seems to have been accompanied by the decreasing independence of calligraphers and their increasing reliance on patronage. Even disregarding such legendary calligraphers as the caliphs 'Ali and 'Uthmān, some evidence suggests that the first calligraphers, that is, those who wrote the majority of Kufic Qur'āns, were learned scholars who were not in the direct employ of sovereigns or princes.[31] Later calligraphers, on the other hand, particularly after Ibn al-Bawwāb, relied greatly or exclusively on princely patronage, culminating in those calligraphers who were employed by the *kitābkhana*.[32] Third, the ranks of Qur'ān calligraphers and book copyists, which were quite distinct in the first three centuries, began to overlap and merge in the tenth century.

Ibn Muqla (886–940)

On the eve of the reforms of Ibn Muqla, Arabic was being written in an ambiguously majestic Qur'ānic script and in an unwieldy variety of secular scripts, mostly used by scribes for writing documents and letters and by booksellers/ copyists for copying various texts. It has been firmly established that contrary to legend, Ibn Muqla did not create any new scripts and certainly was not the inventor of cursive writing, incorrectly referred to today as the *naskh* script.[33] Known primarily as *ṣāḥib al-khaṭṭ al-mansūb* (master of the proportioned script), Ibn Muqla was most notable for inventing a system of proportional writing based on the principles of geometric design (*handasat al-ḥurūf*).[34] The rules for his proportioned writing did not emerge from Qur'ānic Kufic but were ultimately based on book scripts, which were also the subject of the reform.[35] In other words, Qur'ānic Kufic, which by the tenth century had reached a very high standard, was not directly affected by the changes of Ibn Muqla; the reform was intended for the more mundane scripts used by scribes rather than by calligraphers. The result of these reforms, therefore, was not the gradual softening of the angular Kufic script but its supplantation by the redesigned scripts of the copyists.

The system of proportion that Ibn Muqla devised was based on the the dot and the circle (fig. 6). The dot was formed by pressing the nib of the *qalam* (reed pen) on paper until it opened to its fullest extent, after which it was released evenly and rapidly, producing a square on end, or a rhombus. The size of the dot affected only the size of the writing; the relative proportions of letters remained constant for each individual script. Placing dots vertex to vertex, Ibn Muqla then proceeded to straighten the Kufic *alif*, which had been bent to the right, and adopt it as his standard of measurement. The length of the *alif* produced the diamater of a circle that was inscribed around each character, lending it a proportional relationship to all the other characters, thus producing a canon for each script.[36] This innovation allowed a number of systematic methods or templates to be created for each of the six major scripts (*al-aqlām al-sitta*), which, thenceforth, could be produced accurately to scale.[37]

Ibn Muqla, therefore, created order where disorder had been perceived in scribal writing, a feat that earned him heroic stature among later Muslim biographers. Since success is often equated with quality, the success of Ibn Muqla's proportional writing made him the creative genius of the new calligraphy, although he may not have been an especially gifted calligrapher himself.[38] In fact, the emphasis by connoisseurs from medieval times to the present on finding authentic specimens in the hand of Ibn Muqla has diverted attention from a proper investigation of the formula and legacy of his success. The important question, then, is not so much the exact identity of his hand, but rather the impact of his calligraphic reforms on subsquent developments in Qur'ānic and secular scripts.

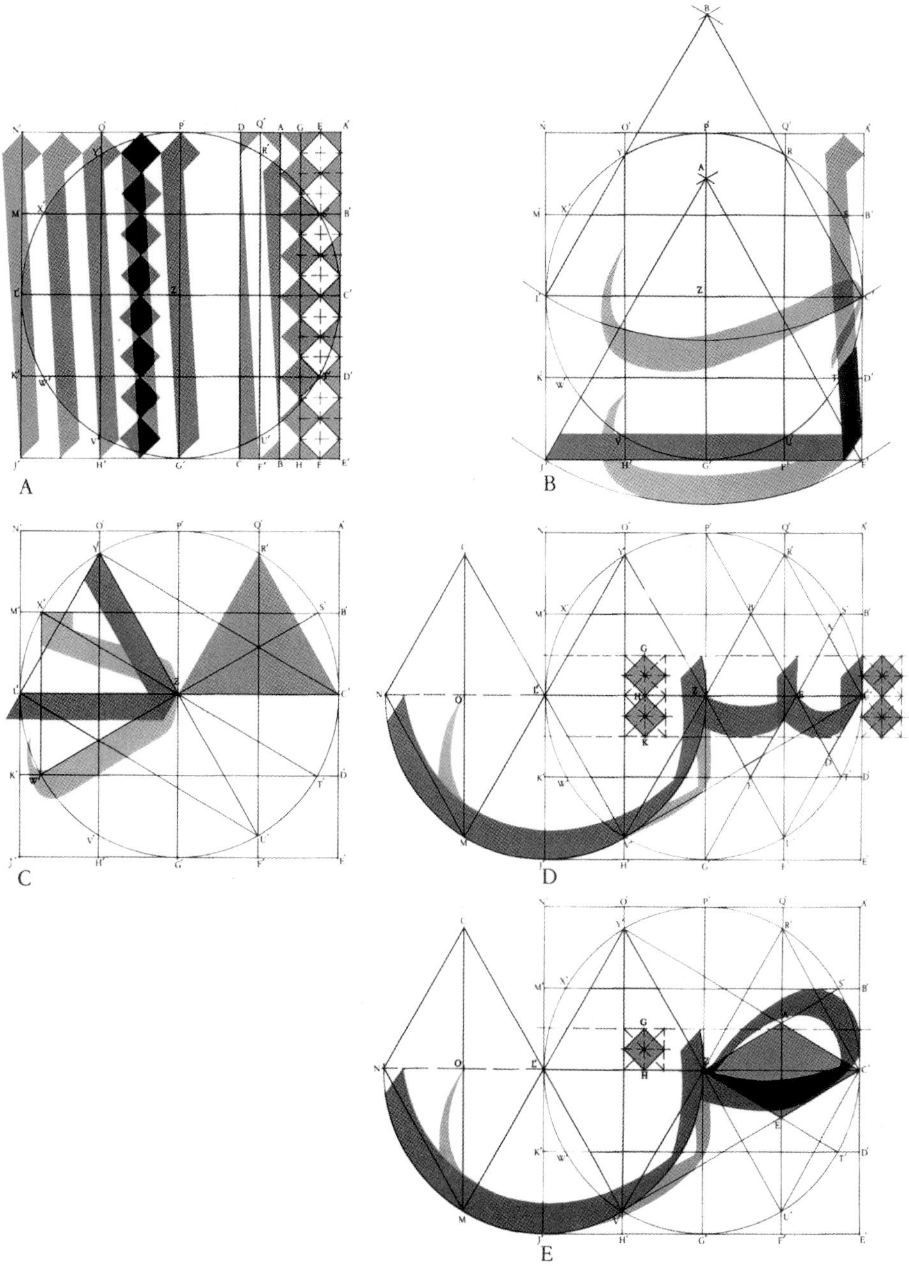

6 Reconstruction of the letters *alif* (*a*), *lām* (*b*), *dāl* (*c*), *sīn* (*d*), *ṣād* (*e*) (after Soucek, "Arts of Calligraphy," based on A. Mustafa, "Scientific Construction of Alphabets").

Reconstructions of Ibn Muqla's alphabet based on his own descriptions produce a script characterized by regularity, verticality, semi-angularity, short sublineal curves, open knots, and the triangular appearance of some characters (fig. 7).[39] In all these respects, this reconstructed script resembles the so-called semi-Kufic script used in many secular manuscripts of the ninth and tenth centuries and in many Qur'āns about a century later (fig. 8).[40] The regularity, even rigidity, of Qur'ānic semi-Kufic might be seen as the result of strict adherence to the geometric precepts of Ibn Muqla. An exercise in restraint, the semi-Kufic has none of the deep sublineal curves of Maghribi Kufic nor the flourishes of later cursive writing.

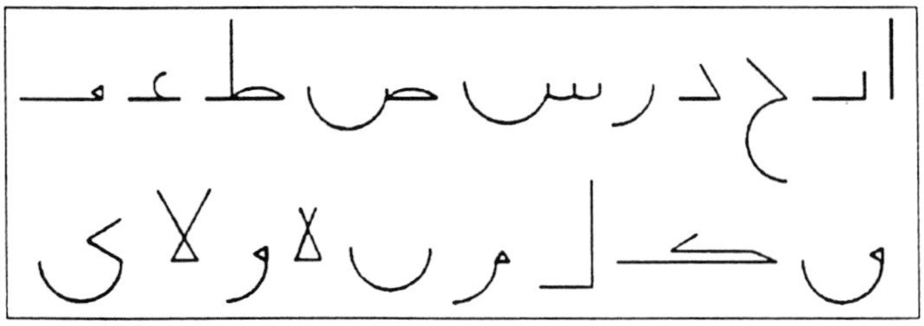

7 Tentative reconstruction of Arabic letter forms according to Ibn Muqla (Abbott, "Arabic Paleography," fig. 1).

The script of Ibn Muqla can be further approximated by examining Qur'ānic fragments and album pages that have been spuriously attributed to his hand (fig. 9). Although certainly not by him and often written two or three centuries after him, these fragments nevertheless display striking similarities both to each other and to semi-Kufic Qur'ānic script. Such consistency is significant even in forgeries, for a forger has to pay due respect to the original he is copying. In this case, there is little doubt that what is being copied is an especially precise form of the semi-Kufic script.[41]

In addition to their distinctive and legible script, semi-Kufic Qur'āns display at least three other features that distinguish them from their predecessors. The first and most important is that they are almost all written on paper instead of vellum. The widespread use of paper, from the late ninth century, in chancery documents and secular manuscripts contributed to the legibility and speed of execution required by scribes and book copiers and promoted the expansion of literacy.[42] Qur'ān manuscripts lagged behind by about one century: in fact the earliest known, dated paper Qur'ān is written in a very upright and regular semi-Kufic script (fig. 10).[43]

Since paper had been used by scribes and book copyists long before it was put to use for Qur'āns, it stands to reason that some of these copyists would have served as mediators between these two realms of writing. Even though the work of Ibn Muqla, the foremost copyist, has been lost, we still have a literary treatise autographed by 'Ali b. Shādhān al-Rāzī, the same calligrapher who wrote the earliest known paper Qur'ān. Entitled *Kitāb akhbār al-naḥwiyyīn al-Baṣriyyīn* (Tales of the Grammarians of Basra) and dated A.H. 376/A.D. 986, this

8 Semi-Kufic Qur'ān on paper, Iran, A.H. 388/A.D. 998. Signed Muḥammad ibn ʿAlī ibn al-Ḥusayn al-Ṣaffār. Istanbul, Topkapı Serai Müzesi Kütüphanesi, HS 22, fol. 56a.

جاء امة رسولها كذبوه فاتبعنا بعضهم بعضا وجعلنهم ا
حاديث فبعدا لقوم لا يؤمنون ثم ارسلنا موسى
واخاه هرون بايتنا وسلطن مبين الى فرعون وملا
يه فاستكبروا وكانوا قوما عالين فقالوا انؤ
من لبشرين مثلنا وقومهما لنا عبدون فكذبو
هما فكانوا من المهلكين ولقد اتينا موسى
الكتب لعلهم يهتدون وجعلنا ابن مريم وامه اية
واوينهما الى ربوة ذات قرار ومعين يايها
الرسل كلوا من الطيبت واعملوا صلحا انى بما تعملون
عليم وان هذه امتكم امة وحدة وانا ربكم فاتقون
فتقطعوا امرهم بينهم زبرا كل حزب بما لديهم
فرحون فذرهم فى غمرتهم حتى حين ايحسبون
انما نمدهم به من مال وبنين نسرع لهم فى
الخيرت بل لا يشعرون ان الذين هم من خشية ربهم مشفقون
والذين هم بايت ربهم يؤمنون والذين هم بربهم لا
يشركون والذين يؤتون ما اتوا وقلوبهم وجلة انهم
الى ربهم رجعون اولئك يسرعون فى

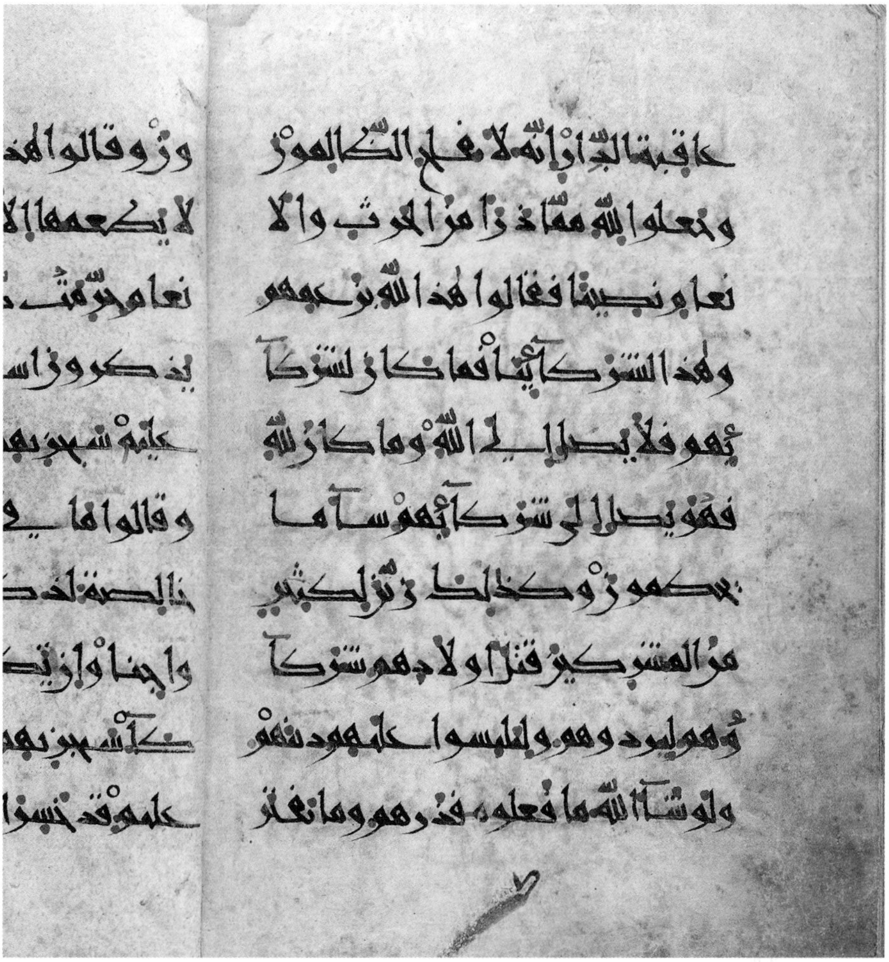

10 Iran, Qur'ān (another part of the same ms. at the University Library in Istanbul [A6758] is dated A.H. 361/A.D. 972). Calligrapher 'Alī b. Shādhān al-Rāzī. Dublin, The Chester Beatty Library, 1434, fols. 22b–23a.

OPPOSITE

9 Iran, Qur'ān fragment on paper, 12th century. Falsely attributed to Ibn Muqla. Dublin, The Chester Beatty Library, Ms. Add.

treatise is written on paper in a reasonably legible, fully vocalized semi-Kufic script, representing the high end of secular manuscripts produced in the late tenth century (fig. 11). Comparing the calligrapher's style in these two manuscripts, we note their overall resemblance despite the greater innovation displayed in the secular manuscript. These two manuscripts, therefore, show the close linkages between Qur'ānic and non-Qur'ānic calligraphy in the aftermath of Ibn Muqla's reforms and demonstrate the existence of copyists who, perhaps for the first time, were also involved in the production of Qur'ān manuscripts. Written about one generation after the death of Ibn Muqla, 'Ali b. Shādhān's Qur'ān represents the direct influence of the master's calligraphic method, the transmission of this method from secular to Qur'ānic manuscripts, and the impact of paper production on both processes.

The second new feature of semi-Kufic Qur'āns is their format: they abandon the horizontal format of Abbasid Kufic and adopt the vertical format of secular manuscripts.[44] The motive for this change has not been determined but is unlikely to have owed to the switch from vellum to paper, since both formats had hitherto been used previously with vellum. More likely, the vertical format of secular manuscripts went hand in hand with the adoption of scripts that had been used primarily in the chancery and in literary manuscripts. The change in format, therefore, could have been simply an outgrowth of the calligraphic change. But it could also have been intentional, serving as yet another way to differentiate the new Qur'ānic manuscripts from their predecessors.

The third feature shared by many semi-Kufic Qur'āns is that they begin with single- or double-illuminated folios that refer to the particular recension of the Qur'ān and give a verse count. So far as we know, this feature did not exist in Abbasid Kufic Qur'āns,[45] but begins with the earliest dated semi-Kufic Qur'ān (972), signed by 'Ali b. Shādhān (see fig. 10). A high percentage of the preserved, complete semi-Kufic Qur'āns produced between 950 and 1100 contain verse-counts, which suggest that this was a prevalent and deeply rooted practice.[46] The content of the verse count varies slightly from one manuscript to the next, but it generally includes the number of *sūras* and words in the Qur'ān. Semi-Kufic Qur'āns, therefore, differ from Abbasid Kufic Qur'āns in their material, format, script, diacritical marks, and verse-count. Despite their superficial similarity to the earlier Qur'āns, they should be considered not as a stage in a continuous evolution from angular to cursive, but rather, as a complete and deliberate departure from past custom.

Although generally discussed in aesthetic terms, Ibn Muqla's innovations primarily affected clarity and legibility, concerns that seem consistent with his role as a state official.[47] His calligraphic reform grew out of earlier trends toward clarity in scribal and manuscript writing, but his efforts in this regard were perhaps the most systematic and pervasive. Engendered within an atmosphere of increasing literacy, brought about by the introduction of paper, this reform was intended to remedy a situation caused by the expansion of literacy.

11 Al-Sirāfī, *Kitāb akhbār al-naḥwiyyīn al-baṣriyyīn*. Calligrapher ʿAlī b. Shādhān al-Rāzī. Iraq/Iran, dated 986. Istanbul, Suleymaniye Library (Šehid Ali 1642), fol. 191a.

It resulted in the creation of a series of templates for the canonical calligraphic scripts, which guaranteed quality and consistency. But this standardization involved a relatively small number of the previously known scripts; those not influenced by the reform were quickly forgotten.

The power implications of this standardization and canonicity are fairly straightforward. Brinkley Messick, in *The Calligraphic State*, expatiates on the links between the introduction of new writing systems and the rise of a new power structure.[48] Specifically, he notes that the switch that took place from organically formed spiral texts to texts with a standardized linear format implied enforced changes in the relation between form and content and between the state and the population. Although the change in modern Yemen from manuscript to print culture is more abrupt and the sources on it more ample, both situations describe a process by which new writing systems are deployed for affirming power and asserting control. The Abbasid reforms entailed such control of the scripts, control of the scribes who had to be retrained in these scripts, and ultimately control of the content—the texts for which these scripts were to be used.

Although contemporary writers directly attribute these reforms to the creative genius of Ibn Muqla, there is no question that their success and quick impact resulted from their adoption by the Abbasid state.[49] As vizier to three successive Abbasid caliphs—al-Muqtadir, al-Qāhir, and al-Rāḍi—Ibn Muqla was deeply embroiled in the politics and intrigue of the Abbasids, especially during the reign of al-Muqtadir (907–932), in his attempt to produce a canonical recension of the Qur'ān.

The need to produce a universal recension of the Qur'ān was strongly felt in the early Islamic period, and it was finally accomplished under the third caliph 'Uthman, when the official recension was finished and all other variants were allegedly destroyed.[50] Only one reader, Ibn Mas'ūd, refused to destroy his version of the Qur'ān or to stop teaching it after the 'Uthmanic recension had been made official.[51] His codex, which differed from the 'Uthmanic recension in several important respects, was later taken over by the Shī'ite Fatimids. As time went on, even the so-called canonical version once more became a source of some confusion because of the ambiguity of the script, as Welch notes, "to the point that it became impossible to distinguish 'Uthmanic from non-'Uthmanic ones."[52]

Under the patronage of Caliph al-Muqtadir, a jurist named Aḥmad ibn Mujāhid produced Qur'ānic codices based on the seven canonical readings belonging to important *qurrā'* of the eighth century. His views, set forth in a book called *Kitāb al-Sab'a*,[53] were adopted by the Abbasid state and made official in the year A.H. 322/A.D. 934. Ibn Muqla was directly involved in the creation and canonization of these Qur'ānic recensions and even in the suppression of the recensions of the two variant readers, Ibn Miksam and Ibn Shanabūdh.[54] Especially noteworthy is the persecution by Ibn Mujāhid and

Ibn Muqla of Ibn Shanabūdh, who had persisted in teaching the Qur'ān of Ibn Mas'ūd. He was brought to trial before a court presided over by the vizier Ibn Muqla, where, after he had been flogged, he completely disavowed his previous position and signed a document stating that in the future he would adhere to the 'Uthmanic text.[55]

This act of al-Muqtadir and his vizier Ibn Muqla was possibly politically motivated. The caliphate and orthodox Islam were at the time under attack from many different sides by heterodox groups of various Shī'ī persuasions. Closest to Baghdad were the Qarāmiṭa, who had occupied Basra and Kufa during the reign of al-Muqtadir and even threatened Baghdad several times. Farther away, but posing a more serious threat to the orthodox caliphate, were the Fatimids, who had conquered central North Africa and Sicily in the first quarter of the tenth century and were pushing eastward. In the face of these overwhelming threats, the caliphate could resort to one of the very few weapons it had left—its nominal position as the safeguard of the Islamic community and enforcer of the correct religion. Establishing canonical recensions of the Qur'ān and creating a new, unambiguous script for these standard versions were acts in keeping with that role.

Even locally, the political implications of this Qur'ānic reform were quite remarkable, for in essence the Abbasid state used trusted members of the administration to try, judge, and punish Qur'ānic scholars who were deemed divergent from their views. Although they were state functionaries with no particular claim to religious knowledge, Ibn Muqla and his cohorts were placed in a position to enforce a particular religious dogma and to punish those who persisted in departing from it. This is a curious situation, though not the first time that the Abbasid state had resorted to such repressive measures: the *miḥna* of Ibn Ḥanbal presents a similar, though ideologically opposite, case.[56] In effect, the trials ordered by al-Muqtadir and conducted by Ibn Muqla demoted traditional Qur'ānic readers and promoted a state version of the Qur'ān that was copied by men of the administration. The fact that the calligraphers of the Kufic Qur'ān were probably drawn from *'ulamā'* circles may have contributed to the ultimate supplantation of their style and manner of writing by the newly canonized calligraphic modes.

Thus, Ibn Muqla was both the calligrapher who created a new calligraphic system that was eventually applied to the Qur'ān and the vizier who enforced the caliphal order to establish a body of canonical Qur'ānic readings. The two roles are undoubtedly related: the adoption of *al-khaṭṭ al-mansūb* for copying the Qur'ān was inspired by the canonization of the text of the Qur'ān. The new script, with its improved orthography and the correct numeration, would have left no doubt in the mind of Muslims that they were reading one of the new orthodox recensions, certainly not a Qur'ān with an aberrant reading. The canonization of the text is made clear and visible by the new canonical script, and the two processes conjoin to reaffirm the absolute control of the content and the form of the Sacred Book by the Abbasid state.

Control is therefore essential to the creation of proportional writing and its application to the Qur'ān: it brought to an end three centuries of Kufic writing. Although the exact processes by which the transfer of scripts from the secular to the religious domain remains incompletely known, the highlights are fairly clear. Three main processes were at work: the reform of scribal writing; the canonization of the Qur'ānic text; and the application of proportioned writing to the Qur'ān. Linked together by webs of power, these processes led to the transformation of the visual form of the Qur'ān. Although little discussed by most modern writers, this was perhaps the most significant artistic innovation of the middle Abbasid state.

Ibn al-Bawwāb (d. 1022)

The second most important stage in the reformation of Qur'ānic calligraphy took place under Ibn al-Bawwāb. All the sources agree that Ibn al-Bawwāb followed the method of Ibn Muqla but further improved it by making the script clearer, more cursive, and more elegant. The thirteenth-century historian Ibn Khallikān said, "Ibn al-Bawwāb revised and refined [the method of Ibn Muqla] and vested it with elegance and splendor."[57] Ibn Kathīr, the fourteenth-century Damascene historian, added that "[Ibn al-Bawwāb's] writing is clearer in form than Ibn Muqla's," and that in the author's time, "all people in all climes follow his method except few."[58]

Only one small Qur'ān has been securely attributed to Ibn al-Bawwāb—the famous copy at the Chester Beatty Library (1431), dated A.H. 391/A.D. 1000–1001 (figs. 12–15).[59] This is the earliest known cursive Qur'ān and undoubtedly one of the first made, since Ibn al-Bawwāb was the first to write Qur'āns in fully cursive scripts. Written on brownish paper in a clear and compact *naskh*, this manuscript is rather easy to belittle: it has neither the majesty and mystery of early Kufic folios nor the grandeur and sumptuousness of later cursive Qur'āns. But it is precisely because it looks so familiar and legibile to the contemporary reader that this Qur'ānic manuscript is in fact so original. In effect, this copy makes a clear and final break with the majestic but ambiguous script of the first three Islamic centuries, replacing it with a robustly cursive and perfectly legible script that survives today.

The two scripts represented in this manuscript—*naskh* in the text and *thuluth* in the opening folios and *sūra* headings—enjoyed great success in subsequent centuries and were imitated by numerous calligraphers. The renowned *naskh* of Ibn al-Bawwāb was actively imitated until near the end of the twelfth century, recalling the wide appeal of Ibn Muqla's calligraphic method.[60] As with Ibn Muqla, the manuscripts closest in date to Ibn al-Bawwāb (before 1100) adhere the most closely to his hand, while those from the succeeding century begin to diverge.

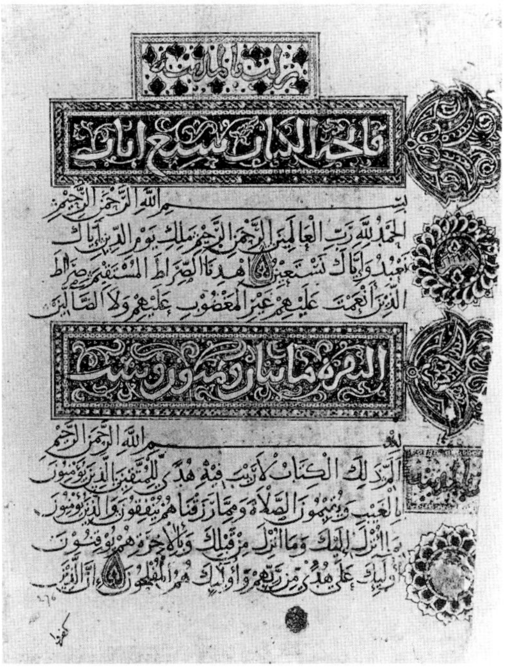

12 Baghdad, Qur'ān of Ibn al-Bawwāb, A.H. 391/A.D. 1000–1001. Signed 'Alī ibn Hilāl Ibn al-Bawwāb. Dublin, The Chester Beatty Library, 1431, fol. 9b.

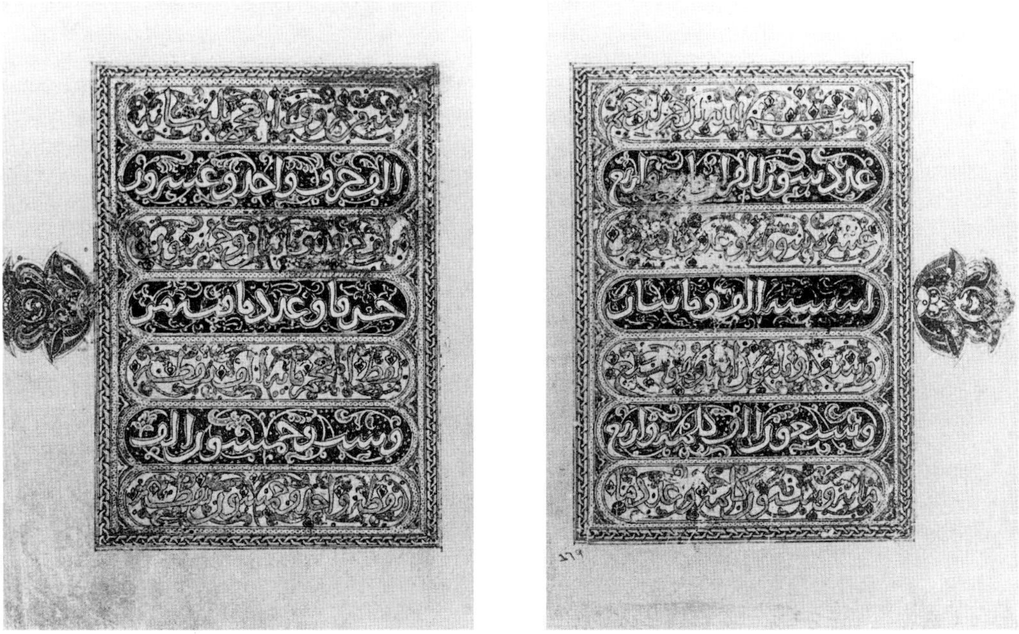

13 Baghdad, Qur'ān of Ibn al-Bawwāb, A.H. 391/A.D. 1000–1001. Verse count. Dublin, The Chester Beatty Library, 1431, fols. 6b and 7a.

14 Baghdad, Qur'ān of Ibn al-Bawwāb, A.H. 391/A.D. 1000–1001. Dublin, The Chester Beatty Library, 1431, fols. 7b and 8a.

15 Qur'ān of Ibn al-Bawwāb, Geometric finispieces. Dublin, The Chester Beatty Library, 1431, fol. 285a.

The *thuluth* used in the statistical pages and the *sūra* headings of the Qur'ān of Ibn al-Bawwāb is no less remarkable than the *naskh* used in the text (figs. 13 and 14). Despite its early date, it shows a number of refinements that remained with Qur'ānic calligraphy for nearly two centuries and which even influence monumental writing. The script is of a type called *thuluth-ash'ar*, appearing here as a fully cursive script, thinly outlined in gold. Although somewhat densely written, this script is especially noteworthy for its clarity and legibility, achieved in part by its totally explicit letter forms and by delicate variations in the thickness of its lines. Perhaps its most distinctive feature is that of interconnection: normally unconnected letters and even independent words are connected smoothly to one another with thin sinuous extensions.

The *thuluth* of Ibn al-Bawwāb, including its idiosyncratic features, was copied by many later Qur'ānic calligraphers and by calligraphers working on architectural monuments.[61] As with Ibn Muqla, Ibn al-Bawwāb's impact was mainly felt in the lands east of Baghdad, although at least one Qur'ān manuscript from North Africa, datable to the late eleventh century, copies his *thuluth* in its *sūra* titles.[62] But despite the great renown of Ibn Muqla and Ibn al-Bawwāb and their immediate influence in the eastern Islamic world, they had virtually no impact on Egypt. No semi-Kufic or early cursive Qur'ān manuscripts are known to have been produced in Fatimid Egypt; the vast majority were in fact made in Iraq and Iran, with Baghdad occupying a position of honor. Geography may have played a role: Baghdad, the center of this calligraphic transformation was, in the period under consideration, better connected with Iran than with Egypt. But the absence of any "reformed" Qur'ān manuscripts from Egypt until the beginning of the thirteenth century must have another explanation, to which I shall return.

It is fairly simple to observe the impact of geometric regularization in the scripts influenced by Ibn Muqla but somewhat more demanding to discern it in the hand of Ibn al-Bawwāb. A clear difference exists between the visible geometry of the semi-Kufic script and the integrated geometry of the proportioned script of Ibn al-Bawwāb, often described as a script without any visible external edges (*allā turā min al-khārij zawāyāhu*).[63] In other words, the rigorous geometric structure of letter forms developed by Ibn Muqla has been assimilated within the new sinuous script. This assimilated geometry pervades a variety of artistic forms in the eleventh century, including geometric strapwork and *muqarnas*. And it can hardly be accidental that these calligraphic and architectural changes occur simultaneously and within the same geographic regions, as I shall demonstrate in the next chapter.[64]

Interestingly, the surviving Qur'ān manuscript of Ibn al-Bawwāb itself contains two double folios with highly developed geometric designs. The full-page illuminations consist of boldly drawn intersecting circles that enclose vegetal designs and other geometric patterns (fig. 15). The other two folios consist of a repeating pattern of octagons that include within them the recension and the verse count of this particular Qur'ān (fig. 13). The overall composition betrays some similarities with much earlier Byzantine manuscripts, in which the polygons enclose figural images rather than words. But in fact these geometric patterns, which are more fully developed in later manuscripts (fig. 16), are much more complex than the Byzantine designs and even contemporary architectural patterns. It is therefore possible to suggest that such interlaced patterns made their first appearance in Qur'ānic illuminations before being transmitted to architectural ornament.[65]

Between about 930 and the first decades of the eleventh century, Qur'ānic calligraphy therefore underwent two decisive changes that completely transformed the physical appearance of the Qur'ān, both as a whole and in detail. The first change led to the creation of a paper Qur'ān written in a crisp, sometimes rigid, script with full diacritical marks, while the second resulted in a variety of fully cursive Qur'āns which have remained relatively unchanged until recently. Palaeographic and artistic details aside, what really distinguishes these Qur'āns from the earlier Kufic ones is legibility. Semi-Kufic Qur'āns are, with the exception of some ornate examples, reasonably legible, while the fully cursive ones can be easily read by any literate person.

Whereas we have been able to link the calligraphic reforms of Ibn Muqla with the politics of the Abbasid state and the canonization of Qur'ānic recensions, the situation is quite different with Ibn al-Bawwāb. This "son of the porter" was evidently a man of humble origins who never occupied an esteemed post under the Abbasids; his highest position seems to have been keeper of the Buyid library in Shiraz. Indeed, his connection with the Buyids has led at least one writer to conclude that "Ibn al-Bawwāb shared the Shī'ite persuasion of his patrons, the Buwayhids."[66] There is, however, absolutely no possibility that Ibn al-Bawwāb was Shī'ite, since his biography in Ibn Khallīkān states that "he died in Baghdad and was buried next to the Imām Aḥmad ibn Ḥanbal."[67] He was, therefore, most likely a Ḥanbalite, and as such, theologically opposed to Shī'ism and a partisan of the Abbasid caliphate.

Given this perspective, is it also possible to connect the calligraphic reform of Ibn al-Bawwāb with the religious politics of the Abbasid state? By the year 1000, when this Qur'ān was produced, most of the Islamic world, including the caliphate itself, was controlled by Shī'ite dynasties. The Fatimids had even proclaimed a Shī'ite counter-caliphate centered in Cairo and were actively agitating for the overthrow of the Abbasids. The resistance offered by the Abbasids, at first feeble, gathered strength during the caliphate of al-Qādir (991–1031), who took advantage of the weakened Buyids to reclaim some of his former authority as the safeguard of the Sunni community. In 1011, he issued a manifesto condemning Fatimid doctrine, denigrating their genealogy, and declaring the Ismā'īlī Fatimids to be among the enemies of Islam.[68] In 1017, al-Qādir attempted—for the first time since the ninth-century caliphate of al-Ma'mūn—to promulgate an official theology that condemned all opposing

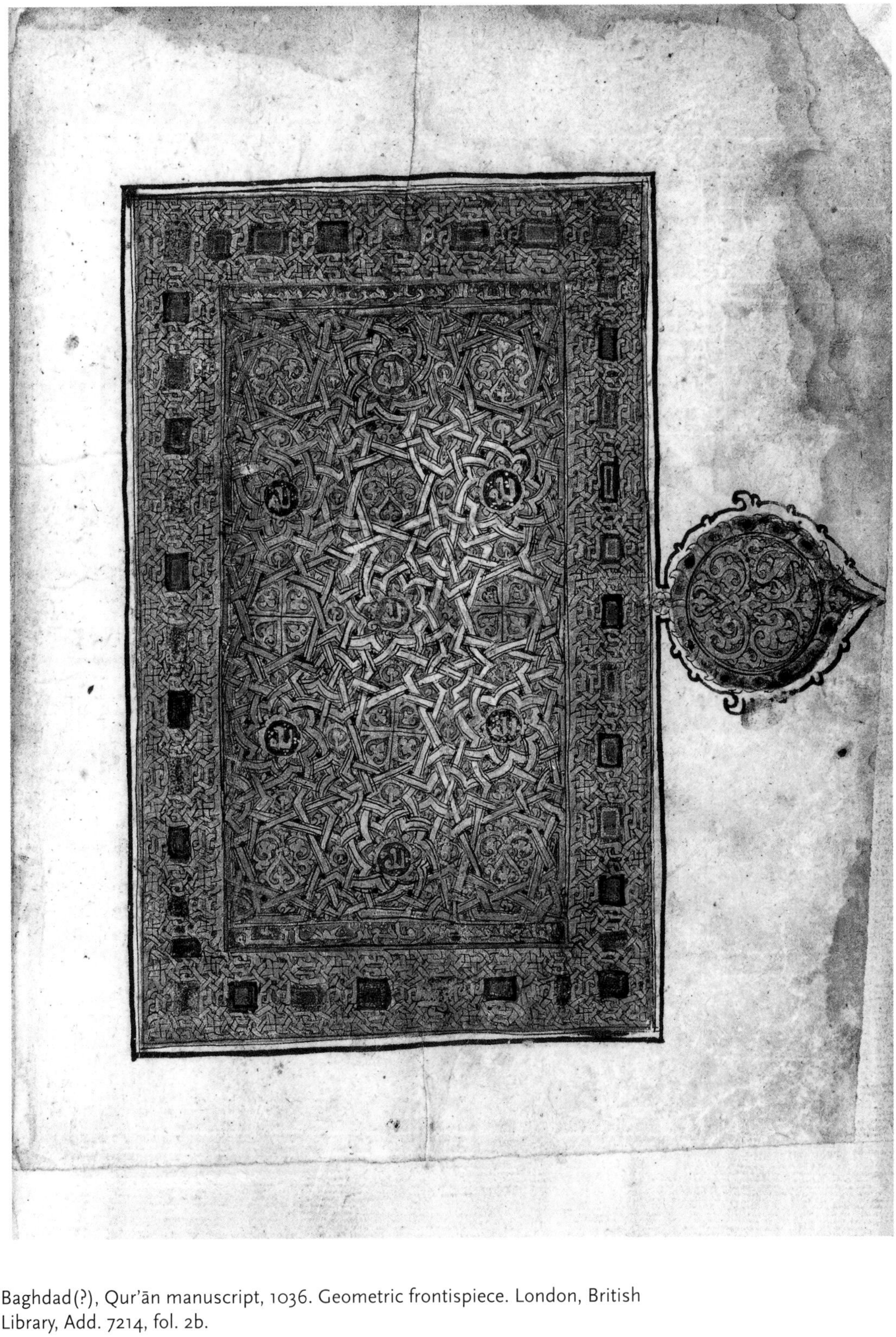

16 Baghdad(?), Qur'ān manuscript, 1036. Geometric frontispiece. London, British Library, Add. 7214, fol. 2b.

doctrines. The so-called *al-Risāla al-Qādiriyya* (Epistle of al-Qādir) took aim primarily at the Mu'tazilī Shī'ites but also numbered much more moderate groups among its enemies. It forbade *kalām* and all other forms of theological argumentation and interpretation. It even mandated the imprisonment, exile, and execution of all those jurists and rulers who persisted in such unorthodox practices.[69]

The cornerstone of the the Epistle of al-Qādir, as explicated by the caliph's chief apologist al-Bāqillānī, concerned the nature of the Qur'ān. First, it was not created in time, as the Mu'tazilīs and other rationalists believed, but simply recorded the eternal words of God.[70] Second, it was uncreated in whatever form it existed: *maktūb* (written), *maḥfūẓ* (memorized), *matluw* (recited), or *masmū'* (heard). It had only one meaning, not the two—a surface meaning (*ẓāhir*) and a deeper reading (*bāṭin*)—that the Mu'tazilīs and Isma'īlīs maintained. Third, the Qur'ān of Ibn Mas'ud, which was used by the Fatimids, constituted an unacceptable alteration of the Qur'ānic text.[71] The first two tenets were related, for a Qur'ān that was created in time can be interpreted with greater freedom than one that is, like God, eternal. And a Qur'ān with two levels of meaning must be interpreted by those who know for those who do not. Conversely, an eternal Qur'ān with a clearly manifest truth cannot be further interpreted, and therefore one had to accept the traditional exigesis presented by the jurists in the first three centuries of Islam. Therein lies the political importance of *al-Risāla al-Qādiriyya*. By closing the door to interpretation after the first three centuries of Islam, and by insisting on the incorrectness of the recension of Ibn Mas'ud, it undermined the religious foundations of the Fatimid and Buyid states and affirmed the legitimacy of the Abbasid caliphate.

The Qur'ān of Ibn al-Bawwāb therefore represents the creation of a perfectly cursive and easily legible script suitable for expressing the clear and explicit nature of the Word of God. Although ultimately based on the script of Ibn Muqla, the uncompromising clarity of the new script must be seen as a direct reflection of the Qādirī creed's insistence on the single and apparent truth in the Qur'ān. Conversely, the reformed Qur'ān was intended to challenge the authority of the earlier Kufic Qur'āns, whose use continued in Fatimid Egypt until the establishment of the Ayyubid dynasty in the late twelfth century.

Very few Fatimid Qur'āns of any description are known, and to my knowledge, only the so-called Blue Qur'ān has been attributed with any degree of authority to the early Fatimid period in North Africa (fig. 17).[72] Scholars have often commented on the archaizing nature of the script, whose unvocalized and undotted letters seem to recall Qur'āns of the previous (ninth) century.[73] In fact, the ambiguity of the script is perhaps further enhanced in this manuscript by the fact that it is written in gold over dark blue. The gold shimmers and seems to flow over the receding blue background, creating an evanescent

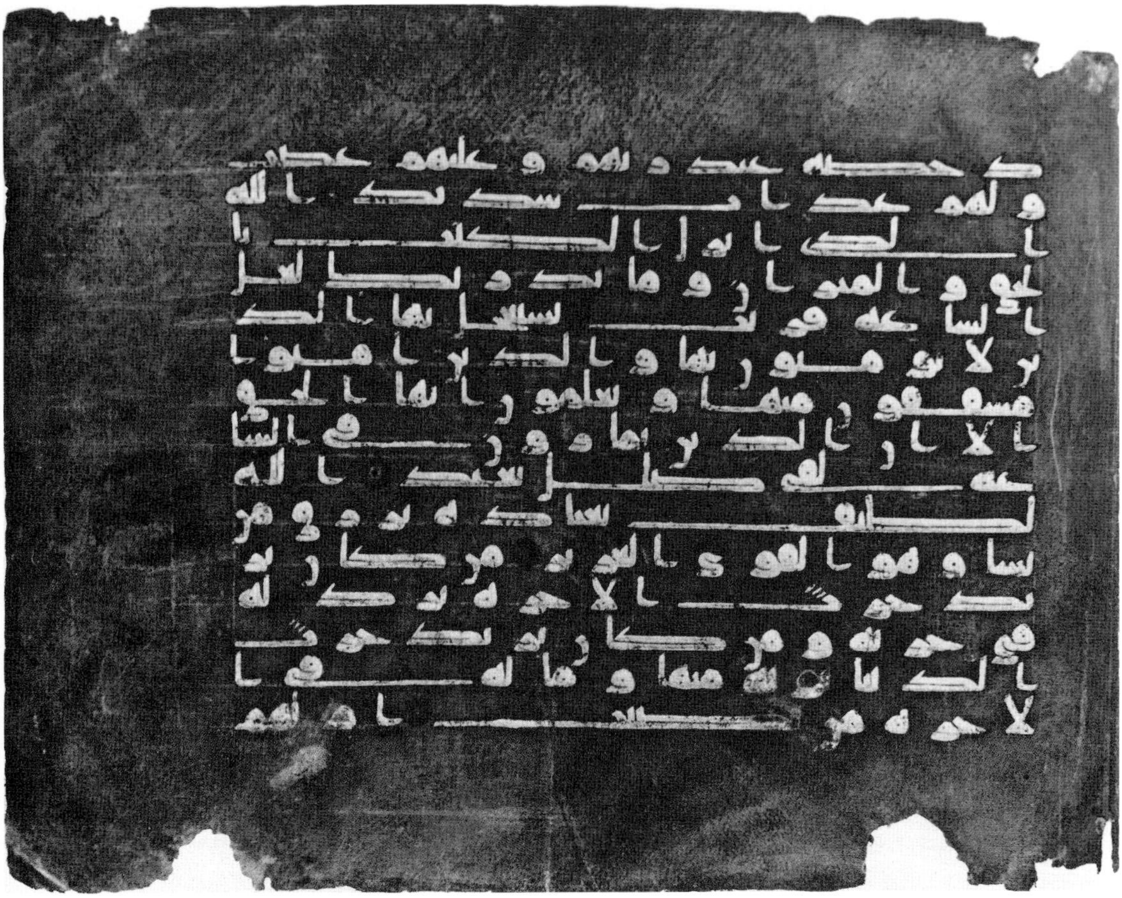

17 North Africa, page from the "Blue Qur'ān," gold on blue parchment. 10th century. Chapter XLII, verses 10–23. Private collection.

effect that seems to affirm the Mu'tazilī belief in the created and mysterious nature of the Word of God. It is difficult to imagine a greater contrast than that between the Blue Qur'ān and the Qur'ān of Ibn al-Bawwāb.

The process described above had important implications for the calligraphers and calligraphy of succeeding centuries. With respect to the calligraphers, it seems clear that the fame enjoyed by Ibn Muqla and Ibn al-Bawwāb in their time and later was attributable not simply to their artistic merit and creative innovations but to the association of their names and creations with the caliphs and princes for whom they worked. They became rubrics of recognition: later calligraphers imitated their style and even forgers attributed works to their names. They initiated the genealogy of calligraphers with whom I began this chapter, but they were not the lone actors that the sources describe them to be. They were rather part of an intricate social, political, and theological construction that shaped their careers and gave meaning to their creative efforts.

As for the new calligraphic style, its popularity, even universality, not long after its creation has clearly diminished its original meanings and symbolic associations. Yet at the time of its inception and particularly its adoption throughout the Islamic world, which had only recently become Sunni, it literally reflected the triumph of a theological view and all its political ramifications. The actual image—not just the content—of the Word became the symbol of the most important principle of the Sunni revival, a movement that redefined the course of medieval Islam.

3

The Public Text

It might be tempting, in the following discussion of the transformation of monumental inscriptions, to follow the basic structure and method of the preceding chapter. After all, the changes in Qur'ānic and monumental writing were nearly congruent in their geographic extent and, though not entirely synchronous, were closely linked in their chronological development. Both transformations were also ultimately motivated by one predominant concern: making the word of God or the statement of a dynasty unambiguous and intelligible to all literate people. Theologically, this preoccupation with clarity and legibility was shown in the previous chapter to be linked with contemporary ideas about the nature of the Qur'ān. Politically, the textual and visual canonization of the Qur'ān proclaimed and symbolized the emergent movement of the Sunni revival, a movement that sought to reaffirm the legitimacy of the Abbasid caliphate and the traditionalist basis of Islamic thought while opposing and undermining contrary beliefs and political systems, in particular those of the Fatimids.

But a few problems and anomalies must be addressed before we directly apply the methods and extend the conclusions of the previous chapter to the following discussion. First, the transformation in monumental writing postdated the Qur'ānic one by about a century, in effect beginning in the second half of the eleventh century. Second, Ibn Muqla's reform of Qur'ānic calligraphy, despite its unparalleled importance, had virtually no impact on monumental calligraphy. Conversely, the scripts of Ibn al-Bawwāb, in particular his *thuluth*, greatly influenced the development of monumental calligraphy for several centuries to come. Third, there are scarcely any texts relevant to the makers and the making of monumental inscriptions, in contrast to the relative abundance of such texts for scribal and Qur'ānic calligraphy.[1] Finally, although public inscriptions often contain Qur'ānic passages, they are rarely exclusively Qur'ānic but more commonly dynastic and historical in content.

But perhaps the most telling differences between Qur'ānic and monumental calligraphy concerns their private versus public natures. Whereas luxurious Qur'ān manuscripts were private possessions with a fairly limited audience and circulation, monumental inscriptions were public and official statements that proclaimed the contemporary concerns of the theocratic dynasties that had commissioned them.[2] In a largely aniconic artistic culture, these public inscriptions were by necessity one of the primary visual means of political and religious expression and one of the few ways for a dynasty to distinguish its reign from that of its predecessor. While most dynasties also resorted to other, more symbolic means of political expression, such as gates, minarets, domes, or even sculpture, public inscriptions remained throughout medieval Islam the chief means for transmitting political and religious messages and for portraying these messages in a dynastically distinctive manner.

The dual nature of calligraphic writing—informative and symbolic, denotive and connotive—has been alluded to in the discussion of Qur'ānic calligraphy, but it acquires greater focus and significance in the study of public inscriptions.[3] The greater prominence of these inscriptions and their expanded audience turned some of them into focal points within the city and possibly into objects for group discussion. It follows that their visuality and receptivity should be essential to their understanding and interpretation, and that their degree of complexity and intelligibility should be engaged instead of being simply resolved into a didactic reading. To ignore the formal complexities of public texts, or to dismiss them, as Ettinghausen does, as "[hindrances to] verbal communication in the modern sense,"[4] is to deprive this art form of its most affective and populist feature.

The case for a semiotic interpretation of calligraphic writing is also not aided by studies that insist on "the immanent and transcendent nature of the Word of God"[5] regardless of the form it may acquire, nor even by others that resort to numerology and "letter symbolism" in order to explain the complexity and ambiguity of some calligraphic styles.[6] More likely, the reception of such inscriptions was specific to content and sensitive to form without necessarily being esoteric and occult. Learned patricians, who were usually quite proficient in calligraphy,[7] were probably able to read the text and appreciate its artistic merit; common people, on the other hand, had only a general idea about the content and form of monumental inscriptions. In other words, aesthetic values such as beauty, skill, complexity, and clarity were inextricably linked with questions of status and power, so that the ability to build, own, or fully appreciate objects or monuments with complex inscriptions became a criterion for belonging to a social or political elite.[8]

Questions of complexity and legibility are therefore central to understanding the ontological factors behind the transformation of public inscriptions in the eleventh and twelfth centuries, from the ambiguous Kufic to the clear cursive scripts. In order to provide a context and a point of contrast for this transformation, I begin by reviewing the problem of the creation of the floriated Kufic script under the Fatimids, suggesting in the process some of the political and theological issues associated with its development. I next trace the subsequent development of cursive scripts from their vernacular origins in Iran to their definitive formulation in twelfth-century Syria, pointing out the role of Nūr al-Dīn in promoting this process. I then follow the spread of highly standardized cursive scripts in the twelfth century in Syria, Iraq, and elsewhere. Finally, I examine the entirely different course of development before the end of the twelfth century in Egypt, which provides an important point of contrast and leads to an interpretation.

Floriated Kufic

Of all the varieties of monumental Kufic, floriated Kufic is perhaps the most elegant, combining as it does angular characters with curvilinear plant forms. In its fully developed form, exemplified by the Fatimid and north Syrian inscriptions, floriated Kufic may be considered the peak of achievement in early Arabic epigraphy. The beauty and inherent complexity of the script have attracted considerable attention that has focused mainly on its origin, development, and deciphering.[9] Most scholars now concur that, despite early sporadic developments, the consistent use of fully formed, floriated Kufic began only in the second half of the tenth century, specifically in the first Fatimid inscriptions of the mosque al-Azhar (A.H. 361/A.D. 972; fig. 18a).[10]

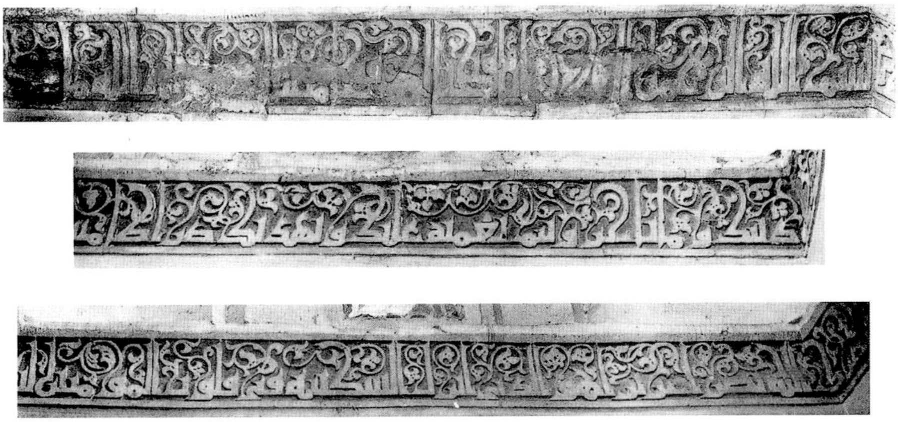

18a Cairo, Mosque al-Azhar, A.H. 361/A.D. 972. Inscriptions in the *maqsūra* (after Flury, *Die Ornamente der Hakim und Ashar*, pl. IV).

These inscriptions and the succeeding ones at the mosque al-Ḥākim (before A.H. 403/A.D. 1013) differ completely from earlier Kufic inscriptions. They introduce an entirely transformed script in which all characters sprout floral tendrils that form an organic unit with letter forms while serving as a decorative filler for the surrounding space (fig. 18b).[11] The ambiguities thus created between text and ornament, foreground and background, are further enhanced by the curvatures, counter-curvatures, knots, and indentations internal to the characters, as described by Sourdel-Thomine.[12] A splendid example of this kind of virtuosity can be seen in the cenotaph of Fātima at the Bab Ṣaghīr cemetery in Damascus, dated A.H. 439/A.D. 1037, in which one scholar has noted the existence of ten different types of the *lām-alif* character (fig. 18c).[13]

18b Cairo, mosque al-Ḥākim. Inscription on the casing of northwest minaret. A.H. 403/A.D. 1001.

18c Damascus, cenotaph of Fāṭima. Inscription on southern face, A.H. 439/A.D. 1047 (redrawn after Moaz and Ory, *Inscriptions arabes de Damas*, pl. ivb).

Following its development under the Fatimids, in the eleventh century floriated Kufic spread outside of Egypt to regions controlled by the Fatimids or subject to their propaganda and influence, including Palestine, Syria, western Iran, and southern Anatolia (fig. 18d).[14] What were the motives for the creation of this script, and what did the newly privileged script mean within the context of early Fatimid propaganda? The creation of a new public form of expression was probably intended to reaffirm the claims to legitimacy of this theocratic state, which had been embroiled from the start in political and sectarian controversy, while also distinguishing it from earlier dynasties. More specifi-

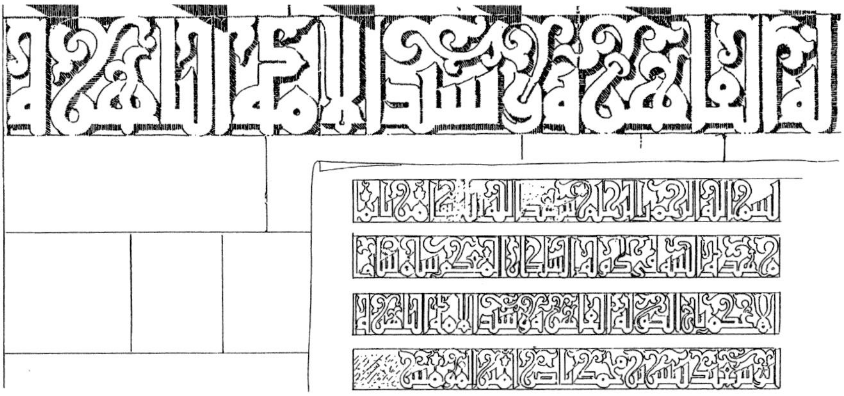

18[d] Aleppo, minaret of the Great Mosque. Uppermost inscription, A.H. 483/A.D. 1090 (Herzfeld, *Inscriptions et monuments d'Alep*, 2: pl LIII).

cally, the deliberate ambiguity of the script and the considerable variation in its letter forms seem to resonate with one of the fundamental tenets of the Ismā'īli doctrine—the distinction between the exterior, or exoteric (*ẓāhir*), and the inward, or esoteric (*bāṭin*), aspects of religion.[15] Specifically, as Madelung observes, "the *ẓāhir* consists in the apparent, generally accepted meaning of the revealed scriptures and in the religious law laid down in them," changing as such with each prophet. The *bāṭin*, on the other hand, "consists in the truths (*ḥaqā'iq*) concealed in the scriptures and laws which are unchangeable and are made apparent from them by the *ta'wīl*, interpretation, which is often of cabalistic nature relying on the mystical significance of letters and numbers."[16] This duality of meaning and the valorization of *bāṭin* over *ẓāhir* was to be challenged by the transformed scripts of the eleventh and twelfth centuries.

Precursors to the Transformation (1030–1150)

Though predominant during the eleventh and first quarter of the twelfth century, floriated Kufic was already being challenged in public inscriptions as early as the first half of the eleventh century. Appearing first in the coinage of the Ghaznavids in eastern Iran,[17] and subsequently in their public inscriptions, monumental cursive writing coexisted with its Kufic counterpart for more than a century. This occurrence is exemplified by a series of cenotaphs of Ghaznavid rulers and princes—beginning with that of Sultan Maḥmūd ibn Sebuktekin (998–1030) himself—that combine floriated Kufic with a perfectly cursive script, often written on a bed of arabesque (fig. 19b).[18] This combination of scripts continues in the epigraphy of the Great Seljuqs, becoming commonplace by the early twelfth century for funerary as well as architectural monuments. Perhaps the finest illustration of this calligraphic virtuosity can be seen in a group of gravestones from western Iran or the Jazīra with different varieties of cursive and Kufic scripts.[19]

19[a] Thuluth according to the hand of Ibn al-Bawwāb, 1000–1001 (redrawn from manuscript CBL 1431).

19[b] Ghazna, fragment of inscription belonging to Abu'l-Muẓaffar Ibrāhīm (1059–1099) (redrawn after Flury, "Le Décor épigraphique ... Ghazna," pl. XIII/1).

19[c] Isfahan, Masjid-i Jāmī, fragment of inscription on north face of south dome, A.H. 478/ A.D. 1086–88 (after Grabar, *The Great Mosque of Isfahan*, fig. 24).

What was the source of this cursive script, which we have so far seen in the epigraphy of the Ghaznavids and the Great Seljuqs? In the absence of any textual evidence to shed light on this development, the specimens themselves must be examined for what they might reveal about their own history. The script of these early examples is a rather squat, highly cursive, and largely unvocalized *thuluth* resting on a bed of arabesque.[20] Though quite legible, it lacks some of the refinements seen in fully developed *thuluth*, such as the pointing of the uprights and the opening of knotted letters. These "deficiencies" could simply be attributed to inexperience in a new style, were it not for the resemblance of this script in sum and in detail to the *thuluth* of Ibn al-

19[d] Marrakesh, Qubbat al-Barūdiyyīn, 1117. Inscription at springing of dome (after Meunié, *Nouvelles Recherches*, fig. 28).

19e Tlemcen (Algeria), Great Mosque. Inscription at springing of dome, A.H. 530/A.D. 1135 (from Marçais, *L'Architecture musulmane d'occident*, fig. 150).

Bawwāb, as seen in the verse counts and chapter headings of his unique manuscript (cf. figs. 19a and 19b).[21] Indeed, this early monumental cursive script emulates an even more specific feature of the style of the great master, namely interconnection; that is, the tendency to connect normally independent characters by a thin sinuous line.

This hallmark feature of the master's script was slavishly copied by many of his students and followers.[22] Its use in the earliest cursive official inscriptions suggests close affinities between Qur'ānic and monumental writing and points to the pivotal importance of the hand of Ibn al-Bawwāb. The adoption of Ibn al-Bawwāb's calligraphic hand for monumental inscriptions of the eastern Islamic world accords perfectly with the widespread influence of his style in the eleventh and twelfth centuries in the lands east of Baghdad.[23] We may therefore conclude that the peculiarities of early monumental cursive inscriptions stemmed less from their underdevelopment than from their slavish adherence to the *thuluth* of Ibn al-Bawwāb, a hand better suited to paper calligraphy.

Why, then, did the Ghaznavids and the Great Seljuqs (fig. 19c) adopt this idiosyncratic hand for some of their public inscriptions? The answer lies partly in politics and partly in theology: the Ghaznavids were staunch Sunnis, loyal supporters of the caliphate, and bitter opponents of its archenemy the Fatimids, who under the al-Ḥakim (996–1021) were ever more active in their Ismā'īlī propaganda. Maḥmūd of Ghazna took every opportunity to recognize and court the favor of his exact contemporary, the caliph al-Qādir (991–1031), receiving in return various honorific charters (*manshūr*), honorific titles, and robes of honor (*khil'a*).[24] It seems, therefore, that the adoption of the calligraphic style of Ibn al-Bawwāb for Ghaznavid and Seljuq monumental inscriptions was an act of symbolic homage to the caliphate and an endorsement of their Sunni views regarding the explicit nature of the word of God.

Nūr al-Dīn (1146–1174)

Whereas in the east the change in public inscriptions from floriated Kufic to cursive was slow and fluctuating, in Syria it was implemented in only a few years. [25] Van Berchem has noted that the change from angular to cursive scripts in Syria was as sudden as it was rapid, having been put into effect within just a few years at the order of Nūr al-Dīn as a "mésure intentionnelle pour la realisation d'un vaste plan, partie d'un reforme."[26] Herzfeld stated the matter even more emphatically by placing this transformation "at a point almost

exactly defined by the year 548 [1153]," when Nūr al-Dīn abandoned the form and content of earlier Seljuq protocols and embraced the changes produced by "the deep movement of the Sunnite reaction."[27] Most recently these observations have been reiterated by Sourdel-Thomine, who concluded that "Nūr al-Dīn ordered the adoption of the cursive script in official inscriptions, to the detriment of the angular script, which without disappearing completely, was reduced to repetitions of ancient types."[28]

Despite the plausibility, even overall veracity, of these conclusions, two important problems complicate the chronological sequence of inscriptions in Syria from the late eleventh to the middle of the twelfth century. First, one early cursive inscription does exist in Syria, in the form of a frieze that appears on the minaret of the Great Mosque of Aleppo, dated A.H. 483/A.D. 1090. Curiously, while all four other inscriptional bands on the minaret are written in floriated Kufic of the highest quality, the cursive inscription is quite mediocre by comparison, displaying perhaps the mason's lack of experience in the new style. Like other contemporary Seljuq inscriptions, it is written on a bed of arabesque and contains no dots or vowel marks. In the absence of a better explanation, I propose that the minaret follows the epigraphic formulas long practiced under the Great Seljuqs, who were ultimately the patrons of this minaret.[29]

The second problem is that Nūr al-Dīn did not use the new cursive style from the very beginning of his reign. In fact, his earliest known inscription at the *mashhad* al-Dikka in Aleppo, dated 1146, is written in a rather simple Kufic style that closely resembles his father's (Zangī) inscription of 1128 on the same building.[30] The poor quality of the inscription, its derivative style and titulary, and the fact that it commemorated a building act on a Shi'ite monument are all symptomatic of the shaky and indefinite start of Nūr al-Dīn's career.[31] His very next dated inscription (A.H. Shawwāl 543/ A.D. February 1149) at the portal of the *madrasa* al-Ḥallāwiyya, however, is written in an excellent *thuluth* script that resembles late Seljuq *thuluth* but without the arabesque background (figs. 20a and b). It is a pleasing and legible style characterized by compactness, pointed uprights and generally open knots, and full use of diacritical and orthographic marks. The character forms are uniform in appearance and display a characteristic tapering in the thickness of the line, a feature already seen in the earliest Ghaznavid inscriptions and even earlier in the *thuluth* of Ibn al-Bawwāb.[32] Except that the cramped space forced the calligrapher to overlap some of the letters, the inscription is very easily legible.

This inscription, in effect, initiates the total transformation of monumental calligraphy for Syria and ultimately also for Egypt. With only two exceptions,[33] all the succeeding inscriptions from the period of Nūr al-Dīn and his Ayyūbid successors are written in the cursive *thuluth* script (fig. 21). We are led to inquire, therefore, what events in the early career of Nūr al-Dīn led him to embark on this fundamental transformation. Although later sources, written under the patronage of Nūr al-Dīn and the Ayyūbids, are deliberately vague about Nūr al-Dīn's early years, a close reading of one of the few preserved Shī'ite histories of the period, Ibn abī Ṭayyi', suggests that like his father, Nūr al-Dīn was initially far more tolerant of Shī'ism and quite ambivalent in the

a

b

20[a–b] Aleppo, *Madrasa* al-Ḥallāwiyya, A.H. 543/A.D. 1149. Inscriptions on the portal.

21 Aleppo, *Maqām* Ibrāhīm in the Citadel. Inscription of Ismā'īl (son of Nūr al-Dīn), A.H. 575/ A.D. 1180.

pursuit of Sunni orthodoxy.[34] His personal and public transformation was catalyzed by two main factors: early and somewhat unexpected successes against the Crusaders and improved links with the Abbasid caliphate. Between 1146 and 1149, Nūr al-Dīn was able to recapture the north Syrian city of Edessa, to aid in defeating the Second Crusade, and to deal a decisive defeat to the principality of Antioch. According to Gibb, "in the eyes of all Islam, [Nūr al-Dīn] had become the champion of the faith and he now consciously set himself to fulfill the duties of this role."[35]

The Abbasid caliph wasted no time in recognizing these victories by bestowing on Nūr al-Dīn various honorific titles, the most important of which was *al-mujāhid* (the fighter for the faith). This title appeared for the first time on the *madrasa* al-Ḥallāwiyya and subsequently became one of his most common epithets. But the caliphate had other concerns than the Crusades, namely, the restoration of Sunni orthodoxy all over the Islamic world, particularly in Egypt, where the Ismā'īlī Fatimids had long posed a political threat and theological challenge to the Abbasids.

The chief apologist for the Abbasid cause at the time was the powerful theologian and vizier Ibn Hubayra, whose call for the unification of Sunni Islam and destruction of the Fatimids found an immediate response in Nūr al-Dīn. The two are known to have corresponded about these matters, and it was at the vizier's urging that Nūr al-Dīn proceeded to wrest Egypt from the hands of the Fatimids in the name of the caliphate.[36] Thus, early triumphs against the Crusades, the machinations of Ibn Hubayra and the Abbasid caliphs, and undoubtedly a personal propensity toward orthodoxy and asceticism all motivated Nūr al-Dīn's pursuit of Sunnism, making him the primary force behind the Sunni revival.

Beginning as a theme subsidiary to the more pressing problem of the counter-Crusade, the revival of the *Sunnah* soon became the central motive of Nūr al-Dīn's policy, and it is therefore legitimate to view all his major acts through this traditionalist reaction. The calligraphic transformation was one of the most visible signs of this broad movement which had lain dormant in Syria during the turbulent decades of the first half of the twelfth century but was now promulgated by the Abbasid caliphs and Nūr al-Dīn. At its most basic, the use of cursive writing for public inscriptions declared, by virtue of its total difference from earlier public inscriptions, the end of the Fatimid epoch and the beginning of a new era. More specifically, the use of a script with demonstrable links to the Abbasid caliphate was intended to reinforce the legitimacy of Nūr al-Dīn's rule in Syria and in all other territory conquered in the name of the caliph. Finally, because it was legible and unambiguous, the new public writing shattered the cherished duality of meaning implicit in Fatimid inscriptions.

The Canonization of the Thuluth of Ibn al-Bawwāb: 1170–1260

By the time of Nūr al-Dīn's death in 1174, the monumental cursive script that he had mandated for Syria had become standard for all public inscriptions, not just in Syria but also in Upper Mesopotamia, Anatolia, North Africa, and Spain. Although it is unlikely that all these regions were following the example of Nūr al-Dīn, it is possible that some of them were, while others received their cultural cues directly from the Abbasid caliphate. Iran, where the change was gradual and intermittent at first, differed from this model of sudden transformation, but by the last quarter of the twelfth century, it had also switched over completely to cursive inscriptions. The only real exception was Fatimid Egypt, to which I will turn after surveying the situations in selected other regions.

Iraq

No early cursive monumental inscriptions have been preserved in Baghdad, which obscures the impact of Ibn Muqla and Ibn al-Bawwāb on their native city. The earliest preserved monumental inscriptions come from the period of the Caliph al-Nāṣir (1180–1225).[37] The situation is a little more encouraging in Mosul, where except for a handful of early-twelfth-century tombstones written in a crude cursive style, the earliest monumental cursive inscription is the one surrounding the inner frame of the *miḥrāb* of the mosque al-Nūrī, dated A.H. 543/A.D. 1148.[38] The inscription, which is written on a bed of arabesque, closely resembles Iranian Seljuq inscriptions of the late eleventh century (fig. 22a). The entire composition of this flat *miḥrāb*, with its friezes of floriated Kufic inscriptions framing an inner cursive inscription, is clearly modeled after

a

b

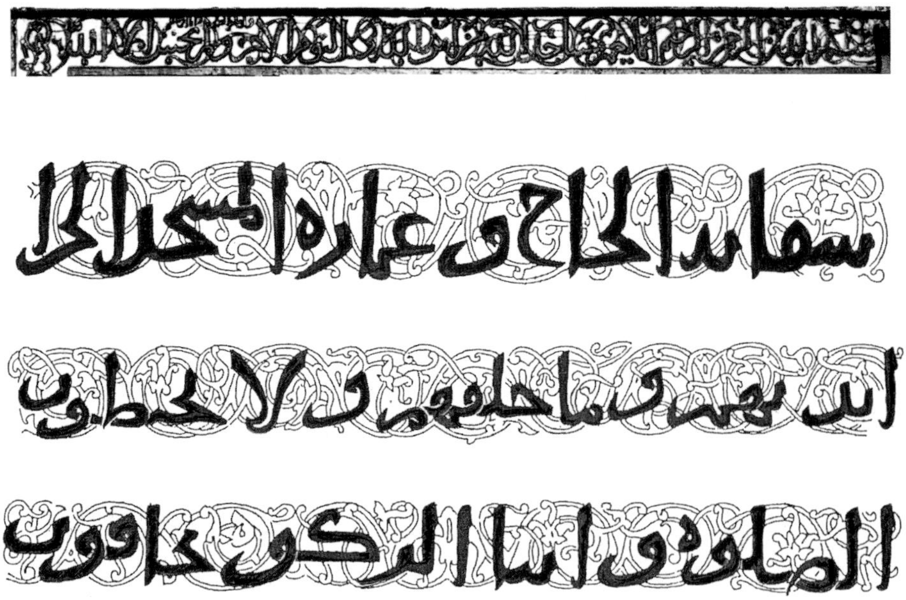

22a–b Mosul, Mosque al-Nūrī. *a. Miḥrāb*, A.H. 543/A.D. 1148, detail of cursive inscription. *b.* Inscriptions on capitals, 1170–72.

a Seljuq Iranian prototype. Interestingly, the *miḥrāb* is signed by a certain Muṣṭafa al-Baghdādī, attesting to the existence of carvers of stone inscriptions from Baghdad.

As in Syria, monumental cursive writing also seems to have been introduced en masse into Mosul under Nūr al-Dīn, who, though never its actual ruler, exercised considerable control over Mosul during the latter part of his reign.[39] The mosque that he founded there between 1170 and 1172 contains numerous inscriptions on the capitals of its massive piers (fig. 22b). Although they generally resemble Nurid inscriptions in Aleppo, these inscriptions still recall early Seljuq cursive inscriptions in their minimal use of dots and their arabesque backgrounds. Other inscriptions from this mosque, possibly dating from the Nurid phase, consist of long friezes in white marble inlaid with black marble.[40] These are somewhat closer to contemporary Aleppine inscriptions in their character form, their use of diacriticals, and their minimal background ornamentation.

Other than these twelfth-century inscriptions, the only pre-Mongol monumental inscriptions in Mosul are those decorating the various shrines erected during the reign of Badr al-Dīn Lu'lu' (1222–1259).[41] The portal to the mosque of the shrine of Imām 'Awn al-Dīn (A.H. 646/A.D. 1248) beautifully displays the great variety of cursive scripts used in Mosul in the few decades preceding the Mongol invasion (fig. 23). The uppermost frieze, serving the function of a cornice, is in monumental *thuluth* (or *thuluth jaliyy*), a large and slow-moving script with minimal overlapping of words and practically no interconnection.

23 Mosul, *mashhad* of Imām ʿAwn al-Dīn, A.H. 646/A.D. 1248. Portal to the *masjid*.

Another large script, rendered in white marble on bluish alabaster, presents the name and titles of Badr al-Dīn across the lintel. This highly attenuated script brings to mind the late Ayyubid inscriptions of Aleppo. The third, and for us most interesting, calligraphic style in this portal is represented by a long frieze that frames the portal on three sides. The inscription, which gives the fairly common Verse of the Throne, is written in a splendid compact *thuluth* style that recalls, even surpasses, the twelfth-century inscriptions in Aleppo.

With no fewer than twelve instances of interconnection, this inscription might be expected to sacrifice legibility for the sake of cursiveness and artistic nuance. Remarkably, however, it remains perfectly legible throughout, a feature that must be attributed to the excellence of its calligraphy and the unobtrusive nature of the interconnections, whose extreme thinness further enhances the tapering and interconnection of the letter forms. It is indeed astonishing that a calligraphic nuance first introduced in the late tenth century should still resonate in monumental writing two-and-a-half centuries later.

North Africa

In North Africa, including Sicily, the floriated Kufic script remained dominant until about the middle of the twelfth century, when it was challenged, both in coinage and on monuments, by cursive scripts.[42] Appearing initially in some Tunisian tombstones from the late eleventh and early twelfth centuries, the style is first seen in a monumental context late in the period of the Almoravids (1056–1147).[43] The earliest cursive monumental inscriptions in North Africa are the two friezes that encircle the bases of the Qubbat al-Bārūdiyyīn Marrakesh (datable 1117) (fig. 19d)[44] and the famous ribbed filigree dome of the Great Mosque of Tlemcen (Algeria), dated A.H. 530/A.D. 1135 (fig. 19e).[45] Both display a highly cursive script that resembles the Seljuq *thuluth* inscriptions found in Ghazna, Isfahan, Aleppo, and Mosul. Like them, these inscriptions also rest on a bed of arabesque, shun vocalization and orthographic marks, and display the characteristic tapering of letter forms.

A more extensive cycle of early cursive inscriptions is found farther west, at the mosque of al-Qarawiyyīn at Fez. These inscriptions belong to the major building phase of the Almoravids, when the entire axial nave of the mosque was rebuilt (1134–43) with a series of *muqarnas* vaults.[46] The cursive inscriptions coexist with many highly complex floriated Kufic inscriptions, resembling in this respect a group of Qur'ānic manuscripts written in the Maghribī script but utilizing the *thuluth* script of Ibn al-Bawwāb for their chapter headings.[47] Seemingly restricted to a medallion above the *miḥrāb* and to short friezes framing the cells of the two *muqarnas* vaults nearest to the *miḥrāb*, these inscriptions are nearly identical to the Tlemcen inscription, except that some of them are written on an unadorned background. The foundation inscription above the *miḥrāb* consists of four short lines of slightly more developed *thuluth* that attempts, though not very successfully, to maximize the feature of interconnection (fig. 24).

The overall crudeness of these inscriptions seems perfectly consistent with the newness of cursive writing in North Africa and with the apparent desire to follow closely an imported model with all its idiosyncrasies. This model was undoubtedly the new calligraphic style in the Abbasid capital, a style that had been formulated by Ibn al-Bawwāb and popularized by his many students. Copying an important symbol of the revived Abbasid caliphate was perfectly consistent with the Almoravids' strong links with the Abbasids, whom they recognized as the spiritual heads of Islam, and who in turn recognized them as rulers of al-Maghreb in the name of the caliph and Sunni Islam.[48] The Moroccan

24 Fez, mosque of al-Qarawiyyīn. Foundation inscriptions above the *miḥrāb*, A.H. 531/A.D. 1137 (redrawn after Terrasse, *La Mosquée d'al-Qaraouiyin*, pl. 51).

historian Abdallah Laroui refers to the Almoravids "as the western counterpart of the Seljuks of the east," both in terms of their political opposition to the Fatimids and their adoption of Ash'arism, the theology that exerted considerable influence on the dominant Maliki school in the first half of the eleventh century.[49] The numerous letters exchanged between Yūsuf ibn Tāshufīn or his son 'Ali and the various Abbasid caliphs attest to the Almoravids' veneration of the Abbasids, whose name was included on the coinage and pronounced during the Friday *khuṭba*.[50] The appropriation of this cultural symbol and its incorporation in the most important mosques of the Almoravids was therefore intended as a sign of homage to the Abbasids and as a means to enhance the legitimacy of the Almoravid state.

Fatimid Egypt

Van Berchem concluded that the inscriptions of the mosque of al-Ṣāliḥ Ṭalā'i', dated 555/1160, demonstrate that the Kufic script was used in historical inscriptions until the end of the Fatimid dynasty, when it was replaced by cursive scripts.[51] Commenting on this transformation, Creswell declared that "henceforth the beautiful decorated Kufic script, the glory and pride of Fāṭimid art, was to be used no more for historical inscriptions but employed solely for decorative bands of quotations from the Qur'ān, and that to an ever decreasing extent."[52] Despite relatively minor objections to these conclusions, they remain as sound today as they were a century ago.[53] Indeed, the earliest public cursive inscription in Cairo is Ayyubid: dated A.H. 575/A.D. 1179, it once belonged to a *madrasa* built by Saladin next to the shrine of Imām Shāfi'ī.[54] Although this inscription has disappeared, it is entirely appropriate that the earliest cursive inscription in Egypt should belong to the shrine of the most important theologian of Sunni Islam, one who was held in special regard by the Ayyubids.[55] The use of cursive inscriptions to commemorate the building of the shrine of Imām Shāfi'ī underlines the fundamental transformation of Egypt under the early Ayyubids.

Fortunately, another inscription from the period of Saladin still remains *in situ* in the Mudarraj Gate of the Cairo citadel (fig. 25). Although dated A.H. 579/A.D. 1183–84, one century after the Seljuq inscriptions in Isfahan and Aleppo and half a century after the Almoravid inscriptions in North Africa and those of Nūr al-Dīn in Syria, this inscription is astonishing in its crudeness and carelessness.[56] With a spindly line, inconsistent letter forms, and neither points nor vowel marks, the script displays none of the refinements that had long been established in cursive monumental calligraphy. This and other inscriptions from the time of Saladin reflect the inexperience of local calligraphers in the new calligraphic style. [57] Indeed, only in the latter part of the Ayyubid period did the quality of monumental cursive inscriptions approach that seen in Syria and Iran.[58]

25 Cairo, citadel. Inscription of Ṣalāḥ al-Dīn on the Mudarraj Gate, A.H. 579/A.D. 1183.

Although the fall of the Fatimids is sometimes attributed to Saladin, I emphasize above that it was brought about by Nūr al-Dīn, who had long planned to overthrow the Fatimids and bring Egypt back into the fold of orthodoxy. Religiously and ideologically, the legacy of Nūr al-Dīn casts an even longer shadow, and there is little doubt that he was ultimately responsible for the dismantling of Fatimid shrines and the replacement of Ismāʿīlī symbols with Sunni ones. It follows that the supplanting of the highly ambiguous, floriated Kufic script by clear and legible cursive scripts implied the acceptance of the Sunni belief in the single and unambiguous nature of the Word of God, whether in Qurʾāns or in public texts. The long-held belief in the dual meaning of the Qurʾānic message, which had been transformed by the Fatimids into an esoteric cult,[59] was visibly challenged by a script whose legibility and accuracy left little room for variant readings and therefore variant interpretations. Without completely doing away with the dual nature of calligraphic writing, the new cursive script shifted the balance decisively in favor of the denotive over the connotive aspects of writing. Subsuming the mystical within the informational and the *bāṭin* within the *ẓāhir*, the new public inscriptions perfectly embodied and eloquently propagated the exoteric and encompassing tendencies of the Sunni revival.

Another dimension of the Sunni-Shīʿī or Ashʿarī-Ismāʿīlī competition for public space, one that is more readily apparent to the casual viewer, was the increase in size and length of inscriptions. Briefly, early Islamic monuments,

26 Cairo, mosque al-Aqmar, 1125.
Inscription on facade.

with the exception of the entirely unique Dome of the Rock, were noticeably devoid of inscriptions, whether interior or exterior. The dearth of inscriptions seems to apply equally to Abbasid mosques, whose inscriptions, with the possible exception of the mosque of Ibn Ṭūlūn, seem to have been restricted to discrete bands across the *miḥrāb* or along an entablature.[60] In any case, there is little question that the Fatimids mark another departure in this arena as well, for they begin with their first mosque, al-Azhar, consistently to use inscriptional friezes to delineate entablatures, frame the extrados of arches, and mark the springing of domes.[61] By the eleventh century, beginning with the mosque al-Ḥākim, these inscriptional bands had migrated from these discrete locations to decorate exterior walls, architectural details, and minarets. This practice, which continues uninterrupted to the end of the Fatimid period, reached an especially high level of execution at the mosque al-Aqmar (1125), where arches, windows, and entablatures are highlighted by inscriptions (fig. 26). In

27 Cairo, complex of Qalawūn, 1285.
Inscription on facade.

view of their similarity to the inscriptional bands (or *ṭirāz*) commonly used on garments since Abbasid times, these inscriptional friezes are often also referred to as *ṭirāz*.

Exposed by virtue of their external location but hidden because of their illegible script, these inscriptions further resonate with the Ismāʿīlī duality of *ẓāhir* and *bāṭin*. The word is made available as a public text, but its message is wrapped within a nearly indecipherable script. The simultaneity of visibility and incomprehension, of inclusiveness and exclusiveness, underlines the intentions of a dynasty that always seemed divided between its messianic and propagandistic intentions and its encrypted messages. The script to which they adhered to the end was not simply illegible to most, but perhaps more importantly, it came to symbolize the very idea of the ambiguous and therefore exclusive nature of hidden truths.[62]

The Sunni dynasties turned this studied formula on its head: they appropriated and further expanded *ṭirāz* inscriptions, but they had them written in a much more easily legible script. The chronology of this development is not altogether clear, but exterior cursive *ṭirāz* bands in Iran begin to appear around the middle of the twelfth century, in Iraq and Syria in the late twelfth century, and in Cairo around the middle of the thirteenth century. The development of these *ṭirāz* bands was accompanied by a very important innovation: they were lowered from their discrete and elevated location as friezes or framing elements and made to cut right across the walls and supports of the building, almost like the cuneiform inscriptions on an Assyrian relief (fig. 27).[63] The increased legibility of the script and the lowering of the inscriptional band conjoin to create an image of a clear and accessible message, which resonates well with the exoteric nature of the word in the new Sunnism.

More specifically, the appropriation of the Qur'ānic script of Ibn al-Bawwāb by the newly emergent Sunni dynasties strongly suggests some awareness of the political implications of this act. Indeed, the public display of a calligraphic style with indisputable links to the Abbasids was intended to recognize the spiritual reign of the caliphate as well as affirm the legitimacy of the dynasty paying homage. This process is paralleled in the diplomatic sphere by the caliph's bestowal of titles and official garments, while in return receiving gifts and having his name included in the coinage and mentioned in the *khuṭbah*. Practiced by most dynasties of the eleventh and twelfth centuries, this reciprocal process aided the greatly weakened but newly assertive caliphate while providing some basis of legitimacy for these arriviste dynasties.

I have argued here and elsewhere that the late Abbasid caliphate was engaged in the production of symbolic forms, and that these forms found wide acceptance in much of the Sunni Islamic world.[64] Often originating in the nonofficial, even vernacular sphere, these forms were systematized in the tenth and eleventh centuries according to geometric processes, producing elegant types that were then used in highly significant contexts. Iconically charged as such, these forms became the veritable symbols of the Sunni revival and the resurgent caliphate and were as a result adopted and further developed by Sunni dynasties in different parts of the Islamic world.

It is a door made of cast brass for the king's palace in the city of Āmid. It is the chèf-d'œuvre, to view it saddles are strapped on. Truly it is the pearl, the orphan, a priceless possession.[1]
— Ibn al-Razzāz al-Jazarı

4

The *Girih* Mode: Vegetal and Geometric Arabesque

For the public at large, Islamic art is defined negatively by its abhorrence of figural representation, and somewhat more positively by its singular preoccupation with the vegetal and geometric ornament, commonly known as arabesque. Even nonspecialists who might be totally uninformed about Persian and Mughal painting or the great monuments of Islamic architecture often have little trouble identifying passages of arabesque ornament as Islamic, Arabic, or Moorish. Curiously, the scholarly reaction to this ingrained interest in Islamic ornament has been largely negative or at best defensive: rather than striving to enhance the public's appreciation of ornament, most historians of Islamic art have attempted to "correct" it by pointing to Islam's rich traditions in figural representation.[2] But these efforts have not radically transformed the public's "misconception" of Islamic art, since its view is formed less by ignorance or even prejudice than by an aesthetic appreciation of features that are not present in the same way or to the same extent in other arts. In fact, the overwhelming preference for Islamic patterns over painting has a long history in European artistic culture, dating back to such orientalizing palaces as the Brighton Pavilion in Bath, Leighton House in London, or Olana on the Hudson River and long predating the academic study of Islamic art. Although these fantastic recreations of Arabic-Islamic environments can be faulted for their essentializing perspective and imperialist subtext, they nonetheless indicate what cultured Western and perhaps non-Western observers valued most about Islamic art.

Rather than once again rehearse the formal development of the vegetal and geometric arabesque, this chapter focuses primarily on its unprecedented development in the middle period as a way of coming to terms with its possible meanings and universal attraction. A historiographical introduction takes into account the opposed positivist and essentialist trends that have dominated this area of study, and the more recent discourse that has attempted to explore the semiotic dimensions of Islamic ornament within accepted art-historical parameters. The chapter argues that despite the ubiquity of ornamental forms in early Islamic art, vegetal and geometric patterns substantially developed during the eleventh and twelth centuries within the context of the Sunni revival. Focusing on a select number of monuments, many from the period of Nūr al-Dīn, during which the arabesque is used in significant ways, I propose a number of interpretations for the early uses of vegetal and geometric arabesque.

The Study of Islamic Ornament

Although scholarly attention to Islamic ornament has not matched the public's enthusiasm for it, this area of study has nevertheless benefited from important, though sporadic, episodes of research. Alois Riegl, the great art historian and theoretician, was the first to analyze vegetal Islamic ornament, proposing that the arabesque represented "the final and logical consequence" of certain tendencies in late antique ornament.[3] Following a strictly formalist method, Riegl traced the gradual and incremental evolution of plant forms from Hellenic naturalism to Islamic abstraction and "infinite rapport," arguing that an artistic intentionality (*Kunstwollen*) underlay this development.[4] *Kunstwollen* aside, Riegl's meticulous attention to minute changes and the overall aesthetic picture provided a scientific foundation for the arabesque as well as integrated it within the body of European ornament.

Although Riegl's separation between the vegetal and geometric varieties of the arabesque has no firm basis in Islamic art, this distinction was accepted by other writers on ornament, including Dimand and Kühnel, possibly because it helped systematize a very diffuse area of study. In fact, in his short monograph *Die Arabeske* of 1949, Kühnel further emphasized this distinction by dealing exclusively with vegetal ornament in Islamic art and restricting the term "arabesque" to vegetal ornament of sufficient abstraction, sinuousness, and interconnection.[5] While these taxonomic studies have helped in presenting the data in a clear and logical manner, they have generally failed to account for periods of highly dynamic development in Islamic ornament, or for the sometimes selective dispersion of ornamental forms in different parts of the Islamic world. Even more seriously, their emphasis on the continuous and autonomous development of forms seems to have prevented them from engaging the question of meaning, except on the most basic and essential level.[6]

Curiously, little serious work was written on Islamic ornament in the pivotal decades of the 1960s, 1970s, and early 1980s, as scholarly attention in the field shifted to monographic and archaeological questions. Regrettably, however, this scholarly vacuum was soon filled by publications, many dating to the Islamic Festival of 1976, in London, that claimed an insider's perspective while making unsubstantiated, entirely ahistorical claims about the alleged meaning of Islamic ornament. There is no need to be derailed by this scholarly genre, whose largely interchangeable statements can be represented by Burckhardt: "... geometric interlacement doubtless represents the most intellectually satisfying form for it is an extremely direct expression of the ideas of the Divine Unity, underlying the inexhaustible variety of the world." [7] We cannot, as historians, concern ourselves with discourses that stand outside of history and that claim superiority to its facts and modes of argumentation.

Reacting to this excess and going back to the formalist outlines laid out by Riegl, Allen in 1988 published a collection of essays, of which the first two attempt for the first time since Kühnel to deal historically with the question of ornament. Two main points are convincingly argued in these chapters. The first is that some early Islamic ornamental styles are closely linked to the lacey vegetal ornamentation that is already present at the Hagia Sophia, and that is generally attributed to "some Asiatic influence."[8] Following the development of this style into the tenth and eleventh centuries, Allen attempts to identify the period when Near Eastern ornament left its late antique moorings and became more characteristically Islamic, or arabesque. Noting that this development did not occur until the eleventh century, Allen argues that contrary to fundamentalist assertions, these ornamental features postdate the rise of the faith by several centuries and cannot therefore be considered part of its essence. Allen next argues that since these developed ornamental forms differ considerably from their early Islamic counterparts, they cannot both be used to define or substantiate a prevailing Islamic ethos based on *tawḥīd*.

But rather than capitalizing on his well-founded conclusions to inquire into the cultural or religious underpinnings of truly arabesque forms, Allen instead uses them as ammunition further to undermine the Islamist view of Islamic ornament. Dismissing the notion that vegetal or geometric arabesque could be linked to theological or intellectual discourses, he argues that "geometry was not necessarily part of a cultured man's education,"[9] a statement which, as Necipoğlu has already demonstrated and as I reiterate below, is not based entirely on fact.[10] In conclusion, Allen proposes that "[vegetal and geometric arabesque] probably conveyed some sort of weak association, but artistically they are principally visual inventions rather than intellectual constructs."[11] As for the existence of parallel developments in calligraphy, of the kind discussed above in chapters 2 and 3, he inexplicably concludes that these "may be fortuitous, since there were many such developments."[12]

Grabar has written extensively on ornament and its role in artistic perception, but his ultimate conclusions regarding its meaning do not markedly differ from Allen's. Dealing simultaneously with the entire Islamic world and with specific instances in which ornament reached an especially high level of expression, Grabar seems unable to commit himself to its potential ontological significance. The pentagonal patterns at the North Dome of the Great Mosque of Isfahan and the fabulous *muqarnas* domes at the Alhambra do lead him to investigate their meaning, but he is more compelled by the eloquence of the texts than by the power of the ornamental forms themselves.[13] Whether linking the Isfahan domes with Omar Khayyam's astronomical theories or those at the Alhambra with Ibn Zamrak's poetry, he invariably valorizes a textual interpretation of specific monuments over an interpretation of the forms themselves.

It might be futile and perhaps unnecessary to summarize Necipoğlu's views on the two-dimensional arabesque since her brilliant investigation of this subject extends over several chapters in her book and includes a plethora of published and entirely original views on its development and meaning within specific historical contexts. Distancing herself from essentialist scholars and critiquing the positivistic positions taken by Allen and even Grabar, she attempts to find a middle ground in which ornament takes on some attributes of meaning without necessarily symbolizing any specific religious attribute or theological question. Although her study primarily focuses on the Timurid and early Ottoman periods, she begins her investigations much earlier, artfully resting her interpretations of later ornament on thorough analyses of the Abbasid period and the epoch of the Sunni revival. Shunning formalism and strict chronology, she adopts an episodic approach to the material, gradually creating a chain of interpretations, or interpretive climates, wherein dynamic developments in ornament are juxtaposed against theological and political discourses. Two such defining moments are discussed for the pre-Mongol period: Samarra ornament in the context of Mu'tazilite atomistic theory, and the full development of the *girih* mode in connection with the theology of the Sunni revival. Concerning the first, she proposes that the Samarra beveled style may have been inspired by the Mu'tazilite atomism, because such a cosmology "could have engendered a new way of representing the material world."[14]

In highlighting the impact of the theological and cosmological tenets of the Sunni revival on visual form, Necipoğlu has in fact accepted and further developed some of my earlier conclusions on the development of the *muqarnas* dome and proportioned scripts.[15] We are in general agreement on the linkage between the Ash'ari occasionalistic view of the universe and the growth of arabesque patterns that dissolve surfaces and volumes while directing a meditative gaze into the transience of the created world and the permanence of the creator. We also agree on the synchronicity of developments in Islamic calligraphy in the eleventh and twelfth centuries (chapters 2 and 3) and the creation of the *girih* (Persian: knot)[16] ornamental mode, a mode of interlaced vegetal forms and interlocked geometric shapes and patterns.[17]

But Necipoğlu expands these conclusions to take into account contemporary reactions to these new developments, linking them with earlier and later discursive formations, particularly Mu'tazilism and the theosophy of eastern Illuminationism (Falsafat al-Ishrāq). Ibn Jubayr's "enthusiastic description in 1182 of Nūr al-Dīn's joined work at the Great Mosque of Aleppo" (p. 102), the aesthetic zeal displayed by the inhabitants of Fez as "they covered over ornaments just the night before the Almohads entered the city" (p. 217), and Ibn Khaldun's comment on the astringent and sobering effect of geometric ornament (p. 103), all serve to ground her discourse in the contemporary intellectual climate while supporting her views about the semiotic dimensions of the *girih* mode. She concludes, therefore (p. 109), that "the new geometric mode seems to have represented a new visual order projecting a shared ethos of unification around the religious authority of the Abbasid caliphate." Only when this symbolic unity had been shattered by the Mongol conquest of 1258 did these original associations of the *girih* mode begin to weaken and had therefore to be compensated for by inscriptions, poetic allusions, and other textual pointers. Necipoğlu therefore concludes (p. 122) that for the post-Mongol period, "these evocative patterns would trigger religious, metaphysical, or mystical speculations, but they were by no means symbolic or iconic 'representations' of them." Occupying "an intermediary zone between the 'decorative' and the 'symbolic'," these two- and three-dimensional decorative patterns only acquired specific meanings through the addition of inscriptions and other contextual factors.[18]

Although the following discussion accepts the interpretive parameters advanced by Necipoğlu and Grabar, it differs from them most obviously in its greater temporal specificity, which focuses the discussion on the pivotal period of the Sunni revival. But my interpretation also departs from Grabar and even Necipoğlu in assessing the value of inscriptions for explaining architectural and decorative forms. This intimate linking of architectural form and epigraphic content has always struck me as a bit tendentious, for, at the very least, such a contention inevitably diminishes the meaning of anepigraphic monuments, such as the tombs of Zumurrud Khātūn in Baghdad or Humayun in Delhi. Even where they exist and where they do make important statements, monumental inscriptions were perhaps intended less as heuristic devices than as an extra layer of meaning that may, but does not necessarily, facilitate or enhance our understanding of architectural forms or monuments. Ultimately, this understanding must be based on a deeper appreciation of the forms themselves and on an appraisal of historical circumstances and contextual factors—such as function, placement, visibility, and so forth.

Early Development of Geometric and Vegetal Ornament

It is generally believed that an entirely original style of geometric ornament first developed in Central Asia under the Samanids in the second half of the tenth century, from where it may have spread by the second half of the eleventh century to Ghaznavid architecture in Afghanistan and Seljuq architecture in central Iran.[19] Characterized by highly textured brick patterns of the type commonly known as *hazār baf*, this ornamental style is the first to utilize the very building material to create an ornamental skin that is both part of and apart from the structure itself. Although *hazār baf* ornament continued to be used all over Iran and even parts of Iraq until the end of the twelfth century, it began to give way by the late eleventh century to a more advanced geometric style mainly characterized by the use of overlaid strapwork and complete star patterns; that is what we refer to as the *girih* mode. The Ghaznavid palaces at Ghazna and especially Lashkar-i Bazār contain excellent examples of overall geometric wall revetment mainly done in carved stucco and, quite rarely, in carved stone.[20] The designs are geometrically simple, most commonly employing a straightforward triangular grid in which interlaced truncated equilateral triangles form between them hexagons that are filled with rich vegetal arabesque (fig. 28). In other, perhaps later, examples the design is outlined in high-relief ribs, a technique also known in northwestern Iran and Baghdad in the late twelfth century.

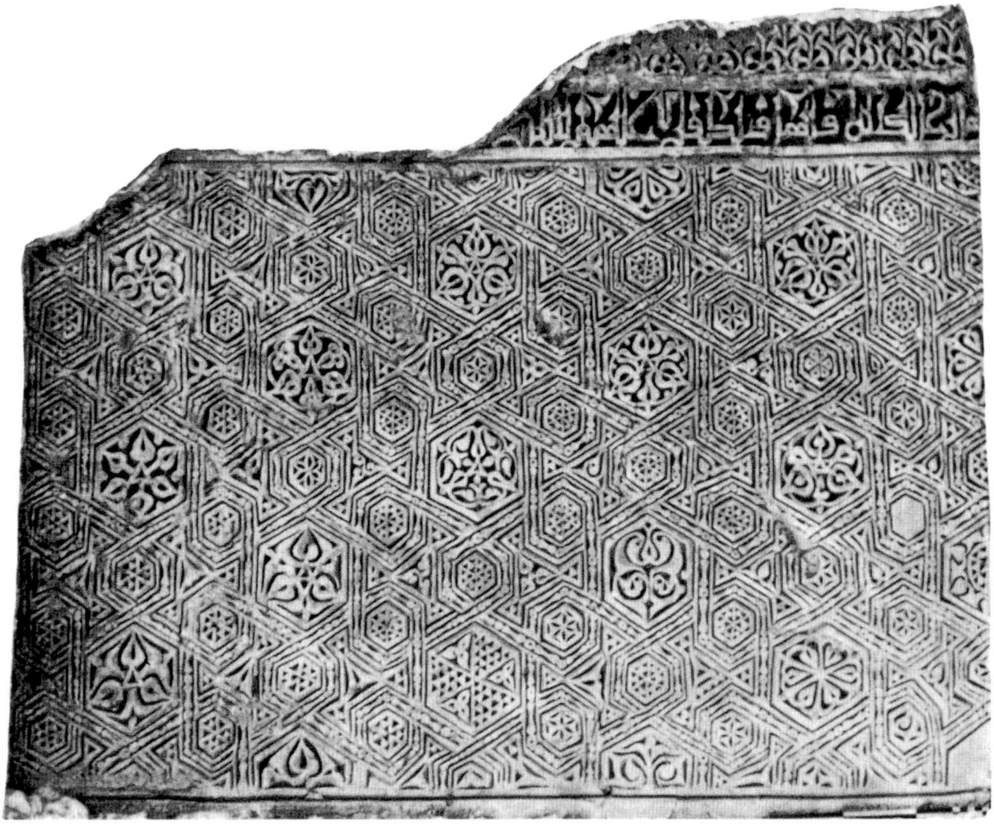

28 Afghanistan, Lashkār-ī Bāzār, Central Palace, 11th century. Geometric ornament (Schlumberger, *Lashkari Bazar*, 3, pl. 150).

29 Ghazna, Afghanistan. Wall paintings of vegetal arabesque (Schlumberger, *Lashkari Bazar*, 3, pl. 40b).

It is somewhat more difficult to trace the development of the vegetal arabesque and to determine the cusp at which it began to look less classical and more properly Islamic. Although some have seen in the Samarran beveled style the first example of true arabesque, this identification is problematic because of the deliberate visual ambiguity of its dense and fleshy foliage, which can often be read simultaneously as leaf or animal forms.[21] Rather, as with *muqarnas* and public inscriptions, some of the earliest true vegetal arabesque designs come from eastern Iran, where fully developed specimens decorated the dados of the late eleventh-century palace at Ghazna and the many marble cenotaphs discovered in that region (fig. 29). The palace decorations are characterized by their advanced degree of abstraction and interconnection, prompting Pope to conclude that "the Ghaznavid style is distinguished by increasing elegance primarily expressed in a rapid development of arabesque design."[22] Fully mature and faultlessly executed, these early specimens of vegetal arabesque suggest that they may have been derived from earlier models, possibly produced in the Abbasid capital, which had in fact supplied Ghaznavid architecture with many of its forms and ceremonials.[23] In turn, Ghaznavid designs would have supplied Seljuq artisans working in stucco and brick with the germinal idea for the vegetal arabesque.

Unlike the many arabesque patterns in Ghaznavid palaces, their nearly contemporary counterparts in Fatimid Cairo developed a different ornamental style using human and animal figures within an elaborate vegetal framework (fig. 30). This type of animated scroll survives in one painted example from Samarra,[24] and this decorative style was probably imported from Iraq under the Tulunids around the same time that the beveled style was also brought to Egypt. In view of its use of animal figures, the *rinceau animé* was restricted to palaces, whereas the beveled style occurs in both religious and palatial contexts—in the latter, sometimes blended with animal figures. Although true overall arabesque is rare in these decorative styles, it does appear in a small group of late Fatimid ivories that depict human and animal figures on a bed of delicate arabesque design.[25] This, in itself, does not necessarily argue for a local invention, but possibly for a stylistic change (whether gradual or abrupt is hard to say) owing to the prevalence of imported forms.

The situation is rather different in Fatimid religious buildings, where vegetal ornament up to the beginning of the twelfth century continued to employ variations of the beveled style (often in woodwork) and a type of Byzantinizing ornament that, despite its density and abstraction, still retained traces of naturalism in its leaf forms and its continuous stems, as well as its containment within framed panels. Other ornamental designs, such as those decorating the *maqsura* of al-Azhar mosque, are stylized trees that recall similar palm and palmette trees used at the Dome of the Rock and even earlier in Byzantine architecture (fig. 31).[26] Such continuities with Byzantine art coincide with the well-documented connections between the Fatimids and Byzantium in architecture and ceremonials.[27]

Fatimid Ornament

The *girih* mode of arabesque ornament, which by the eleventh century had already become common in the eastern Islamic world, is relatively rare in Fatimid art before the second half of the twelfth century. It did, however, exist both in its geometric and especially in vegetal varieties, in a handful of outstanding woodwork examples, specifically two wooden *minbars* and two wooden *mihrabs* from the late Fatimid period.[28] The first *minbar* is none other than the one commissioned by Badr al-Jamālī for the shrine of the head of al-Ḥusayn at Ascalon, but which was subsequently moved by Saladin to *maqam* Ibrahim at Hebron, where it remains. Dated to A.H. 484/A.D. 1091–92, this is one of the earliest examples of wooden strapwork that is composed of individually cut geometric shapes and also one of the earliest *minbars* with well-developed vegetal arabesque designs inscribed within a simple geometric framework.[29]

Indeed, the technical and ornamental originality of the Hebron *minbar* has led most historians to conclude that it is not an Egyptian product but most

30 Three wood panels, previously at the western Fatimid Palace, late 11th century. Cairo, Museum of Islamic Art.

likely one made by Syrian craftsmen, or under strong Syrian influence.[30] Although quite plausible, this conclusion can only be retroactively substantiated, since the earliest examples of Syrian marquetry postdate the Hebron *minbar* by several decades. On the other hand, it seems amply clear that this new style of woodworking did not completely supplant the earlier style, which was largely derived from the Samarran beveled style; rather, the two styles coexisted until the middle of the twelfth century if not beyond. For example, a *minbar* made in 1106 by the son of Badr al-Jamālī is completely devoid of geometric strapwork, decorated instead by large rectangular panels carved in the beveled style.[31] Furthermore, the astonishing *minbar* at Qūs (dated A.H. 550/A.D. 1155–56) also seems quite intrusive, for it is not succeeded by comparable examples until the late twelfth century, when, as we shall see below, at least one Syrian woodworker was brought to Egypt.

Technically, the Hebron *minbar* as well as the three other late Fatimid examples mentioned above are characterized by a relatively simple triangular grid, mainly consisting of hexagons and regular or elongated six-pointed stars. None are based on square grid or radial grids, and none exhibit the interlocking of triangle- and square-based shapes that becomes common in slightly later Syrian woodwork. The most notable feature of these wooden *minbars* and *miḥrabs* is not so much their geometric ingenuity, but rather their happy combination of simple geometric patterns with an astonishing wealth of vegetal

ornament. This felicitous accord is nowhere better represented than in the niche of the *miḥrāb* of Sayyida Nafisa (1145–46; fig. 32) or especially in the backrest of the Qūs *minbar*.[32]

Thus, it seems that whereas the vegetal and especially geometric *girih* mode was largely absent from Cairene imperial monuments, it had decisively made its way into subimperial monuments or those outside the capital. This dichotomy of Fatimid artistic patronage has been discussed by Bloom, who argues that such intrusive forms as *muqarnas* transition zones were primarily used in nonroyal domes whose links with popular piety may have facilitated their use of ornamental forms that had not yet found their way to imperial foundations.[33] Although the situation is much clearer in the case of *muqarnas* vaulting—

32 *Miḥrāb* of Sayyida Nafisa (1145–46). Cairo, Museum of Islamic Art.

OPPOSITE

31 Cairo, mosque al-Azhar, 972. Stucco ornament in the *maqsura*.

which is absent from Fatimid imperial domes but fairly common in lesser foundations—the dichotomy might be extended with some reservations to the use of the two-dimensional *girih* mode of ornament.

The *Girih* Mode in Baghdad and the Post-Seljuq States

Returning to Baghdad, we must once again deplore the near-absence of any surviving monuments there before the late twelfth century, making it difficult to trace the development of the arabesque in what may have been its generative center. Despite the dearth of evidence, Necipoğlu has argued for the centrality of Baghdad in the development of the arabesque, suggesting that examples in eastern Iran may be a distant reflection of a metropolitan style that had largely, though not completely, disappeared.[34] Citing the geometric arabesque on the full-page frontispieces of the Qur'ān of Ibn al-Bawwāb, made in Baghdad in 1000, she proposed that "the *girih* mode could have made its first appearance in manuscript illumination" and that manuscripts could have facilitated the transfer of patterns to different parts of the Islamic world. While no definitive evidence for this thesis exists, one is nevertheless struck by the advanced arabesque designs of these frontispieces, whose interlacing hexagons that contain within them *thuluth* calligraphy on a bed of arabesque were not seen for nearly a century in architecture and woodwork (see figs. 15 and 16 and pp. 47–48).

Further clues to the centrality of Baghdad in the development of medieval Islamic ornament may be retrospectively traced from the later structures that have survived there. Several preserved Baghdadi monuments from the late twelfth and first half of the thirteenth century —including the mausoleum of Zumurrud Khatun, the Abbasid Palace, and the *madrasa* al-Mustanṣiriyya—demonstrate an astonishing level of design and craftsmanship in their unique combination of geometric ornament, *muqarnas*, and carved brick decoration (fig. 33; see figs. 62–64 and pp. 122–124). This level of excellence bespeaks a vigorous and deeply rooted tradition that may date back to the time of Ibn al-Bawwāb, if not before.

While more still needs to be written about Baghdad, Syria's role in the development of the arabesque and its transmission to Egypt remains even less defined. Here several late eleventh- and twelfth-century examples of both vegetal and geometric arabesque survive, and their high degree of craftsmanship and complexity attests to Syria's pivotal importance in this branch of Islamic art. One of the first medieval structures in Aleppo, the minaret of the Great Mosque of Aleppo (dated 1090), contains outstanding examples of vegetal arabesque, which are deeply carved in the rudimentary *muqarnas* cells of its uppermost zone. While both the *muqarnas* and the carved decorations on it represent the translation of eastern designs into stone, the clarity and geometric rigor of these decorations can also be attributed to northern Syria's excellent stone masonry and its still-vibrant links with late antiquity (fig. 34). This con-

33 Baghdad, *madrasa* al-Mustansiriyya, 1242.
Tripartite facade of the mosque with carved brick decoration.

tinuity can also been seen in the dense and deeply carved arabesque designs covering the entablature and cornice of the Qastal al-Shu'aybiyya in Aleppo, built by Nūr al-Dīn in 1150 (fig. 35). The astonishingly complex arabesque, far exceeding anything known in Iran, is given a sense of balance and coherence by the use of a classicizing beaded molding that frames and unifies the vegetal ornament. It appears, therefore, that as with *muqarnas* vaulting, an eastern design has been rationalized in Syria into a more rigorous and coherent form, refinements that are also seen in other aspects of medieval Syrian architecture.[35]

Curiously, however, this manner of arabesque carving in stone all but disappeared in Syria in the second half of the twelfth century, its last flourishing being the spectacular arabesque designs at the Great Mosque of Harran, which was entirely rebuilt around the end of the reign of Nūr al-Dīn in 1174.[36] Fragments remaining *in situ* and at the nearby Urfa Museum attest to a high level of craftmanship and design, and to a measure of continuity with the architecture

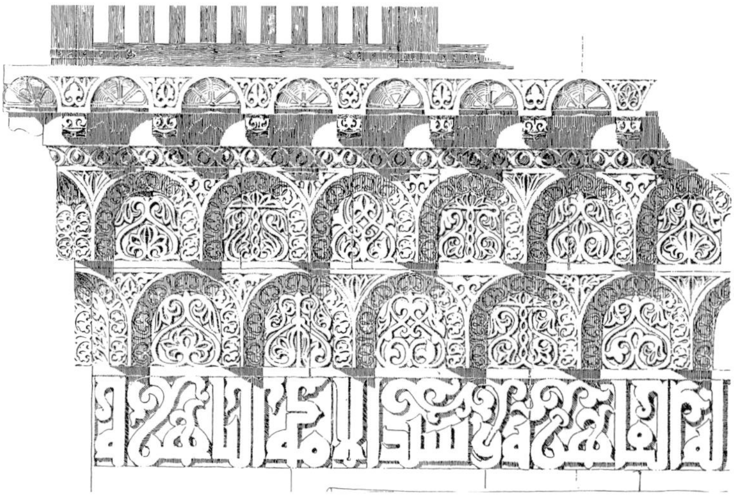

34 Aleppo, minaret of the Great Mosque, 1090. Uppermost zone (from Herzfeld, *Alep* 3, pl. LXII).

of Aleppo and of late antiquity (fig. 36). The arabesque ornament is especially noteworthy for its precision and deep carving in several layers, a feature also seen in contemporary stonework in Mosul. This style of carving resembles contemporary woodwork.

Harran aside, the richness of the vegetal arabesque gave way in the second half of the twelfth century to the relative austerity of geometric strapwork and stone *muqarnas* vaults.[37] But it did continue in the more pliable media of plaster and especially of wood, medium of the unqualified twelfth-century masterpieces of the *girih* mode. Perhaps not coincidentally, some of the finest works from this period were commissioned by Nūr al-Dīn for his various institutions in Aleppo, Hama, Damascus, and even Jerusalem. These include the doors of the *bīmāristān* al-Nūrī in Aleppo (c. 1150) and in Damascus (1154); the wooden

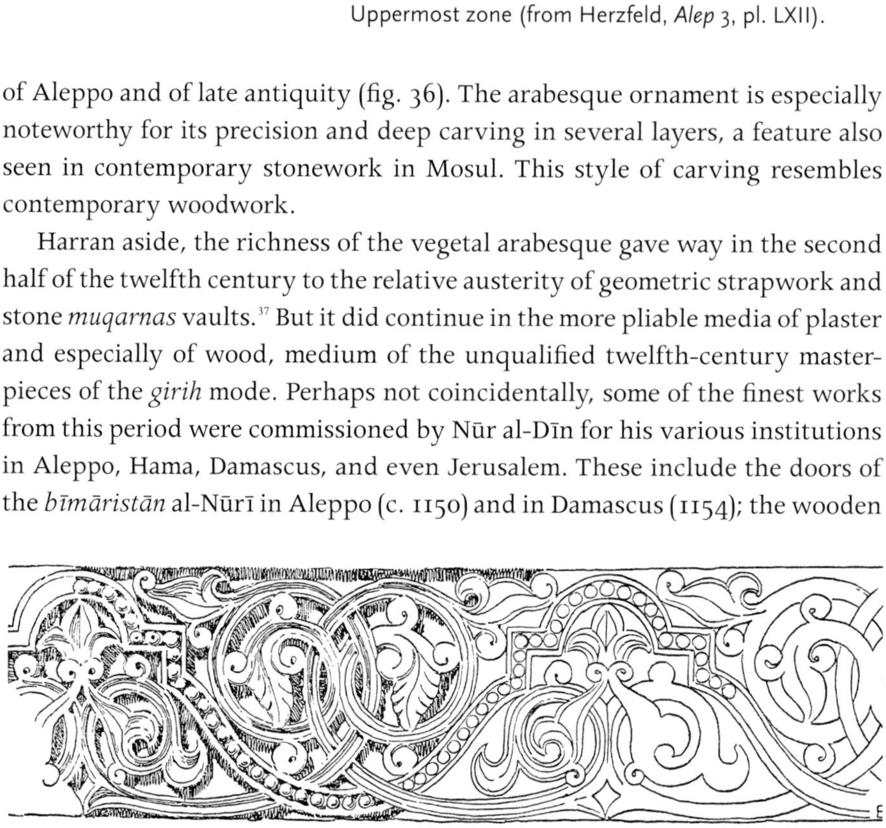

35 Aleppo, *qasṭal* al-Shu'aybiyya, 1150. Arabesque scroll on cornice (after Herzfeld, "Damascus II," fig. 8).

OPPOSITE

36 Harran (Turkey), Great Mosque, c. 1180. Capital with deep arabesque carving (presently at the Urfa Museum).

miḥrāb previously at the *maqam* Ibrahim at the Aleppo citadel (1165); the wooden *minbars* at Hama (1163) and the one designed for the Aqsa mosque in Jerusalem (1168); and Nūr al-Dīn's own cenotaph in his *madrasa* al-Nūriyya (1172).[38] The first specimen, which has been seriously damaged in recent years, is a double door whose apparent simplicity belies the cleverness and rarity of its design and construction (fig. 37).[39] Unlike the geometric patterns on later doors, which are either applied to a bronze sheathing or else composed marquetry style, this example is entirely made of undecorated wooden pieces (triangles, parallelograms, and trapezoids) that are affixed to the door frame, completely covering it with a repeating design based on a triangular grid. The technique, which is not known in other doors, is akin to inlay work, except that the wooden pieces are large and of the same material and color as the door itself. In both these respects, it is perhaps closer to the Iranian *hazār baf* brick technique, which, though entirely unknown in Syria, may have been transmitted through other more transportable means.

The large wooden doors at the *bīmāristān* al-Nūrī in Damascus are pivotal, both for their advanced geometric and vegetal ornaments and for the known identity of their maker (fig. 38). The double door is made of wood sheathed in bronze, to which brass nails are fixed to form an overall geometric pattern. The design, which covers the entire door except for a narrow inscriptional frieze at the top, is a fully developed star pattern based on a triangular grid. Its primary unit is a six-pointed star inscribed within a hexagon, which is surrounded by six five-pointed stars whose external sides form a larger hexagon. Five such units are used: two in each leaf and one in the middle of the door, with half on each leaf. The door knockers are placed over two of the five-pointed stars of the central unit. When the door is closed, the design on both leaves can be read as a single composition focused on the large star in the exact middle of the door.

The logic, originality, and beauty of this geometric design testify to the genius of its maker, *al-muhandis* (the geometer) Abu'l-Faḍl b. 'Abd al-Karīm Muḥammad al-Ḥārithi (d. A.H. 599/A.D. 1202–3), who, according to Ibn abi Uṣaybi'ah, made this door and most of the others that once existed in the *bīmāristān*. He was known as a carpenter, stonemason, and geometer or engineer who had studied Euclid and the Almagest in order to excel in his crafts. Interestingly, he also read astronomy and medicine as well as *hadīth*, grammar, and poetry and even wrote treatises in science and literature.[40] In other words, he was an artisan, a scientist, and a man of letters, a combination that, although questioned by many writers on Islamic art, may have been fairly commonplace in medieval Islam.[41]

The now-lost *miḥrāb* at *maqām* Ibrahim in the Aleppo citadel is undoubtedly one of the great masterpieces of Islamic woodwork and of design in the *girih* mode (fig. 39). Rising to a height of about three meters, it consisted of a deep niche covered by a hemispherical conche and flanked by a wide frame of wooden marquetry. With the exception of a small passage of rather archaizing

37 Aleppo, *bīmāristān* al-Nūrī, c. 1150. Wooden door with inlaid wood marquetry.

38 Damascus, *bīmāristān* al-Nūrī, 1154. Wooden door sheathed in copper and ornamented with brass nails.

vegetal scrolls in its spandrel, the *miḥrāb* is entirely made of wooden marquetry, whose complex geometric strapwork encloses the most delicate vegetal arabesque fillets and a few passages of floriated Kufic inscriptions. These are almost exclusively Qurānic, but they also give the name of the carpenter, Ma'ālī b. Sālim , and the date of its completion in A.H. 563/A.D. 1167–8.[42]

Three different design grids are used ingeniously: a triangular grid in the niche; a square grid for the flanking frames; and an astonishingly complex pentagonal grid for the conch, constructed to fit perfectly within the hemispherical surface. In both the niche and the flanking frames the design is no longer simple repetitions of hexagons, as at Ghazna or Fatimid Egypt for example, but now consists of several interlocking forms that create a more complex geometric pattern. Herzfeld, who seems to have witnessed the woodcarvers' craft in its last days in Mosul, said that such designs are locally referred to as *tafṣīl makhbūṭ,* literally "mingled composition," but most likely refer to geometric interlaces with several interlocking shapes.[43] The frame design, for example, emanates from an eight-pointed star whose points are extended to contain between them irregular hexagons that develop into pairs of regular octagons placed below and above the stars. The paired octagons contain in between them a fourth shape made up of the two adjoined halves of a six-pointed star, an unexpected shape in a square grid. A more ingenious combination of grids exists in the niche, whose emphatic triangular grid contains square forms, such that the overall design can simultaneously be read diagonally as diamonds enclosing six-pointed stars and vertically as a series of staggered squares that enclose little diamond shapes. By expertly manipulating the borders around the generative units of this design, the artisan was able to create an interlaced pattern whose astounding complexity does not obscure its modular construction. Such rationalization of geometric ornament occurred first in Syria and is not known elsewhere at this early date.

These designs are considerably more advanced than anything previously attempted, whether in Egypt or even in Iran, and they focus attention once again on the dynamic changes in architecture and design that took place under Nūr al-Dīn. The complexity and variety of the design, the openwork carving of the arabesque fillets, and the inclusion of inscriptions within it all distinguish this *miḥrāb* from its smaller Fatimid predecessors and point to a creative school of geometers-woodcarvers who were active in Aleppo between the twelfth and the first half of the thirteenth centuries. The *miḥrāb* is signed by Ma'āli ibn Sālem, a prominent Aleppine woodcarver whose progenitors were responsible for important works in Aleppo and Cairo, including the *minbar* for Jerusalem and the cenotaph of Imam Shāfi'ī in Cairo (see fig. 44, and p. 96).

The *minbar* at Hama has long since lost its stairs and the flanking walls, which would certainly have carried geometric designs. The upper structure, which is entirely original, consists of the usual chair with three arched openings and a backrest, crowned by an elaborate entablature that surrounds a

small dome (fig. 40). Only the backrest contains a geometric pattern, a simple design that encloses the *shahāda* within two cartouches. But the highlight of this *minbar* is the vegetal arabesque patterns that decorate the three open arches and the frieze and cornice above them. The arabesque is deeply carved in overlapping and interlacing levels. Despite its complexity, it maintains perfect rhythm and clarity, as well as some sense of organic unity due in part to the smooth, convex section of the vegetal stems, which soften the linearity and abstraction of the overall design.

The *minbar* commissioned by Nūr al-Dīn for the Aqsa mosque in Jerusalem marks the peak of creativity of the Aleppo school of woodcarvers. The *minbar* is dated twice, to A.H. 564/A.D. 1168 and 572/1176, suggesting that it was begun by Nūr al-Dīn but perhaps not completed until the brief reign of his son al-Ṣāliḥ Ismāʿīl (figs. 41–43).[44] There is no doubt, however, that Nūr al-Dīn was the motivating force behind its construction and that it was designed to fulfill the dream of liberating Jerusalem, which had preoccupied him since the beginning of his reign in 1146. As is well known, Nūr al-Dīn died with his dream

OPPOSITE

39 Aleppo, *maqam* Ibrahim in the citadel. Wooden *miḥrāb*, A.H. 563/A.D. 1168 (Herzfeld, *Inscriptions et monuments d'Alep* 3, pl. XLVI).

RIGHT

40 Hama, mosque al-Nūrī. *Minbar*, A.H. 558/A.D. 1163.

unfulfilled, and the completed *minbar* remained at the Great Mosque of Aleppo, where Ibn Jubayr saw it in 1182. It was finally transported to Jerusalem in 1187, a few months after its liberation by Saladin, who realized Nūr al-Dīn's ambition by placing his votive structure in its intended place at the Aqsa mosque in Jerusalem.[45]

The *minbar* was signed by four different artisans: Ḥāmīd b. Ẓāfir, Abu'l-Ḥasan b. Yahyā, Abu'l-Faḍā'il b. Yahyā, and Salmān b. Ma'ālī, all from the village of Akhtarīn in the vicinity of Aleppo, the latter most likely the son of Ma'āli b. Sālem, who had made the *miḥrāb* at the Aleppo citadel in 1168. Others from the same family were also responsible for important works in Cairo and perhaps elsewhere.

This was one of the best executed and most famous *minbar* ever made. The recent analysis of its geometric patterns, preliminary studies for building a replica, shows that it contained twenty-five different geometric patterns in its various panels in addition to vegetal arabesques, openwork, *muqarnas*, and inscriptions.[46] Every surface, including even the risers of the steps and the inside walls of the bannister, is perforated with patterns, producing a rich, varied, and not entirely resolved effect. Triangular, square, and radial grids are represented; and some patterns combine two grids, a feature we already

41 Jerusalem, Aqsa mosque, *minbar* of Nūr al-Dīn, A.H. 564/A.D. 1169 (destroyed by fire in 1968). (The Creswell Archive, No. C5005: Ashmolean Museum, University of Oxford.)

42 Jerusalem, Aqsa mosque, *minbar* of Nūr al-Dīn, eastern side. A.H. 564/A.D. 1169. (The Creswell Archive, No. C5006: Ashmolean Museum, University of Oxford.)

43 Jerusalem, Aqsa mosque, *minbar* of Nūr al-Dīn: detail of ornament. (The Creswell Archive, No. C5009: Ashmolean Museum, University of Oxford.)

encountered at the *miḥrāb* of *maqām* Ibrahim. Though perhaps lacking the overall unity and harmony often characterizing *minbars* of the Mamluk period, this specimen represents an unprecedented richness of patterns that had not been previously combined in one object.

The unsurpassed excellence of the woodcarvers of Aleppo in the twelfth century is further confirmed by the fact that at least one of them practiced his craft in Cairo. Two commemorative caskets commissioned by Saladin—those of Imam al-Shāfi'ī (dated A.H. 574/A.D. 1178)[47] (fig. 44) and Imam al-Ḥusayn[48]—are signed by 'Ubayd b. Ma'ālī, who must be the son of Ma'ālī b. Sālim, the maker of the Aleppo *miḥrāb* and therefore a brother of Salmān b. Ma'ālī, the chief artisan of the *minbar* of Jerusalem. It seems likely that 'Ubayd moved to Cairo in the early 1180s, where he continued to practice the family craft under the patronage of Saladin and his successors. Both caskets are carved on all four vertical faces in bold geometric patterns, framed by inscriptional bands and enclosing rich vegetal arabesque. In fact, it seems likely that the relative simplicity of the geometric strapwork was necessitated by the size and complexity of the vegetal arabesque fillets.

The artisanal transmission from Syria to Egypt leads to two conclusions. First, it seems likely that, as with the *muqarnas* and proportioned cursive writing, the *girih* mode, which is largely intrusive in Cairene art and architecture before the end of the Fatimids, was at least partly introduced from Syria in the early Ayyubid period.[49] And second, once again Aleppine woodwork and woodworkers are important in disseminating geometric patterns to outlying regions. Neither of these conclusions, however, in any way minimizes the role of paper or pattern scrolls as equally plausible means of transmission for geometric and vegetal designs.

The later development of the two-dimensional *girih* mode is outside the confines of this study, and, at any rate, Necipoğlu's study of it is definitive. But I would like to end this analytical discussion by citing a little-known specimen that once formed part of the elaborate paneling of the *maqām* Ibrahim in the Aleppo citadel. This was a double door, datable to the restoration of Toghril in A.H. 616/A.D. 1219, that once led to a small chamber in the eastern side of the building (fig. 45). Unlike the *miḥrāb* itself, the pattern on this door is purely linear; it was never intended to have fillings. Herzfeld's description of it remains unsurpassed: "It is the most complicated design ever produced by that branch of art. The almost unsolvable problem of a design based on horizontal groups of eleven-pointed stars is solved by alternative intercalation of a parallel group of twelve-pointed and one of ten-pointed stars between them."[50] Standing at the peak of wooden geometric ornament, these panels point the way simultaneously to Anatolia and Mamluk Egypt, where patterns were expanded in size and perhaps improved in quality. But they do not match the creative intensity of Syrian woodworkers of the Zangid and Ayyubid periods.

In his book on automata, written at the beginning of the thirteenth century,

44 Cairo, shrine of Imam al-Shāfiʿī. Wooden cenotaph of Imam al-Shāfiʿī, A.H. 574/A.D. 1178.

al-Jazari describes and illustrates a massive bronze door that the author himself designed for the palace at Āmid (Diyarbakir) of the Artuqid prince al-Malik al-Ṣāliḥ Nāṣir al-Din Muhammad, to whom the manuscript was dedicated (fig. 46).[51] The description and the illustrations are exemplary in their clarity and concision, describing how the design was conceived, the wooden elements cut, and especially how the brass elements were cast into individual shapes. Perhaps most interesting for us is that the author makes a point of describing his pattern as the intersection of two linear systems, hexagonal and octagonal, with various other fillings and incidental shapes between them. He then adds with no little pride that "in this *shabaka* there are no half or quarter stars nor any incomplete pieces, except for two half stars."[52]

Al-Jazarī, who was himself a geometer, toolmaker, and a visionary, reminds us of his predecessor al-Ḥārithi (the designer of the *bīmāristān* doors) in that both spanned the distant worlds of the artisans and men of the word. They, and perhaps others like them, chose to situate their creative efforts in the middle ground between theory and practice, creating models and templates

45 Aleppo, *maqām* Ibrāhīm in the Citadel. Analysis of wooden window panels, c. 1230 (after Herzfeld, *Inscriptions et monuments d'Alep* 1, fig. 56).

46 Al-Jazari, *Kitāb fī ma'arifat al-ḥiyal al-handasiyya* (Book on the Knowledge of Ingenious Mechanical Devices), Diyarbakir, 1206. Istanbul Topkapı Serai Müzesi Kütüphanesi, Ms. 3472, fols. 167r and v.

for later artisans and enriching the science of geometry through experimentation. Furthermore, such practical geometers may have served as mediators for the understanding and appreciation of geometric designs by patrons and their limited circle of courtiers.[53]

Conclusion

This chapter has examined particular strands in the vegetal and geometric arabesque, following them from their roots to their ultimate fruition as developed specimens of the *girih* mode. It shows that the earliest examples of overall geometric patterns were produced in eastern Iran in the tenth and eleventh centuries, first as brick *hazār baf* and subsequently as carved and molded stucco geometric patterns. But despite the preponderance of archaeological evidence from eastern Iran, I generally concur with the scholarly view that such developments may have occurred first in Baghdad, and that examples in Samanid and Ghaznavid Iran are distant echoes of a vanished metropolitan style.[54] Arguing for the precedence of Baghdad in the creation of geometric and vegetal arabesque are the treatises of theoretical and practical geometry that were produced there in the tenth century—in particular that by al-Buzjānī (d. 998)[55]—and several extant Qur'ānic frontispieces with intricate geometric and vegetal interlaces, of which those in the Qur'ān of Ibn al-Bawwāb are the earliest known specimens of fully developed geometric interlaces. Other related Qur'āns, produced in Baghdad or Iran in the eleventh and early twelfth centuries, also contain frontispieces with increasingly complex geometric designs, further attesting to the centrality of Baghdad and, more generally, to the importance of paper designs in the dissemination of arabesque.

The flourishing of the *girih* mode in Syria under Nūr al-Dīn parallels the introduction of *muqarnas* vaulting and proportioned cursive writing from Baghdad and their subsequent rationalization and monumentalization. Though long noted by Herzfeld, Syria's role in the development of the geometric and vegetal arabesque has been virtually ignored by most writers, who have adopted a mechanistic mode for the transmission of artistic forms, without sufficiently appreciating the unprecedented importance and centrifugal effect of the patronage of Nūr al-Dīn. Indeed, as noted above, the spread of the *girih* mode to Egypt after the Ayyubid takeover owes a great deal to the pivotal period of Nūr al-Dīn and his immediate successor Saladin. These developments also coincide with the introduction of *muqarnas* vaulting, cursive public inscriptions, and even the four-*iwan* plan—all forms that had enjoyed an extended period of development in Iran, Iraq, and Syria before being brought to Egypt.

Was the two-dimensional arabesque, therefore, symbolic? Did it convey any meanings beyond the normative associations generally supported by ornament, including emphasis or dissolution of forms, hierarchy or intermingling of orders, or just plain decoration? The case for any specific meaning for the two-dimensional *girih* seems weaker than for public inscriptions or for *muqarnas* vaulting and fourfold plans. Overall, the arabesque seems to lack the intentionality of use, profound iconographic associations, and close links with Abbasid Baghdad that could be demonstrated for the other forms. Its very ubiquity and use in myriad contexts also seem to undermine any specific symbolic associations.

But arguing for at least some signification is the appearance and intense development of the two-dimensional *girih* in regions and monuments that are closely linked with the Sunni revival. These include middle Abbasid Baghdad, Ghaznavid and Seljuq Iran, Zangid and Ayyubid Syria, Seljuq Anatolia, and North Africa under the Almoravids and Almohads. Furthermore, this otherwise smooth dispersionary model is once again interrupted by Fatimid Egypt, whose ornamental styles continued well into the twelfth century to demonstrate a sustained preference for contained decorative friezes and framed floral ornaments, with fairly limited examples of overall arabesque ornament. Indeed, with the exception of some notable specimens that seem intrusive in Fatimid art, the *girih* mode only entered Egypt with the Ayyubids and reached its fullest development under the Mamluks.

Also supporting the possibility of meaning in the geometric and vegetal arabesque is that, particularly in its earlier examples, it was used with a sense of decorum, a studied sense of applying the appropriate ornamentation to various objects or architectural forms.[56] We note that ornament in the *girih* mode was applied to objects of cultic or symbolic value—including Qur'ān frontispieces, portals, *minbars*, *miḥrābs*, and cenotaphs—before it eventually spread to nearly every type of object and monument. Furthermore, the specimens discussed above demonstrate that whereas vegetal, geometric, or even *muqarnas* ornament often coexisted in one and the same object or monument, they were used with a sense of order that accounted for place, context, and function. Thus, a dense mass of vegetal arabesque was deemed appropriate for cenotaphs or *miḥrābs*, where it might refer to the garden of Paradise awaiting the deceased or the observant worshipper.[57] Geometric ornament, with or without vegetal arabesque fillets, was most effectively used for doors and door frames, *minbars*, minarets, and more rarely, domes. Combining the purity and austerity of geometric principles with the celestial allusions of star-patterns, geometric ornament reflected the ordered universe, whose atomistic and occasionalistic structure was created and sustained by divine intervention, and stimulated passion for the divine creator. Likewise, the strength and vigor of geometric ornament would have enhanced the image of power and authority that *minbars*, minarets, and even portals were intended to project, while also calling attention to their founders. Finally, *muqarnas*, as we shall see below, was most commonly applied to portal vaults and domes.

These specific domains constituted the creative center of the arabesque well into the fourteenth century. The intimate association of the *girih* mode with religiously significant objects clearly worked in both directions: it reaffirmed the symbolic potency of these objects while also enhancing the religious dimension of arabesque ornament. The simultaneity of association stands at the heart of an ornamental system that entirely consumes the object it covers.

The canopy of the roof, consisting of hemispheres joined to the heaven-like ceiling, offers a variegated spectacle; closely packed angles project inward and outward; the beauty of the carving is extraordinary, and wonderful is the appearance of the cavities which, overlaid with gold, produce the effect of a rainbow more colorful than the one in the clouds.[1]

— Nikolaos Mesarites

5

Muqarnas Vaulting and Ashʿarī Occasionalism

Muqarnas, also called stalactite or honeycomb vaulting, is one of the most original and ubiquitous features of Islamic architecture. It appears in a variety of building materials, including stucco, brick, stone, and wood, and is applied with great versatility to various architectural forms, such as cornices, corbelled transitions, capitals, vaults, and domes. Furthermore, *muqarnas* enjoys a broad historical and geographic span and was especially dominant between the eleventh and fifteenth centuries in the central and western Islamic world. Its ubiquity, distinctive appearance, and effective use enriched and unified Islamic architecture in the middle period.

Muqarnas has been defined variously as "an architectural form," "a vaulting system,"[2] "a decorative device,"[3] "an immensely flexible combination of three-dimensional units,"[4] or even as "an echo of the motion of heaven in the terrestrial order."[5] But none of these definitions seems adequate; in fact, their choice of terms and points of emphasis inevitably skew the evidence and valorize certain directions of research over others. Until we have gathered more facts about the *muqarnas* and investigated its various formal and ontological parameters, it might be more prudent to postpone a final definition and simply present a working definition based on formal features. I, therefore, tentatively define *muqarnas* as a decorative or structural system in which tiers of repeated small units with discrete geometric shapes are corbelled to form a stairlike or concave pattern or form.

Despite its ambiguity, this definition makes it immediately clear that *muqarnas* cannot be discussed independently from the forms to which it was applied and which have been transformed through its application. Specifically, the following discussion of *muqarnas* domes and vaults cannot be singlemindedly focused on the *muqarnas*, but must also take into account both the nature of the architectural forms to which it was applied and the synthesis that results from such an application. This basic distinction between the concept of *muqarnas* and the forms to which it was applied might seem so straightforward as not to warrant discussion, but most contemporary scholarship has conflated the two components and, in so doing, obscured the significance of the *muqarnas* phenomenon. This simple act of differentiation requires a view of the *muqarnas* dome (or any other *muqarnas* form for that matter) not as an essential component in Islamic art, but as one that was produced through the application of a new concept to well-known architectural forms.

This chapter begins, therefore, with a discussion of the etymology of the word *muqarnas* and the earliest uses of *muqarnas* forms before focusing on the development of the true *muqarnas* dome. The likely origin of this form in Baghdad and its adoption by Nūr al-Dīn and the Sunni dynasties of North Africa once again point to the peculiar "center-periphery" model explored in the previous chapters. The early use of *muqarnas* vaulting in palatial and religious settings adds an important dimension to the iconography of this form and provides further clues to its interpretation.

Etymology

One of the main difficulties encountered in the above discussion of the two-dimensional arabesque is that the usual silence of the sources about its development is compounded by the lack of a specific indigenous name for it.[6] Our discussion of the *muqarnas*, therefore, is already more advanced because of the availability of a term whose antiquity at least matches the specific forms to which it has been applied. Early studies on the etymology of the word *muqarnas* have yielded conflicting and inconclusive results. Herzfeld has proposed an etymology based on the Greek word *koronis*, capstone or cornice, proposing that *muqarnas* was a corruption of the earlier classical term.[7] Although this etymology does not occur in Arabic or Persian dictionaries, and the term *muqarnas* has no early architectural signification, this derivation has been widely accepted, possibly because it conforms to the connection of Islamic architecture with a classical past.[8] Rosintal first proposed the highly unlikely meaning "stiff" or "frozen" but later opted for a less naive but equally problematic etymology derived from the Arabic verb *qrn* (*qarana* = join), which made *muqarnas* "a joined form."[9] This etymology, however, assumes a derivation of the term from the standard triliteral verb root *qrn*, when the root is clearly the quadriliteral *qrns*.

More recently, Marçais[10] and Golvin[11] promoted the derivation given by the Persianist Kasimiriski, namely, that *muqarnas* describes a form with setbacks arranged in tiers.[12] This meaning resembles one among several given by Ibn Manẓur and Fīrūzābādī (d. 1415) that defines *muqarnas* as a form with stepped or serrated edges, such as fringed leather or a decorative awning.[13] The same meaning is also given to the closely related term *qarnasah*, which is most likely an earlier noun form of the quadriliteral verb *qrns*. Also found in some Arabic and Persian dictionaries is the related term *qirnās* or *qurnās*, generally denoting the part of a mountain that projects outward, much as the nose projects from a human face.[14] Finally, Heinrichs very recently published an etymological study of the *muqarnas* in which he argues against both the classical derivation from *koronis* and the Syriac derivation from *mqarnas*, favoring instead an Arabic etymology derived from *qurnās*.[15]

Interestingly, both *qarnasa* and *qurnās* allude to some of the main features of *muqarnas* as an architectural form, including subdivision and unsupported projection. Significantly, however, these terms do not describe an architectural form or suggest that these features can be discerned in existing architectural forms. Thus, the term *qarnasa* must have predated the existence of the architectural form to which it was eventually applied. Moreover, *qarnasa* or its past participle, *muqarnas*, was used to describe specific architectural forms through the semantic expansion of a relatively obscure and very limited term.[16]

A similar slippage between term and referent is observable in literature. The quadriliteral root *qrns* is first used in the noun form *qarnasa* or in the passive verb form *qurnisa* or *qurnisat*, which describes the action of applying *qarnasa* to an object. Interestingly, the earliest recorded usage occurs in an eleventh-century Andalusian text that describes the dome of a garden pavilion: *wa-qurniṣat samā'uha bil-dhahab wa'l-lazaward* (Its dome was "decorated" with gold and lapis lazuli).[17] It is unlikely that the poet in this instance is describing a true *muqarnas* dome, since the form was not known in Andalusia for another century. Rather, he is probably referring to an especially intricate ornamental pattern for which the more mundane verbs of decoration (e.g., *nqsh* or *zkhrf*) did not seem adequate. A similar ambiguity informs the descriptions of the late twelfth-century traveler Ibn Jubayr, who uses the noun *qarnasa* and the adjective *qarnasiyya* but does not speak of *muqarnas* as such. Furthermore, he applies these terms somewhat generally to forms today called *muqarnas* and to those that more closely resemble geometric ornament or openwork carving (e.g., fig. 41).[18]

The use of the term *qarnasa* to designate both geometric ornament and *muqarnas*-like forms equally, as well as the rarity of the term *muqarnas* in early sources, have both etymological and formal implications. Etymologically, it seems clear that the term *muqarnas* began its expanded semantic life not as a noun but rather as an adjective describing a form or an object with *qarnasa*, perhaps even a great deal of *qarnasa*. As the past participle of the verb *qarnasa*, *muqarnas* stands grammatically midway between an adjective and a noun, designating an object that is totally imbued by the verb it contains and, according to Heinrichs, "a man-made product."[19] We may therefore imagine that a particular decorative style had developed into something altogether new, outpacing the evolution of an appropriate term to describe it. For some time, *qarnasa* sufficed to describe these new forms and other less developed ones. But the vivid and striking appearance of fully developed stalactite forms must have required a more specific term; the term *muqarnas* was therefore fabricated.

Although *muqarnas* was eventually used as an independent noun denoting specific architectural forms, its grammatical construction inevitably recalls its adjectival dimension. Situated at the cusp of being and becoming, its etymological uncertainty closely parallels its architectural manifestation as a set of forms that have undergone transformation. Indeed, the etymological evidence so far presented suggests that *muqarnas* can no longer be considered as a specific and discrete form, but must be regarded as a geometric system that can be applied to a variety of architectural forms, transforming them in the process into characteristically subdivided forms. This makes the search for origins all the more problematic, for the most interesting issue is not so much the earliest occurrence of *muqarnas* forms, but rather the earliest manifestation of significant forms that have been substantially or entirely transformed by the application of *muqarnas*. The most significant of such forms was without doubt the dome, followed later by the portal vault.

Origins

Was the creation of *muqarnas* forms a case of radical innovation, or one of gradual development whose origins date back to early Islamic art? Gombrich has repeatedly warned art historians against interpreting change in premodern art in terms of radical innovation, insisting that "nothing comes out of nothing" and that "it is much easier to modify, enrich or reduce a given complex configuration than to construct one in the void."[20] In a similar vein, Kubler has proposed that "the human condition admits invention only as a very difficult tour de force."[21] These important conclusions do not imply that continuity necessarily leads to uniformity and lack of innovation, nor that significant transformations are not possible within tradition. Rather, by emphasizing the prerogatives of tradition and the difficulty of outright invention, they impel us to uncover intention and meaning in periods of epochal transformation and to acknowledge the cumulative effect of incremental change in creating a period style. In Islamic art, where decoration is often not just the frame but the subject itself—and this truer for *muqarnas* vaulting than for perhaps any other decorative scheme—a greater degree of innovation should perhaps be expected.

A study of *muqarnas* vaulting should focus simultaneously on the earliest occurrences of this decorative system and on those crucial junctures when a particular architectural form is so subsumed by subdivision (or *qarnaṣa*) that it must be described as *muqarnas*. This is not simply a matter of idle speculation, for in domes *muqarnas* was first rather discretely applied only to the transition zones before completely subsuming the entire form. Perhaps the earliest recorded *muqarnas* forms are several concave triangular stucco units discovered by excavation at Nishapur and datable to the tenth century. Although their reconstruction by Wilkinson as a tripartite squinch remains conjectural,[22] an in situ tripartite squinch is documented for the first time in the mausoleum of 'Arab-Atā at Tīm (Central Asia), dated A.H. 366/A.D. 976–7 (fig. 47).[23] The smooth brick dome rests not on the usual arched squinch, but on a transition zone that has been subdivided into three smaller triangular cells arranged in two rows. The effect is not so much of *muqarnas* as of a dome that is well integrated with its substructure by means of a somewhat less obtrusive transition

47 Tim (Uzbekistan), mausoleum of Arab-Ata, 978. Section (after Ettinghausen and Grabar, *Art and Architecture of Islam*, fig. 223).

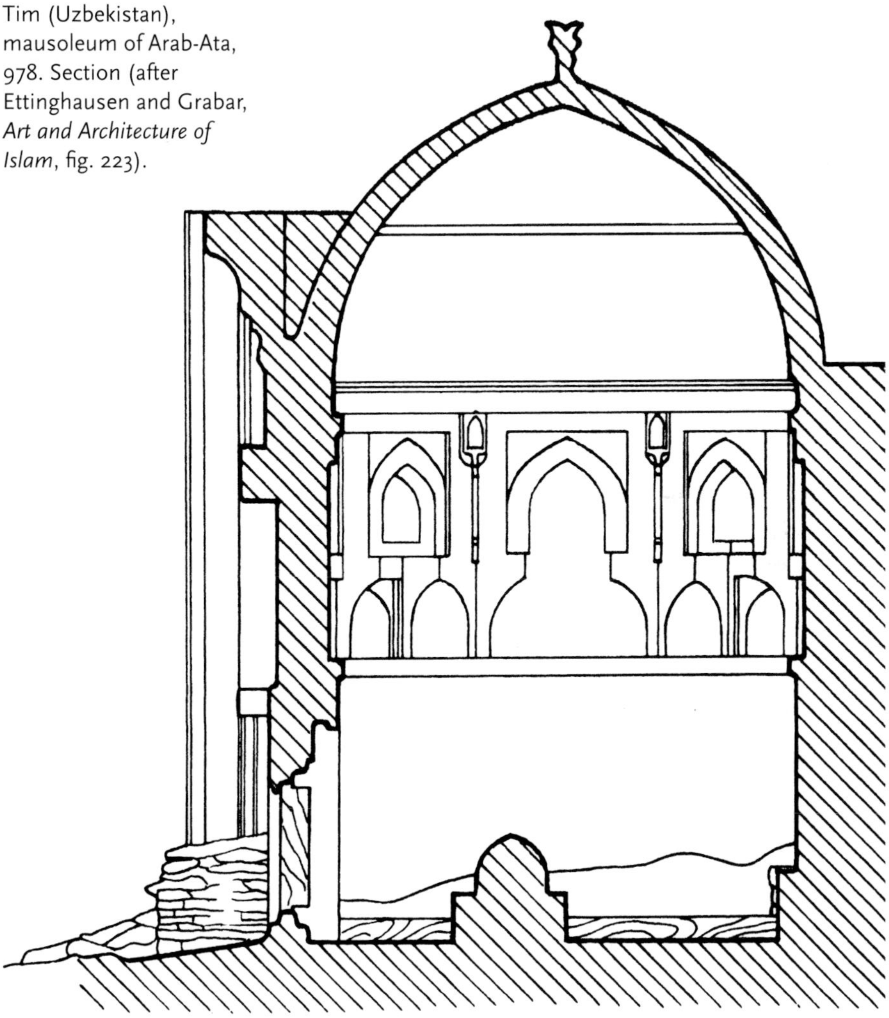

zone. Grabar has nevertheless concluded that "what we find here is the first architectural use of a uniquely Islamic theme, the *muqarnas*,"[24] a conclusion that has been widely accepted until quite recently.[25]

Perhaps the development of this differentiated squinch culminated in the Seljuq domes of the late eleventh and early twelfth centuries, the most accomplished of which is without doubt the famous North Dome at the Great Mosque of Isfahan (fig. 48). The process of integrating the dome with its substructure is further developed here as the outlines of the differentiated squinch continue the ribs of the engaged piers and propel them to the enormous pentagon inscribed in the smooth dome surface. Such domes continued to be built in central Iran virtually unchanged until the fourteenth century, as for example in the Great Mosque at Veramin, dated 1322–26. In other words, the division of the squinch zone into three or five elements was not taken any farther to produce the divided domes and vaults characteristic of *muqarnas*. Thus, although the squinch zone was first differentiated in Iran, it does not necessarily follow that the *muqarnas* dome or portal vault were also first created there. The multiplication of the squinch zone was probably the germinal idea of the *muqarnas*, but the creation of characteristically *muqarnas* spaces cannot simply be construed as a by-product of this incipient development.

Early *muqarnas* forms are also known in two other places, North Africa and Fatimid Egypt, and it is to them that I now turn. Excavations at the eleventh-century site of Qal'at bani Ḥammād in Algeria yielded two types of fragments of potential interest for the history of the *muqarnas*. The first, a group of ceramic parallelepipeds fluted on three or four sides, have been reconstructed as clusters of pendants which may have hung from the corner of a flat roof.[26] But this reconstruction is not universally accepted, and in any case this unique form seems to stand outside the line of development of the *muqarnas*. The other fragments are made of stucco and consist of a few concave triangular cells alternating with brackets. Multiplied, these cells might have constituted a *muqarnas* vault resembling those found later in other parts of North Africa or even Norman Sicily.[27] Dating from around the mid-eleventh century, these fragments are perhaps the earliest extant remains of a true *muqarnas* vault, attesting to its possible early use in a palatial context. But this discovery is also problematic, since such an important development is unlikely to have occurred in a remote region of the Islamic world. Golvin proposes to solve this problem by suggesting an Iranian influence, unaware that such *muqarnas* vaults were not used in Iran for about two more centuries. A much more likely source, as I shall point out below, is Iraq, specifically Baghdad.

OPPOSITE

48 Isfahan, Great Mosque, North Dome, 1086. Transition zone.

49 Cairo, shrine of Sayyida Ruqayya, 1135. *Muqarnas* transition zone of dome.

A number of small mausoleums and squat minarets in southern Cairo and upper Egypt, all dating from the late eleventh and twelfth centuries, contain transition zones and in some instances exterior cornices, which are subdivided and elaborated to varying degrees (fig. 49). Some of the later and better developed mausoleums, such as that at Sitti Ruqayya, actually approximate the appearance of a fully developed *muqarnas* zone. Although these shrines date from the Fatimid period, Jonathan Bloom has demonstrated that they were built not by Fatimid caliphs or viziers, but by lesser patrons, including patricians and women of the court. As products of local piety, not caliphal patronage, these shrines and minarets displayed greater inventiveness and external borrowing than caliphal foundations. Structures commissioned by Fatimid caliphs, such as the dome added by al-Ḥāfiẓ to the mosque al-Azhar in 1135, continued to the very end to employ smooth domes on plain squinches (fig. 50).

Creswell regarded these Egyptian *muqarnas* pendentives as "entirely a local creation,"[28] but Bloom has argued convincingly that they were most likely

50 Cairo, mosque al-Azhar, Dome of al-Ḥāfiẓ, 1135.

inspired by domes and minarets that once existed at the Ḥaram of Makka. Four domes (*qubbas*) at the Ḥaram are described by Ibn Jubayr as having *qarnasa*: the *qubba* above the sacred spring of Zamzam, the qubba al-ʿAbbāsiyya, the so-called qubba al-Yahūdiyya,[29] and the *qubba* at Bab Ibrāhīm. The description of the last dome, which was built by Muḥammad ibn Musa, al-Muqtadir's governor in Mecca in the early tenth century, is especially noteworthy: "Over the portal is a large dome (*qubba*), remarkable because it is almost as high as the adjacent minaret (*ṣawmaʿa*). Its interior is covered with marvelous plaster work and *qarnasi* carving that defy description. The exterior is also made of carved plaster, resembling interlaced drums."[30] Although a fully developed *muqarnas* dome probably did not exist at this early date, the description of this attenuated dome does coincide in part with the domes and minarets found in upper Egypt. Bloom further argues that since Mecca is more the recipient rather than the creator of architectural forms, the dome and the *qarnasa* work described by Ibn Jubayr probably originated elsewhere, perhaps Baghdad.[31]

Imam Dur and Baghdad

Unfortunately, very few early medieval structures survive in Baghdad, including the numerous palaces of the caliphs and the various shrines that are known to have dotted the landscape. A combination of natural disasters, invasions, and poor building material has conspired to wipe out the traces of nearly all structures built before the late twelfth century.[32] By a happy coincidence, however, an interesting eleventh-century mausoleum survives some 70 kilometers north of Baghdad, and it possibly sheds light on similar structures that once existed in the capital. This is the shrine of Imam 'Abdullāh at Dur, commonly known as Imām Dur, a village located at the northern end of the once sprawling suburbs of Samarra (fig. 51).[33]

The shrine was built in A.H. 478/A.D. 1085 by Muslim ibn Quraysh, prince of the 'Uqaylids, an Arab Shī'ite dynasty that controlled parts of upper Mesopotamia just north of the Abbasid domain. The structure was originally intended to contain the remains of Imām Abū 'Abdullah Muhammad b. Mūsā, an alleged son of the fifth Shī'ī Imām, but some sources state that the founder himself was also buried in it.[34] It stands today, as it did originally, as a solitary building, but a mosque and other structures seem to have been annexed to its eastern side at a later date.[35] The shrine consists of an elongated cube with battered walls and engaged corner buttresses topped by a conical dome whose external faceting clearly reflects its inner form. Checkered brick decoration (*hazār-baf*) covers the buttresses and the friezelike zone just below the springing of the dome, which also encloses the name of the builder (Abū Shākir ibn abi'l-Faraj ibn Nāsuwayh) in a cartouche above the northern entrance. Each portion is about 12 meters high, making the 24-meter-tall dome a prominent feature in the utterly flat landscape.

Internally, the square chamber (7.85 meters per side) is transformed into an octagon by four squinches and four arches (fig. 52). A succession of four more eight-celled tiers with cells of decreasing size, each with a 45-degree rotation, makes up most of the dome, which is topped with a little cupola. It would have been quite feasible to build a smooth dome just above the first squinch zone, but a deliberate choice was made to continue the intricate layering of *muqarnas* tiers until the desired height and complexity had been achieved. The layering of diminishing and multiply-profiled cells makes the dome appear insubstantial, as the play of light on its intricate surfaces dissolves its mass. Such visual display, which is one of the most important features of the *muqarnas* dome, distinguishes it from the hemispherical Seljuq domes that rest on *muqarnas* squinches.

A form at this level of development, situated as it is in a tiny village, suggests the existence of earlier models in an urban center. This center can only be Baghdad, the still-vibrant capital of the Abbasids and Sunni Islam, and a city that was witnessing a measure of cultural revival and political independence

51 Dur (Iraq), shrine of Imām Dur, 1085. Exterior.

52 Dur (Iraq), shrine of Imām Dur, 1085. Interior.

that had begun with the stridently Sunni leadership of Caliph al-Qādir (991–1031). Thus, the *muqarnas* dome erected by Muslim ibn Quraysh was most likely inspired by a domical type that had originated in Baghdad and may have become quite common there by the second half of the eleventh century.[36] Two paintings from the fifteenth and sixteenth centuries show bird's-eye views of Baghdad with numerous *muqarnas* domes, suggesting that the form was a common feature of the cityscape in the late medieval period.[37]

North Africa and Sicily

The next dated examples of *muqarnas* domes come not from Baghdad, nor from anywhere in Iraq, but from such diverse places as Marrakesh, Fez, Palermo, and Damascus. I have already noted the tentative beginnings of *muqarnas* vaulting in central North Africa around the middle of the eleventh century; by the middle of the twelfth century, it was everywhere. The earliest example is

the enigmatic *qubba* al-Barūdiyyīn in Marrakesh, datable to the reign of the second Almoravid ruler ʿAli b. Yusuf (1107–43), more specifically 1117 (fig. 53).[38] The *qubba*, which has been excavated and restored since its discovery in 1947, stands today several meters below street level as a decorated dome that rests on a rectangular, rather than square, understructure, measuring 7.30 by 5.50 meters at the base for a total height of 12 meters.

The *qubba* is an astonishing structure, decorated on its exterior and interior in the most inventive and flamboyant manner.[39] The exterior is horizontally divided into three zones separated by moldings and merlons: open arched doors on the first level; arcaded galleries on the second; and a carved dome on the third. The architect used the unequal sides of the rectangle as an opportunity to display his repertory of arched doors and windows—pointed, horseshoe, trilobed, and foliate, all set within a recessed frame (*alfiz*) in the Andalusian manner. The decoration on the dome itself is divided into two zones: the lower with closely spaced interlacing arches, and the upper with chevrons surrounding a large seven-pointed star that emanates from the center (fig. 54).[40]

Viewed as a plan (fig. 55), the dome seems to rest on an octagon rotated within a larger octagon that is surrounded by an eight-pointed star made by the intersecting ribs of two rotated squares. But this impression vanishes when one views the *qubba* directly or through its section (fig. 56). What in plan appear as continuous ribs are in fact four arch-shaped squinches and four arches in the middle of each side, which are surmounted by another level of shallow squinches rotated at 45 degrees. Only when the lines of these two layers, which are quite distinct in the section, are flattened in plan do they appear as intersecting ribs. This is an important point and a striking difference between this dome and the domes at Cordoba, to which it is often compared, whose continuous ribs contrast with these superimposed squinches.

53 Marrakesh, *qubba* al-Bārūdiyyīn, 1117. Exterior view.

54 Marrakesh, *qubba* al-Bārūdiyyīn, 1117. Detail of dome exterior.

55 Marrakesh, *qubba* al-Bārūdiyyīn, 1117. Plan (after Meunié et al., *Nouvelles Recherches*, fig. 15).

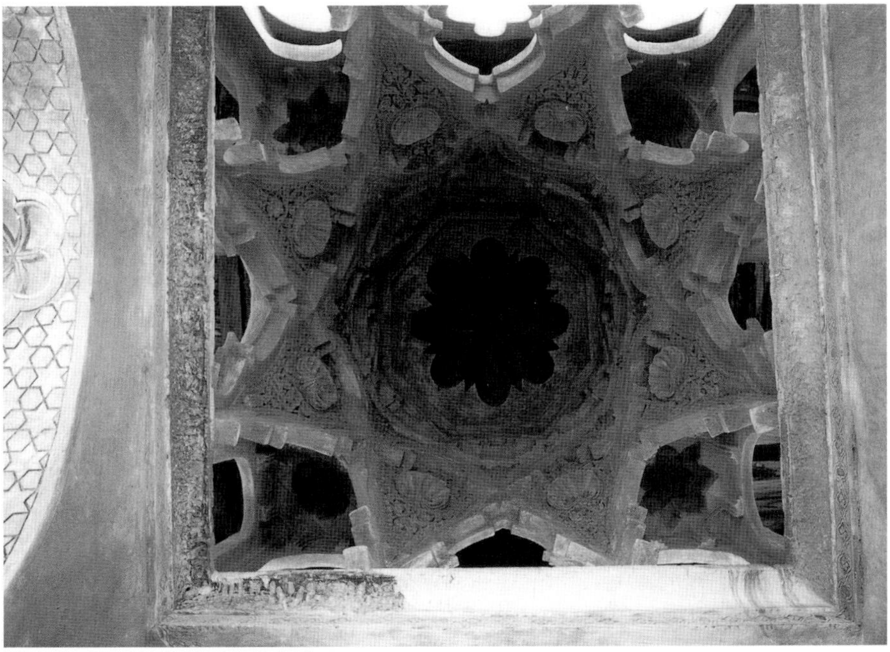

56 Marrakesh, *qubba* al-Bārūdiyyīn, 1117. Dome interior. (Photograph: D. Fairchild Ruggles.)

Internally, the *qubba* consists of four zones separated by moldings: a long plain zone that contains the arched entrances; another long zone with two levels of superimposed arches; a short zone with eight *muqarnas* squinches; and an eight-lobed and ribbed dome on top. The four corner bays with their little *muqarnas* domes can be glimpsed through the arches, producing an unusual three-dimensional effect. The complexity of the layered and seemingly interlaced arches, the *muqarnas* corner domes, and the richness of the vegetal ornament create an opulent and mysterious effect that has never been surpassed by other domes in North Africa. Although not a *muqarnas* dome as such, the *qubba* seems impossible without some knowledge of such domes. In effect, it appears as a synthesis of the ribbed domes of Cordoba and the *muqarnas* domes of Baghdad, a cultural duality that parallels it patrons' links with al-Andalus and the Abbasid caliphate.[41]

This unique dome is linked to Baghdad in several important ways. Its attenuated form, which is not known in Andalusian architecture, recalls the overall shape of such *muqarnas* domes as Imām Dur (cf. figs. 56 and 52, pp. 112–14). The geometric star patterns decorating the soffits of its arches are also intrusive in the Maghreb and point to an eastern source, while the *muqarnas* elements in its little domes point directly to Baghdad. Finally, as noted above, the cursive inscription encircling the springing of the dome is the earliest one in North Africa, and unquestionably represents a borrowing from Baghdad.[42] More than a mere dome above an ablution fountain (if that indeed was its original function[43]) the *qubba* was most likely an act of homage to the Abbasid state and a symbol of acceptance of the occasionalistic theology actively endorsed by the Abbasids. I shall return below to these two points.

Two other Almoravid monuments with early *muqarnas* further underline the significance of borrowings from the Abbasid caliphate. The Great Mosque at Tlemcen (1136) contains a ribbed filigree-stucco dome that rests on *muqarnas* squinches and is capped by a *muqarnas* cupola. In the mosque of al-Qarawiyyīn at Fez, the entire roof of the axial nave was rebuilt in 1134–43 and equipped with several outstanding specimens of *muqarnas* vaulting that display an astonishing variety despite their early date (fig. 57).[44] All these vaults are made of carved stucco and suspended from a wooden gable roof, a building technique that continues for several centuries in North Africa and Spain. This Almoravid rebuilding of the most venerable mosque in Fez, therefore, completely shunned the Cordoban features still present at the *qubba* al-Bārūdiyyīn (fig. 56) and embraced the Abbasid mode of *muqarnas* vaulting. Thus, it seems abundantly clear from these three examples of Almoravid architecture that this Sunni Berber dynasty was primarily responsible for introducing *muqarnas* vaulting into North Africa, thereby planting the seed for the significant developments to be seen later at the Alhambra palace and all over North Africa.

57 Fez, Great mosque of al-Qarawiyyīn. Almoravid rebuilding of the axial nave, 1134–43. *Muqarnas* vault (Terrasse, *La Mosquée d'al-Qaraouyin*, pl. 32).

58 Damascus, *bīmāristān* al-Nūrī, 1154. Portal.

59 Damascus, *bīmāristān* al-Nūrī, 1154. Vault over vestibule.

The Domes of Nūr al-Dīn in Damascus

In Syria, the earliest use of *muqarnas* vaulting dates to the period of Nūr al-Dīn, who had used it in his two most important buildings, his hospital *bīmāristān* (1154) and funerary *madrasa* (1168). The *bīmāristān* al-Nūrī in Damascus presents an innovation that must have been startling at the time of its foundation and is still impressive: a *muqarnas* vault in the hood of the portal (fig. 58). This is the earliest known *muqarnas* portal vault and the only one made of stucco; all later ones are made either of stone or brick. The portal leads to a vestibule, which is covered by a *muqarnas* vault and flanked by two niches, also covered by *muqarnas* vaults (fig. 59). Like the slightly earlier vaults of the Qarawiyyīn mosque at Fez, these vaults are made of stucco and suspended from the load-bearing roof by a wooden framework. Their use of

60 Damascus, *madrasa* al-Nūriyya, 1168. Mausoleum of Nūr al-Dīn, exterior.

pendant elements and eight-pointed stars also recalls the Qarawiyyīn and suggests that they are both similarly based on an Iraqi prototype. Indeed, in the case of the *bīmāristān*, the connection is even stronger, for both the dome type and the institution of the hospital itself were based on a Baghdadi prototype.[45]

The mausoleum of Nūr al-Dīn, dated A.H. 563/A.D. 1168, represents a more fully developed example of a Mesopotamian *muqarnas* dome in Syria, a form more noted for its overall influence than for its exact replication (fig. 60).[46] In addition to being functionally related to Iraqi examples, it also resembles them in its single-shell brick rather than double-shell stucco construction, such that its interior articulation is reflected on its exterior. But in this Damascene version, extradorsality is only possible in the upper half of the dome, since its lower half is encased in a square enclosure. On the interior, however, this separation is barely visible, and the dome presents a fully integrated effect with *muqarnas* corbelling springing simultaneously from the four corners and from eight small *muqarnas* colonettes that flank the windows at the base of the square (fig. 61). By gradually expanding the corner squinches and contracting the number of intervening cells, the vault is transformed first into a nearly octagonal zone that turns in the uppermost zone into a circle topped by a small, gored cupola.

Two conclusions may be derived from these two important monuments. First, *muqarnas* vaulting clearly spans the divide between religious and secular architecture, for we have already seen it used in mosques, palaces, a *madrasa*, and a hospital. The multifunctionality of architectural and decorative forms and the permeability of the religious-secular barrier are both common-

61 Damascus, *madrasa* al-Nūriyya, 1168. Mausoleum of Nūr al-Dīn, interior.

place in Islamic architecture, but the specific case of *muqarnas* vaulting deserves further attention (see p. 124). Second, Nūr al-Dīn's use of the *muqarnas* dome for his illustrious hospital and his own mausoleum parallels his adoption of cursive writing around the same time, and the two phenomena clearly indicate his overriding interest in Abbasid architectural forms. This interest, as noted above, coincides with his theological and political connections with the Abbasid caliphate, the source of legitimation and the safeguard of the Sunni community.[47]

Back to Baghdad

Although I have argued for a Baghdadi origin of the *muqarnas* dome sometime in the early eleventh century, I have also noted the absence of any monuments in Baghdad dating before the end of the twelfth century. Fortunately, a handful of monuments have been preserved in Baghdad from the late twelfth to the first half of the thirteenth century, and some of these are especially noteworthy

OPPOSITE

62 Baghdad, mausoleum of Zumurrud Khātūn, c. 1200. Exterior.

63 Baghdad, mausoleum of Zumurrud Khātūn, c. 1200. Interior.

RIGHT

64 Baghdad, Abbasid Palace, c. 1200. Detail of *muqarnas* vaulting.

for their carved brick arabesque and outstanding *muqarnas* vaults. The shrine of Zumurrud Khātūn, built by Caliph al-Nāṣir (1180–1225) has perhaps the most graceful profile and one of the most integrated interiors of all conical *muqarnas* domes (fig. 62). An octagonal base with intricate geometric decoration supports a tall, conical brick vault whose interior articulation is fully displayed on the exterior, producing the appearance of a pinecone. On the interior, the dome springs from an extremely unobtrusive squinch zone, which transforms the octagonal base into a *muqarnas* dome of sixteen cells (fig. 63). Seven tiers of sixteen cells make up the majority of the dome; their number is cut to ten in the last three tiers. Each cell contains a tiny opening covered by thick glass.

The second monument is the so-called Abbasid Palace, sometimes called the *madrasa* al-Sharābiyya.[48] Regardless of its original function, this monument contains some of the richest and finest carved brick ornament and one of the most original uses of *muqarnas* vaulting in Islamic architecture, that is, a continuous vault over the narrow corridor between the courtyard arcade and the eastern rooms (fig. 64). The *muqarnas* cells begin at the piers and end in small vaults capped with eight-pointed stars, such that the entire corridor is turned into a series of interlinked little *muqarnas* vaults, a remarkable achievement that has no parallel in Islamic architecture. The sophistication and innovation seen here and at Zumurrud Khatun testify to a long tradition of arabesque design and *muqarnas* vaulting in this city of vanished glory and give further credence to Baghdad's instrumental role in the formulation of these techniques.

To summarize, then: incipient *muqarnas* decoration first occurred around the late tenth century in eastern Iran, where it was used to articulate the squinch zones of domes or the exterior cornices of minarets or domes. Sometime in the eleventh century, most likely in Baghdad, *muqarnas* was first applied to significant architectural forms, including the dome and portal vault, producing highly distinctive forms that stand apart from the more common, two-dimensional arabesque decoration. Once developed, *muqarnas* vaulting quickly spread to North Africa by the 1130s and to Damascus by mid century,

possibly motivated by political and religious factors. By the late twelfth century, *muqarnas* vaulting was everywhere, except in Egypt, where its use in official monuments did not begin before the thirteenth century. Finally, despite the absence of early *muqarnas* in Baghdad, the few remaining structures from the end of the twelfth century speak, by virtue of their outstanding merit, of a deeply rooted tradition of *muqarnas* vaulting.

Interpretation

Two medieval descriptions of *muqarnas* vaulting elucidate contemporary interpretations through their direct empathetic reading of this form. Curiously, both accounts are written by Christian monks, who employ the well-established mode of Byzantine *ekphrasis* to describe what to them must have been quite extraordinary buildings. The first account, by Nikolaos Mesarites, was written in honor of the so-called Mouchroutas (Arabic *makhrūṭ*, cone), a structure founded in the middle of the twelfth century during the reign of Manuel I (1143–1180) and adjacent to the principal throne room of the Imperial Palace in Constantinople.[49] The description makes it abundantly clear that the Mouchroutas was a conical *muqarnas* vault, possibly intended as a reception vestibule for visiting Seljuq dignitaries. Interestingly, the building was founded by John Comnenus, a high-ranking official of Turkish lineage, being the grandson of John Axouch, a Seljuq Turk captured as a boy by the Byzantines in 1097." After revealing that the building was the work "of a Persian [i.e., Seljuq] hand," Mesarites proceeds with the following description:

> The canopy of the roof, consisting of hemispheres joined to the heaven-like ceiling, offers a variegated spectacle; closely packed angles project inward and outward; the beauty of the carving is extraordinary, and wonderful is

> the appearance of the cavities which, overlaid with gold, produce the effect of a rainbow more colorful than the one in the clouds. There is insatiable enjoyment here—not hidden, but on the surface. Not only those who direct their gaze to these things for the first time, but those who have often done so are struck by wonder and astonishment.[50]

The second *ekphrasis* is in the form of a homily by the monk Philagathos in praise of the *muqarnas* ceiling of the twelfth-century Capella Palatina in Palermo. Extending for the entire length of the chapel's nave, this *muqarnas* vault is made of wood that has been covered with plaster and painted in myriad figural and nonfigural designs. Philagathos' description ignores the paintings and focuses on the most unusual part of this vault:

> You do not tire of contemplating the roof, a cause of wonder and marvel to those who see or hear about it. Embellished as it is with delicate carvings, which are executed as differently shaped coffers and shining with gold from all sides, it imitates the clear sky of heaven, illuminated by the choir of the stars.[51]

Three observations can be made about these two texts. First, although both writers are undoubtedly men of learning, they put their textual learning aside and opt for, even to cherish, a direct appreciation of the dome. Mesarites emphasizes the surface "not hidden" enjoyment, which can be derived from gazing upon this dome; both writers advise a long and sustained meditation on their intricate surfaces. While deemphasizing figural representation, both writers also dwell on the geometric construction of the vaults, the richness of their gilding and surface decoration, and hence, their great beauty. Informed more by contrasts to Byzantine domes than by comparisons to Islamic ones, these twelfth-century descriptions, in their empathy and freshness, have not been superseded by contemporary interpretations.

The second observation has to do with the effect and allusive power of this sustained meditation. Joy, "insatiable enjoyment," is certainly the primary effect, and it is directly induced in viewers who observe the exquisite geometric surfaces of the domes. For more informed viewers, this immediate enjoyment leads to wonder, marvel, and astonishment, for the domes are linked in their minds with other wondrous devices (*'ajā'ib*) of medieval courts. Furthermore, these *muqarnas* vaults produce the effect of "a heaven-like ceiling ... a rainbow more colorful than the one in the cloud," and "the clear sky of heaven, illuminated by the choir of the stars." In sum, the effect proceeds from instant joy to wonder to heavenly allusion.

Third, despite the similarity of the descriptions, these were in fact very different vaults. While both had *muqarnas* vaulting, one was a secular structure, while the other covered a royal chapel. In fact, in addition to their functional difference, the vaults may have originated in different formal types whose history is still incompletely known, a point to which I shall return.

For contemporary writers, the question of meaning in *muqarnas* has led to quite polarized interpretations, ranging from the usual fanciful readings by essentialist scholars[52] to the rejectionist or ambivalent views of most art historians. Allen, adhering to positivist methodology, proposes that geometric ornament and *muqarnas* "are primarily visual inventions rather than intellectual constructs," since, according to him, visual accuity and the appreciation of geometric forms were not among the necessary traits of the Muslim learned class.[53] Grabar, on the other hand, suggests that *muqarnas* was one of "a set of neutral forms whose only purpose was to please." He adds, however, that "these forms could be charged through external vector like inscriptions into becoming iconophoric; they *could* become carriers of visual and other meanings, but such messages were not inherent to the forms."[54] Unlike the direct reading of the two medieval observers above, Grabar's analysis defers appreciation, placing it behind a veil of inscriptions. In other words, a direct, empathetic reading of the form has been lost in the process of interpreting monumental forms through texts.

Of all contemporary writers, Necipoğlu pays the closest attention to the semiotic dimension of *muqarnas* vaulting and especially to its description and appreciation by Christian and Muslim observers alike.[55] While noting the absence of written sources on "the specific associations of two- and three-dimensional geometric patterns during the Sunni revival," she produces numerous later references in Arabic and especially Persian literature that speak metaphorically of the stellate compositions in *muqarnas* vaults, invariably comparing them to "the celestial sphere" and "the starry heaven."[56] These rich but nonspecific references lead the author to propose that *muqarnas* vaulting was not a symbolic representation but rather "a loosely interpreted analogy" of the heavens. More generally, she proposes that two- and three-dimensional geometric forms inhabit "an intermediary zone between the 'decorative' and the 'symbolic.'"[57]

The Secular Dimension

While agreeing with the general thrust of Necipoğlu's interpretation, I am still intrigued by a few instances in which the *muqarnas* dome seems to have been used somewhat more deliberately, possibly as a symbolic form. Are these instances mere aberrations? Does their symbolism reside merely in their historical context and inscriptions? Or are they perhaps the primary motivators, the Gombrichian schema or primary model of what later became commonplace forms? While we may include most *muqarnas* domes and vaults under Necipoğlu's "intermediary zone," a few singular examples—some secular, others religious—resist such classification. Among the secular domes, I would single out those built by the caliph al-Muqtadir in Mecca, the Almoravid *qubba* al-*Bārūdiyyīn*, and the Byzantine Mouchroutas. Unique by virtue of their early date and unusual location, these structures may point to a deeply rooted Abbasid tradition of dome building that predated *muqarnas* but was eventually influenced by its development.

This Abbasid tradition of nonreligious dome building may well be traced to their famous dome *qubba* al-Khaḍrā', located at the center of Madinat al-Salām.[58] But such an investigation would take us too far afield, so I propose to begin a few centuries later with the Abbasid dome at Bab Ibrāhīm in Mecca. This was an unusual dome, whether in terms of form or function. Functionally, it did not serve any of the purposes for which domes had previously been intended, namely as a *miḥrāb* dome within a mosque or as a shrine or mausoleum. Rather, it seems to have been something of an imperial structure, a monument declaring the presence of the Abbasids in this sacred precinct.

Formally, the dome according to Ibn Jubayr was distinguished by its height, the intricate *qarnasi* plaster carving on its interior, and the interlaced circular arches on its exterior.[59] To my knowledge, only one extant dome contains these three features: the *qubba* al-*Bārūdiyyīn* in Marrakesh; in fact it is the only extant dome that is decorated with interlaced arches on its exterior. As suggested above, the early use of geometric ornament, *muqarnas* vaulting, cursive writing in this dome, and its overall attenuated form all point to Baghdadi influence, suggesting that the *qubba* al-*Bārūdiyyīn* might have been intended as an act of symbolic homage to the Abbasid caliphate. Moreover, its formal similarity to an early Abbasid dome, built in the most sacred spot for the Muslims, further enhances this linkage and imbues it with an aura of sanctity. In other words, the *qubba* simultaneously refers to the Abbasid caliphate and to their pious acts at the Shrine of Mecca, allusions that coincide perfectly with the Almoravids' political and religious orientation.

These two domes also indicate the existence of a hitherto unnoticed monumental type: a tall dome, ornamented on its interior and exterior, that may have been produced in Baghdad in the late ninth or early tenth century. Sometime in the eleventh century this dome was probably decorated with *muqarnas* vaulting, further enhancing its distinctiveness and decorative appeal and possibly referring to a dominant theological concept, to which I shall turn below. By the beginning of the following century, this dome seems to have become an emblem of Abbasid rulership, a sign of homage to their secular and religious authority, and a reflection of their wealth and luxury. For one or all of these reasons, the Almoravids and perhaps other dynasties copied this dome, using it as an annex to a palace or as a garden pavilion.

Viewed from this perspective, the Byzantine Mouchroutas of the mid-twelfth century becomes less enigmatic. This was, after all, a conical *muqarnas* dome, founded and built by men of Seljuq ancestry in order to serve a royal ceremonial function. Although personal motives of pride and identity may have played a role in this foundation, it could only have been admitted into the very heart of the Byzantine Imperial Palace with some knowledge of its Abbasid significance and appreciation of its exotic qualities. In all likelihood, this dome was built as a sign of homage to another imperial realm and as a supreme example of the wondrous artifacts that were circulated in the medieval period.

Despite their paucity, these instances strongly suggest that a type of ornamented conical dome sometimes carried a high and specific symbolic charge, perhaps the reason for its subsequent widespread use in palaces and garden pavilions. In time, it seems likely that the specifically Abbasid associations of the *muqarnas* dome would have been diminished or lost, while it continued to be appreciated for its increasing formal complexity, exotic appearance, and possible astral associations.[60] The frequent use of *muqarnas* vaulting in the palaces and kiosks of the twelfth-century Norman kings of Sicily and the fourteenth-century Nasrids of Granada nicely fits such a hypothesis. The prototype of a lavishly decorated, *muqarnas*-encrusted domical space seems to be at the foundation of La Zisa, La Cuba (or *al-qubba*), and other Norman pavilions, but these elements were probably used for their broadly imperial and distinctly exotic effect, rather than as an act of homage to the Abbasids.[61]

The Alhambra stands at the end of this continuum, having benefited from more than three centuries of development in *muqarnas* vaulting and thus displaying certain continuities as well as some significant departures (fig. 66). Its outstanding *muqarnas* domes were appreciated, much like earlier ones, for their ingenious construction, technical refinements, and exotic form—elements that were intended to produce awe and amazement in the viewer, much like such other wondrous devices (*'ajā'ib*) as unusual fountains, water clocks, and automata.[62] These devices would also have identified their owners as members of the aristocracy, which is another important reason for their wide, cross-cultural circulation. Moreover, these domes embodied an astral or otherwordly dimension, often alluded to in poetry, which may be grounded in theological discourse. Grabar has argued against this possibility, interpreting this astral symbolism in the light of Roman dome iconography and maintaining that these *muqarnas* domes (and others) were in fact "pleasure domes" devoid of any specifically Islamic values. He concludes that "the Muslim world rejected the Christianization of the dome."[63] But did the Muslim world necessarily reject the "Islamization" of the dome?

The Religious Dimension

Obviously, a different interpretation is required to explain the equally widespread use of *muqarnas* vaulting in religious and quasi-religious buildings, including mosques, mausoleums, and *madrasas*. Or conversely, a religious or theological interpretation of the *muqarnas* dome seems warranted, if only to address its frequent comparison, by Muslim and Christian observers alike, to "the celestial sphere" or "the starry heavens."[64] What is the basis of this metaphorical allusion to the dome of heaven? What did these chroniclers, poets, or homilists see in these domes that led them to such spectacular comparisons? It was certainly neither historical context nor epigraphic evidence—the mainstay of interpretation in Islamic architecture—since none of these writers paid any attention to such questions. The answer must reside in the domes themselves, in the specific composition and manipulation of their formal features, and in the metaphorical allusions that these features elicited.

Functionally, early *muqarnas* vaulting is associated with two types of religious or pious monuments: the freestanding mausoleum and the mosque, most commonly as a *miḥrāb* dome or *maqṣūra*. As with palace architecture, both of these functional types had been associated with domes long before the invention of *muqarnas* vaulting. Mausoleums and shrines have used domes since early Islam, a practice whose roots can be traced in several directions: early Christian martyria, Sassanian *jahār-tāq*, and Arab and Turkish funerary practices. Despite the differing typologies available for mausoleums in each region of the Islamic world and the factors impinging on their development, the domed cube was by far the most widespread form for mausoleums.[65]

Early domed shrines in Islam have long been associated with Shī'ism, and although this idea has recently come under attack, it is still largely valid.[66] I propose above that the great intensity of Shī'ī ceremonials and the institutionalization of these commemorations in the second half of the tenth century provoked a visceral reaction among the Sunni populations of Baghdad and the cities of Khurasan. Unable to curb these practices, the Sunnis reacted by staging others of their own, including the creation of domes, as a countermeasure against Shī'ī commemorations.[67] Although there were always other reaons to build shrines, the politics of identity and the rivalry between Shī'īs and Sunnis unquestionably underlay this phenomenon, accounting in particular for the most significant of these foundations and for their increasing visual distinctiveness.[68]

This rivalry may also account for the proliferation of domes within the format of the traditional hypostyle mosque. Some early mosques, particularly those built by the Aghlabids of North Africa in the ninth century, acquired a single dome covering and highlighting the bay in front of the *miḥrāb*. In fact, the Great Mosque of Qayrawan, first built with a single dome in 836, had a second dome in 862 at the beginning of its axial nave.[69] In the following century, the Fatimids continued this practice and even added two more domes at both ends of the *qibla* wall, as seen in the mosques al-Azhar (967) and al-Ḥākim (990) in Cairo.

Not to be outdone by the Fatimids or any other Muslim dynasty, the Spanish Umayyad caliph al-Ḥakam II began in 962 to expand the Great Mosque at Cordoba, adding to it a veritable mosque in its own regard, with a dome at the beginning of the axial nave and a three-dome *maqṣūra* at its end.[70] Even more than their unusual number, these domes stand out for their structure and appearance for, unlike most earlier smooth or gored domes, they are ribbed (fig. 65). Structurally, ribs span the corners and extend laterally across the dome, creating smaller compartments that are easier to span. Visually, the domes present two paradoxes: a fragmented surface that is unified by the overall geometry, and a solid construction whose stability is belied by excessive decoration and by the seemingly unsupported projection of the ribs. Indeed, the same paradoxes also describe the interlacing arches beneath these domes, whose solid antique columns and reassuring massiveness are contradicted by their ambiguous design and gravity-defying composition. Although neither domes nor arches were ever attempted again in quite the same manner, their visual ambiguity, though not their structural ingenuity, exerted considerable influence on the later architecture of the Almoravids and Almohads.

Whether in shrines or in mosques, the politics of identity and difference apparently accounts for the proliferation of domes and for what might be called their "Islamization." As Sunni piety strived to demonstrate its difference from Shīʿī practices and as Muslims continued to search for other ways to distinguish themselves from Christians (as in al-Andalus, for example), they seem to have searched for modes of expression that reflected their own particular creed and world view. And since the dominant movement in the eleventh and twelfth centuries was that of resurgent Sunnism, this particular creed (with all its inner diversity) claimed ascendance in visual expression and succeeded in effecting significant transformations in art and architecture. Contemporary Shīʿītes, with the exception of the Fatimids, simply followed suit at first, before eventually producing a visual identity that reflected their own beliefs and rituals.

How, then, was the dome transformed in this epoch, and how does its transformation reflect or embody a cosmological perspective that might be linked with the theology or theologies of the Sunni revival? The early examples of *muqarnas* vaulting in religious contexts examined above should suffice to establish the main features of its design and the characteristics of its usage in this context. These are the shrine of Imām Dur (1085), the Almoravid vaults at the mosque al-Qarawiyyīn (1135–40), the *bīmāristān* of Nūr al-Dīn (1154), and the mausoleum of Nūr al-Dīn (1168). Regardless of their technical differences—the first and fourth are made of brick, the second and third of stucco—these *muqarnas* domes (and many others) share some basic features. First, the entire dome, or most of it, is made of small but distinct cells consisting of discrete geometric shapes, leaving only the uppermost portion as a smooth or scalloped cupola serving as a lantern. Second, all structural features or normally load-bearing elements such as squinches, pendentives, arches, and colonnettes are diminished by fragmentation and integration with the body of the dome. Third, carved stucco, paint, or glazed tiles are often used to embellish the

65 Cordoba, Great Mosque. Expansion of al-Ḥakam II, 962–67, Villaviciosa dome.

cells, further enhancing their fragmented effect. Fourth, whenever possible, windows are used, although in double-shell constructions, they are ony possible at the base and the lantern.[71] Fifth, the domes sometimes, but by no means always, spring above an inscriptional frieze.

What led the Muslim architect in this period to abandon the hemispherical dome with its age-old symbolic associations and take up this fragmented conical vault? What meanings were intended that differed from those inherent in the hemispherical dome, and how did this new form carry these meanings? If we accept, as the medieval critics did, that these meanings primarily reside in the form itself, then we are entitled to base our interpretation of the *muqarnas* dome on its formal manipulations, visual effect, and metaphorical allusions. Thus, the fragmentation of supports and surfaces into small interrelated segments would imply a particular attitude about the nature of matter, while the application of this process to the entire dome would suggest a particular conception of the dome, or its referent, the universe. Furthermore, the insubstantial, precarious, and ever-changing appearance of these domes might allude to the ephemerality of human efforts, the transience of the material world, and the permanence of the Creator.

Muslim philosophers and theologians devoted considerable thought to the nature of matter and the universe and their relationship to God. Even the most rationalist Muslim theologians rejected the Aristotelian concept of an eternal cosmos because it contradicted the Islamic conception of God as the only absolute and eternal. According to M. Fakhry, from early on and "with hardly a single exception, the Muslim theologians accepted the atomic view of matter, space and time and built upon it a theological edifice over which God presided as absolute sovereign."[72] Accordingly, matter was neither eternal and immutable nor infinite in composition but rather composed of particles which cannot be divided any further (*al-juz' alladhī lā yatajazza'*). Although the rationalist Mu'tazilis were directly involved in the creation of this atomistic cosmology, they nevertheless curbed its potential dogmatism by accepting the existence and mediation of autonomous agents of natural law as well as considerable freewill for human thought and actions.

The Ash'arīs of the tenth and eleventh centuries took over this atomistic cosmology and pushed it to its natural extremes, making it a cosmology of occasionalism, or a theory of atoms and accidents. Abu Bakr al-Baqillānī (d. 1013), the chief Ash'arī theologian before al-Ghazzālī, argued that the world, which to him was everything other than God, was composed of atoms and accidents. Accidents could not endure within matter (*jawhar*) for longer than an instant, but were continuously being changed by God. It follows, then, that the attributes of matter (color, luminosity, shape, etc.) are transitory accidents that change according to the will of God, and that even the preservation of matter—the collocation of its atoms—requires the continuous intervention of God.

The occasionalism of al-Baqillānī therefore ascribed to God not only the first act of creation but also the unending process of preserving the created world from one instant to another. Through a continuous process of annihilation and recreation, God alone can guarantee the order and consistency of the universe by preserving the accidental combination of atoms. This cosmology embodied the wisdom and knowledge of an omnipotent God, who had directly created the universe in time and without any intermediaries, and who was continually involved in maintaining its order, balance, and coherence. This theory differed from the Muʻtazilī, Ismāʻīlī, and even Shīʻī views of the universe, which, in varying degrees, held to the belief that the universe was an external emanation existing independently of God and subject to its own natural law. In sum, occasionalist theology was intended constantly to remind us that God is present and active in all things, and to suggest to us that this world here below would be only a discontinuous chaos but for the Divine Presence.[73]

The parallels between occasionalistic cosmology and the *muqarnas* dome are very striking indeed, displaying on the macro and micro levels ideas of fragmentation, impermanence, and imminent collapse. Indeed, the seemingly complete confluence between the attributes of occasionalism and the perceptual properties of the *muqarnas* dome suggest that the *muqarnas* dome was intended as an architectural manifestation of this thoroughly orthodox Islamic concept. In order to represent an occasionalist view of the world, a fragmented and ephemeral-looking dome was created by applying *muqarnas* to its entire surface, from transition zone to apex. This procedure creates a comprehensive effect intended to reflect the fragmented, perishable, and transient nature of the universe while alluding to the omnipotence and eternity of God, who can keep this dome from collapsing, just as he can keep the universe from destruction.

The likely origin of the *muqarnas* dome in Baghdad in the early eleventh century coincides with the triumph of Ashʻarī thought and occasionalistic cosmology. More specifically, during the pivotal period of Caliph al-Qādir, his chief theologian and apologist, al-Bāqillānī, as previously mentioned, wrote treatises and issued manifestoes opposing Muʻtazilī theology and Fatimid rule as well as valorizing Sunni traditionalism and Abbasid rule. The *muqarnas* dome might thus have been created during this time of heated debate as a symbolic manifestation of an occasionalist universe and a distinctive emblem of the resurgent Abbasid state, the safeguard of the Muslim community. Whether this development took place first within the context of Abbasid palaces in Baghdad or as a dome covering the shrine of an important Sunni theologian cannot be determined. But for reasons already explored above, the precise circumstances of this development are perhaps less important than the fact that the *muqarnas* dome from very early on was employed as a highly charged symbolic form in both secular and religious contexts.

Other than Necipoğlu, whose interpretation of the *muqarnas* dome does not radically differ from what I propose above, only Grabar has offered an interpretation of it. His ideas stem largely from his careful analysis of perhaps the two most famous *muqarnas* domes, namely those crowning the halls of the Abencerrajes and the Two Sisters at the Alhambra Palace (fig. 66). Built in the second half of the fourteenth century—that is, nearly three centuries after the first documented *muqarnas* dome—these domes push the concepts of fragmentation, ephemerality, and unsupported projection beyond any logical limits. The combination of a wide variety of tiny cells with a high proportion of pendants, the intricate composition, the use of color, and diffuse lighting all help create gravity-defying and ever-changing domes that summarize three centuries of artistic development.

Yet Grabar does not base his interpretation of these magnificent domes on their form but rather on richly evocative poetic and prosodic texts, some of which are inscribed on the very walls supporting these domes:

> The hand of the Pleiades will spend the night invoking God's protection in their favor and they will awaken to the gentle blowing of the breeze.
>
> In here is a cupola which by its height becomes lost from site; beauty in it appears both concealed and visible.
>
> The constellation of Gemini extends a ready hand [to help it] and the full moon of the heavens draws near to whisper secretly to it.
>
> It is no wonder that it surpasses the stars in the heavens, and passes beyond their furthest limits.
>
> For it is before your dwelling that it has arisen to perform its service, since he who serves the highest acquires merits thereby.
>
> You would think that they are the heavenly spheres whose orbits revolve, overshadowing the pillar of dawn when it barely begins after having passed through the night.

As with earlier Christian descriptions of *muqarnas* domes, this poem extolls the celestial qualities and heavenly associations of these domes, whose various components have left their terrestrial tethering and joined the orbits of stars and constellations. As Grabar emphasizes, this description goes even farther, comparing the domes to the rotating dome of heaven, a concept dating back to classical antiquity but still resonating in medieval times.[74] This brilliant interpretation is obviously specific to the domes of the Alhambra and can neither be projected backward onto earlier *muqarnas* domes nor be used to impute an absence of meaning to other domes that cannot sustain such an interpretation. Rather than undermining our Ash'arī reading of the *muqarnas* dome, Grabar's interpretation actually embellishes it by giving it a new dimension acquired in the intervening two or three centuries of development.

66 Granada, The Alhambra Palace. *Muqarnas* dome over the Hall of the Two Sisters, 1356–59.

To summarize briefly, the *muqarnas* dome was created in an atmosphere of heightened religious dogmatism and intense political opposition to the Fatimids. Just like the proportioned scripts of Ibn Muqla, it was simultaneously intended to pay homage to the Abbasid caliphate and to embody the central cosmological tenets of the Sunni revival. Despite its great ubiquity after the twelfth century, it was not known in early Islamic architecture and not very significant in its later phases, but epitomized certain transformations that took place during its middle period.

Other investigations into later *muqarnas* domes may yield new nuances or layers of meaning, but such investigations will probably confirm rather than contradict the interpretations presented in the preceding pages. Such a claim might sound rigid, even pretentious, since architectural forms have historically been employed to achieve manifold expressive effects and since the geometric complexity of the *muqarnas* dome seems to invite a multiplicity of interpretations. On the contrary, the *muqarnas* dome, despite its sometimes astounding complexity, is in fact a closed and finite system, whose meaning lies not in allegorical narratives from a sacred text nor in images that provide a window onto another world, but in the intricacies of the form itself. It restricts perception to the immediately tangible universe and directs meditation toward an all-powerful God.

It is perhaps not coincidental that in the conservative religious climate of later Morocco, *muqarnas* domes continue to be elaborated along traditional lines to produce spaces that can only be described as stifling and oppressive.[75] In the more liberal and expansive world of the Timurids, on the other hand, *muqarnas* vaulting is soon relegated to a secondary position, as filler decoration within the more flexible system of ribbed vaulting.

Now, all Syrian vaults are executed in the best masonry. Numerous elements of each zone are sculpted out of one block, the size and shape of which is determined by considerations of stability. ... The driving force was the transposition of original Iraqian brickwork into Syrian stone masonry, which had never ceased to be the living inheritance from antiquity in Syria.[1]

6

Stone *Muqarnas* and Other Special Devices

This chapter discusses stone *muqarnas* vaulting and other fragmented or destabilizing forms in Islamic architecture, investigating their stereotomic qualities as a key to understanding their effect and possible meaning. It therefore continues the discussion in the previous chapter on *muqarnas* vaulting, but shifts the focus to stone *muqarnas* vaults and other exotic effects, such as foliate arches and pendant vaults, which were generally developed through the translation of eastern brick and stucco forms into stone. As with proportioned writing and the *muqarnas* dome, Baghdad also looms large in this investigation, not so much as a direct source of influence, but rather as a distant memory or a golden age to which the petty dynasts of the eleventh and twelfth centuries aspired. The following discussion will therefore attempt to investigate the meaning of these forms within their architectural context and in relation to their possible imperial or pious associations.

The first issue is technical, entailing the translation of brick and stucco motifs into cut stone. This process was neither straightforward nor unproblematic, for the effects possible in brick and especially stucco were difficult if not impossible in stone, where questions of stereotomy (cutting stone into three-dimensional forms) and support must receive urgent consideration. The ensuing process, therefore, involved not direct transmission but translation from one artisanal tradition to another. This process introduces important modifications in the nature of the *muqarnas* vaulting and leads to significant developments in stone masonry.[2]

The second point of investigation addresses the overall effect achieved by the various forms discussed in this chapter: foliate arches, pendant vaults, *muqarnas* vaults, and polychrome interlaced spandrels. If these forms have one feature in common, it is the wondrous effect produced by their destablizing appearance, an impression that was closely linked to their excellent craftsmanship. This effect may have led Cordoban and Syrian craftsmen and their patrons to develop these forms in the first place, thereby creating the first distinctively "Islamic" architectural forms in stone.

But the success of these exotic forms and wondrous effects and their dispersion over most of the Islamic world was perhaps also linked to two other factors that merit further investigation. First, many of these forms were incipiently known in Abbasid architecture of the ninth century, so their monumentalization in the succeeding centuries raises interesting problems in terms of center-periphery or caliphal-medieval relations. And second, as with the *muqarnas* dome, the possibility that these forms may have held some religious significance cannot be entirely dismissed.

Foliate Arches

One might argue that the simplest, most stable, and most easily comprehended support system is that of the post and lintel. Whether in their primitive form at Stonehenge or at the height of their refinement in Doric temples, post-and-lintel or generally trabeated systems exhibit a sense of firmness and repose that cannot be matched by any other support system. The arcuate system, on the other hand, contributes a dynamic element to the architecture while slightly obfuscating its static nature, as viewers must explain for themselves the functioning of the arch and the stress of vertical and horizontal forces. But once that is done, the arch, particularly in its most logical, semicircular form, can be read as a reasonably stable element of support. Interestingly, neither the trabeated nor the semicircular arcuate system enjoyed much popularity in Islamic architecture, which from the start strived to create a distinctive manner of expression that was ultimately based on destabilizing and mystified support systems.

Such exotic forms are first seen in the early Abbasid period, although their ancestry may date to the brick and stucco architecture of Sassanian Iran and Mesopotamia.[3] The Arch of Ctesiphon or Tāq-ī Kisra, one of the buildings that most influenced Islamic architecture, was once decorated with a polylobed molding prominently displayed on its fronting arch (fig. 67a). Several centuries later, the same form is seen at the early Abbasid palace al-Ukhaidir (c. 765), prominently displayed on the voussoirs of the arches of the so-called Court of Honor and the two entrances to the palace mosque (figs. 67b and c).[4] Although these foliate moldings are undoubtedly influenced by the great molding at Tāq-ī Kisra, they differ from it in their deeper profile, which actually extends into the intrados of the arches. Even more deeply carved polylobed moldings, simulating the effect of a foliate arch, can also be seen at some of the later palaces of Samarra, including al-ʿĀshiq and al-Jiṣṣ, both about 870 (fig. 67d).[5]

Brick and stucco foliate arches were first transformed into stone in the western Islamic world, possibly in the *maqṣūra* dome of Great Mosque at Qayrawan, dating to the rebuilding of 836.[6] This intermediary example notwithstanding,

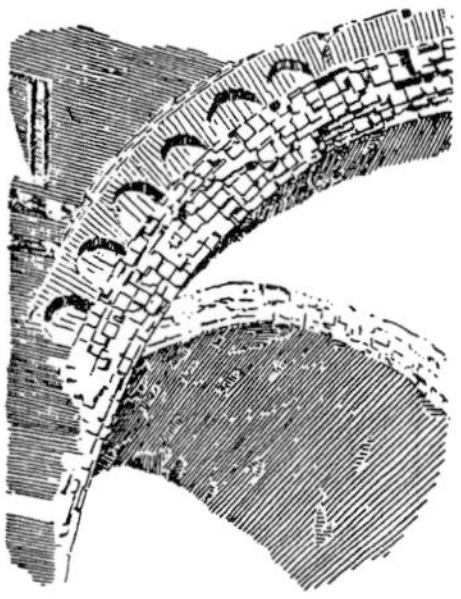

a

b

c

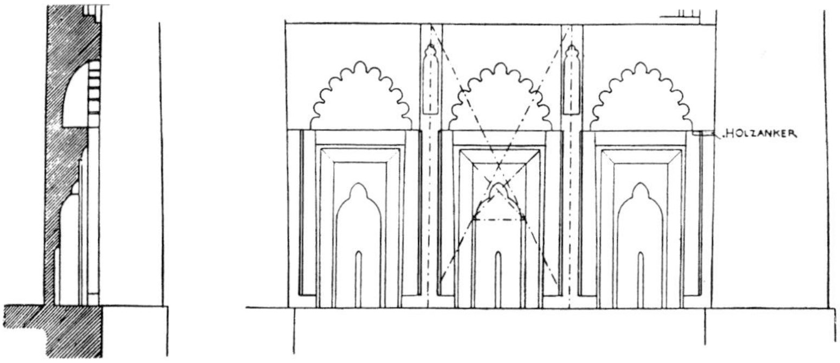

d

67 Polylobed moldings

[a] Iraq, Arch of Ctesiphon, 5th century. Molding on exterior arch (drawing: Herzfeld and Sarre, *Reise* II, fig. 172).

[b] Iraq, Ukhaidir Palace, c. 775. Mosque entrance with polylobed molding (drawing: Creswell, *EMA* 2, fig. 59).

[c] Iraq, Ukhaidir Palace, c. 775. Court of Honor, upper story (drawing: Creswell, *EMA* 2, fig. 61).

[d] Samarra, Qaṣr al-ʿĀshiq, c. 850. Exterior windows with polylobed moldings (drawing: Creswell, *EMA* 2, fig. 258).

the 962 addition to the Great Mosque of Cordoba seems completely surprising. The arches and vaults of this phase have been meticulously analyzed by Ewert and brilliantly interpreted by Dodds but without completely resolving their strident originality and mysterious composition.[7] Never before—and perhaps never again—did Islamic architecture project such contrast between actual stability and apparent instability and such tension between structure and ornament on so massive and magnificent a scale as this (fig. 68). For the first time, the polylobed blind arch has become fully articulated as a five-lobed arch that is free to support a second or even third zone above it or to intersect with other similar arches to produce some of the most dazzling effects in architecture.

But this precocious and largely unique architectural and stereotomic development remained localized in the Iberian peninsula, extending in a much less forceful manner only in the following two centuries to North Africa, where it blended with other eastern influences.[8] In other words, the similar architectural forms that began to appear in Syria in the second half of the twelfth century and somewhat later in southern Anatolia did not owe to Cordoban influence but were localized attempts to reproduce Abbasid architectural forms in stone. Though separated by about two centuries, the two phenomena are related in their assimilation of eastern brick forms into the local stone tradition.

What developments, if any, had occurred in eastern Islamic brick architecture in the intervening two centuries, and what impact did these have on Syria? Curiously, despite the remarkable transformations of the vegetal and geometric arabesque and of *muqarnas* vaulting, the support system itself underwent relatively minor changes. For example, the portal to the Jorjir mosque in Isfahan, dated about 985, is surmounted by a slightly pointed arch framed by a well-articulated, though entirely conventional, foliate arch. As for mosques of the Seljuq period, the significant changes in their plans and *miḥrāb* domes were not matched by their arch forms and support systems, which retained a traditional form recalling earlier mosques.

There are, however, two structures in Raqqa on the Euphrates—the enigmatic Baghdad gate and the mosque of Nūr al-Dīn of 1166—that contain interesting examples of lobate moldings. The Baghdad Gate (fig. 69), previously dated to the late eighth century but now more plausibly redated to the twelfth century, contains a blind arcade with deep lobate arches, whose pronounced profile and complete integration with the body of the gate recall Seljuq vaulting of the late eleventh century.[9] The use of polylobed blind arches at the

68 Cordoba, Great Mosque, expansion of al-Ḥakam II, 962–67. Foliate and intersecting arches.

69 Raqqa (Syria), Baghdad Gate, 12th century(?). Detail of blind arcading.

mosque of Nūr al-Din at Raqqa (A.H. 561/A.D. 1165–66) is somewhat less dramatic but perhaps more significant because these arches are placed at the courtyard facade of a large and important mosque (fig. 70).[10] The two arches flanking the axial nave of the mosque are both framed by trilobed arches, while the remaining arches are framed by alternating pointed and square arches. The depth of the blind arches and the fact that they spring from engaged colonnettes in the composite piers give them the appearance of a freestanding trilobed arch.

Lobate moldings in stone began in Syria in the late eleventh century, precisely the time when Syria returned to the forefront of Islamic architecture. The earliest examples occur in the minaret of the Great Mosque of Aleppo, dated 1090, where a variety of polylobed moldings frame the four sides of the shaft and connect its four corners. The fourth zone, for example, is decorated with a pair of seven-lobed blind arches on each face of the shaft (fig. 34, p. 86). Although we have already seen such blind arches in brick architecture, they are here made from continuous moldings that traverse the four faces of the minaret and even interconnect at the corners, in a manner already seen in northern Syria as early as the fifth century.[11] Thus, the first important example of medieval Syrian architecture represents a true fusion of new eastern ideas with an age-old style of outstanding stone masonry, a style capable of change within a prescribed tradition.

70 Raqqa (Syria), mosque of Nur al-Dīn, 1163. Arches of the prayer hall.

Some of the most splendid examples of this synthesis can be seen in the hinterland of Aleppo in present-day Turkey, specifically at the Great Mosques of Harran and Dunaysir (Kiziltepe). As discussed above, some of the arabesque designs at the Great Mosque of Harran date to its complete rebuilding by Nūr al-Dīn and Saladin between 1174 and 1180 (see above, p. 85). In addition, this mosque contains outstanding examples of early *muqarnas* capitals and trilobed moldings found side-by-side and often on the same member with vestiges of classical design, including architraves on brackets, dentillated moldings, and quite naturalistic grapevine ornament. Some preserved architrave fragments, for example, are sculpted in the form of brackets that support a cornice made into a succession of deeply carved trilobed moldings filled with exquisite vegetal arabesque (fig. 71).

The Great Mosque of Dunaysir, built in 1204, contains fewer classical elements but more developed lobate moldings and foliate arches, particularly in its courtyard facade and main *miḥrāb*. The monumental central entrance to the sanctuary is crowned by a bichrome foliate arch flanked by two external *miḥrābs* and two sets of three windows, all framed by foliate moldings (fig. 72). While these continuous moldings are made to simulate the appearance of a foliate arch, the one framing the main entrance is a true arch whose voussoir blocks are partly embedded in the masonry behind it. Thus, in addition to its decorative framing function, this arch also displays to great advantage the destabilizing effect of foliation, which is made more apparent by the use of stone of two different colors.[12] This elaborate portal is echoed on the interior by an axial *miḥrāb* whose scalloped conche is framed by a deeply set foliate arch that bears a Qur'ānic inscription (fig. 73). It seems clear from this significant use of the foliate arch—at the main entrance to the sanctuary and at the *miḥrāb*—that this previously palatial form was intended to highlight these two architectural elements and emphasize their spiritual dimension.

A few other examples from Aleppo and Diyarbakir will illustrate the spread of foliate arches and their continued use in palatial and sacred contexts. The so-called *maṭbakh* al-'Ajamī, a rare survival of an early thirteenth-century aristocratic residence, preserves an especially elaborate specimen of a foliate arch (fig. 74). This arch, which frames the northern *iwan* of the palace, consists of a double row of alternatingly pendant and recessed voussoirs, staggered so that the pendants of the rear voussoir can be seen between the pendants of the front voussoir, creating a luxurious and wondrous effect. Interestingly, a similar effect is conveyed by the arches of two *madrasas* at Diyarbakir: al-Zinciriyya and al-Mas'ūdiyya, both dating to the end of the twelfth century (fig. 75). In both *madrasas*, the *iwans* are framed by foliate arches whose pendant voussoirs closely resemble the pendant arch at the *maṭbakh* al-'Ajamī. These *iwans* are flanked by trilobed and pendant arches whose stereotomy and design also recall Aleppine architecture, links further confirmed by the Aleppine origin of the builder of the Mas'udiyya, Ja'far b. Maḥmūd al-Ḥalabī.[13]

72 Dunaysir (Turkey), Great Mosque, 1204. Central entrance to prayer hall.

73 Dunaysir (Turkey), Great Mosque, 1204. *Miḥrāb.*

OPPOSITE PAGE

71 Harran (Turkey), Great Mosque, c. 1180. Entablature fragment (presently at Urfa Museum).

74 Aleppo, *maṭbakh* al-'Ajamī, c. 1230. Main *iwan*.

75 Diyarbakir, *madrasa* al-Zinciriyya, 1195. Northern *iwan*.

Pendant Vaults

Whereas foliate arches occurred sporadically in Abbasid and Andalusian architecture before attaining their popularity in the twelfth and thirteenth centuries, the same is not true for pendant vaults, which seemingly appeared suddenly in the latter part of the twelfth century. Their absence in brick architecture is not hard to explain, for the effect of suspension is nearly impossible in brick. Rather, pendant vaults stem directly from the stereotomic tradition that had previously yielded foliate and trilobed arches, some of which certainly produced the effect of suspension in their voussoir blocks. The main development displayed by pendant vaults over foliate arches is that in the former, the suspended keystone is also made to support a double or triple vault behind it.

The earliest extant example of an Islamic pendant vault may well be the portal vault of the *madrasa* al-Nūriyya al-Kubra of 1168, which also contains the mausoleum of Nūr al-Dīn with its famous *muqarnas* vault. The double groin vaults of the portal are fronted by two small arches with a pendant keystone that is today unnecessarily shored up by a later arch, thus spoiling the effect of suspension. This effect is, however, clear in the portal of the *madrasa* al-ʿAdiliyya, which was begun during the reign of Nūr al-Dīn but not completed until A.H. 620/A.D. 1223–24 (fig. 76).[14] The pendant vault of the ʿAdiliyya shows considerable development over its obvious model, evident on the exterior in the much heavier suspended keystone and the trilobed, instead of plain, arches flanking it. This complexity extends to the two vaults behind the keystone, small *muqarnas* vaults each ending in an eight-lobed cupola. Though partly distinct and separated by a median line that extends to the midpoint of the keystone, the two vaults appear united by the *muqarnas* faceting and integrated within a single geometric system.

Our last example of a Damascene pendant vault at the *madrasa* al-Qillījiyya (A.H. 651/A.D. 1253–54) is poorly preserved, all the more regrettable since it shows further development of the principle. Instead of two vaults set within a rectangle, the portal vault of this *madrasa* has four corbelled vaults set within a square. According to Herzfeld's reconstruction, this vault would have comprised two pendant keystones: one in the facade, which has survived (fig. 77), and another at the intersection of the four vaults, now obscured by a partition wall.[15] The latter pendants would have appeared as a fully suspended keystone, creating a tour de force intended "to dazzle the inexpert observer."[16] While the

76 Damascus, *madrasa* al-ʾĀdiliyya, 1223. Portal vault.

77 Damascus, *madrasa* al-Qillījiyya, 1253–54. Portal, detail of pendant keystone.

architect certainly intended to create a wondrous object, it is noteworthy that he also chose to inscribe the *shahāda* (declaration of faith) precisely on the outer suspended keystone.

A fourth and final example comes from the Ayyubid palace at Qal'at Ṣahyūn (recently renamed Saladin), which illustrates once again the permeability of the sacred-secular divide in Islamic architecture (fig. 78).[17] The portal of this early thirteenth-century palace displays two striking innovations: it comprises three, instead of the usual two, pendant vaults; and these vaults are entirely made up of *muqarnas* cells, thereby creating a fully unified effect. The shallow portal is covered by three small half-domes with two pendant keystones, all resting on two tiers of *muqarnas* cells. A masterwork of Syrian stereotomy, this intricate vault is made up of stone blocks that have been volumetrically cut into various complex shapes and then assembled like a large three-dimensional jigsaw puzzle.[18]

Despite their spectacular destablizing effect, pendant portal vaults never quite caught on in Ayyubid architecture and, with few exceptions, did not become part of the vocabulary of Mamluk architecture.[19] This in part results from the difficulty of their design and construction. But it is perhaps more intimately related to two other factors: the increasing preference for *muqarnas* vaults for the portals of all religious and secular institutions, and a changing aesthetic that favored overall ornamentation with smaller elements rather than a single dominant feature. The artisanal showmanship of the twelfth and first half of the thirteenth centuries was to take second place to the increasing uniformity of the fourteenth century.

Stone *Muqarnas*

Chapter 5 discussed the origin and development of *muqarnas* vaulting as well as advancing interpretations of its secular and religious icnonography. Here I am mainly concerned with stone *muqarnas* vaulting: its nearly universal use in portal vaults from the end of the twelfth century; its design and stereotomy; and its possible significance. Syrian stone *muqarnas* has not been studied as thoroughly as Iranian *muqarnas*, so that relatively little is known about the typology and stereotomy of this outstanding feature of medieval Islamic architecture. Herzfeld's classification of these vaults as a "Mediterranean" and an "Iranian" type is but a start, for it deals primarily with the transition zones of these vaults, not with their geometric design and stereotomy.[20] Écochard was the first to address stereotomy in medieval Syrian architecture, and his perceptive analysis of the three-dimensional design of the stone blocks that comprise *muqarnas* and pendant vaults remains to be continued.[21]

The recent computer-based analysis by al-Asad goes a long way toward interpreting indigenous two-dimensional drawings of *muqarnas* vaults and the processes through which these drawings could be tranformed into three-

78 Qal'at Sahyūn (Syria), Ayyubid palace, early thirteenth century. Portal.

dimensional vaults.[22] But these drawings refer exclusively to Eastern brick vaults and cannot be extended to stone *muqarnas* vaults, where stereotomy and support are much more urgent matters. Thus, whereas a two-dimensional plan would have sufficed to convey design ideas to Iranian builders, Syrian artisans had in addition to follow specific guidelines about the cutting of the individual stone blocks. Needless to say, such drawings or models are entirely lacking for Syria, so it is necessary to depend on the various geometric and stereotomic schemes proposed by Écochard and others. Most commonly, these geometric schemes rely on the rotation of polygons within a circle inscribed in the square created by duplicating the half square of the vault. The rotation of these polygons resulted in a complex web of intersecting lines and star patterns, all ultimately emanating from the center of this imaginary circle, or in reality from the center of the scalloped dome that usually caps Syrian *muqarnas* vaults.

This limited analysis of stone *muqarnas* vaulting in Ayyubid Syria demonstrates that it was an exacting process demanding the collaboration of a master mason and a small group of highly skilled craftsmen. It was also a costly process because of the need to use the finest limestone and the high probability of waste. Thus, stone *muqarnas* vaulting was an important technical achievement and a fine luxury product, ranking among the greatest accomplishments of Syrian architecture in the middle period. Its use in the façade of a monument was a mark of distinction and a statement of status; it sometimes hid quite ordinary structures.

The earliest stone *muqarnas* portal, not surprisingly, is from Aleppo—the portal of the *mashhad* al-Dikka, which was added to the earlier building in A.H. 585/A.D. 1189 during the reign of al-Ẓāhir Ghāzī (fig. 79).[23] This is the earliest stone *muqarnas* portal vault in Syria and perhaps in the entire Islamic world, which once again points to Aleppo as the center for stereotomic innovation in Syria and the surrounding region. Furthermore, since the simple design and large blocks of this vault totally differ from stucco and brick *muqarnas* vaults, it seems safe to conclude that the Aleppine *muqarnas* vault was an indigenous development, inspired by the concept of the *muqarnas* but not in any way modeled after earlier stucco and brick vaults.[24]

Nearly all Syrian *muqarnas* portal vaults before the end of the thirteenth century conform to a single type with two basic variations in the form of the transition zone, pendentive, or squinch. Although the first subtype seems to be earlier, the two coexisted for a few decades before the squinch subtype became completely dominant (fig. 80). Beyond the transition zone, the two types are nearly identical, generally consisting of three (or quite rarely four) tiers of staggered *muqarnas* cells and brackets that support a scalloped half dome. The individual stone blocks are externally carved into a relatively small number of three-dimensional shapes, including plain concave triangles or brackets, concave triangles flanked by two brackets, and brackets flanked by two concave triangles. In later, more developed examples, the concave triangles might

79 Aleppo, *mashhad* al-Dikka, 1189. Portal.

80 Aleppo, *madrasa* al-Ẓāhiriyya, c. 1200. Portal vault.

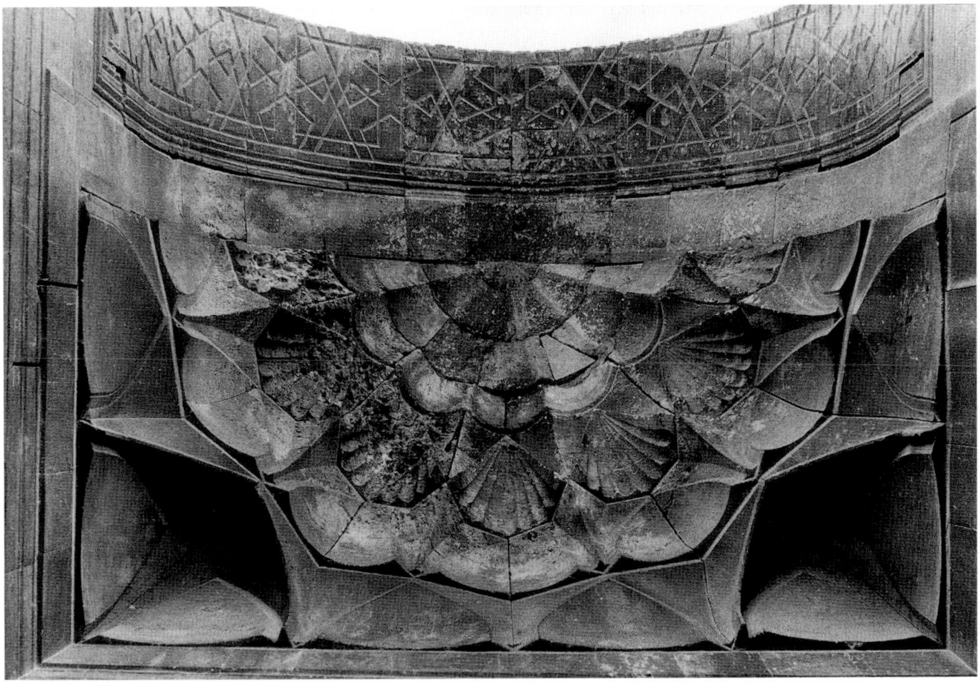

81 Aleppo, *qastal* al-Shu'aybiyya, 1150.
Entry to mosque.

be carved as a scalloped shell, the brackets might project as pendants, and star-shaped stones might be inserted in the squinches and elsewhere. But despite these additions and the decreasing size of individual cells, later stone *muqarnas* followed much the same principles first set forth in Aleppo, except in a few specimens whose lacelike complexity has little to do with stone and more with Timurid stucco vaults.[25]

Polychrome Interlaced Spandrels

The last exotic and destabilizing device created by the artisans of Aleppo is the so-called stone interlace, which is best exemplified by a wonderful series of polychrome interlaced spandrels, usually placed over *miḥrābs* and portals. Although not nearly so prevalent as *muqarnas* vaulting, interlaced spandrels are known in Anatolia, Syria, Palestine, and Egypt between the thirteenth and fifteenth centuries, and occasionally later. In some respects, these masonry interlaces recall joggled voussoirs, from which they might in fact have developed. In both, stone, often in two or three colors, is cut into angular or curvilinear profiles and fitted together to form a two-dimensional passage of interlocking masonry. The two differ mainly in complexity and size: interlaced spandrels follow quite complex designs carried out over the much larger area of the spandrel. I therefore begin with a short discussion of joggled voussoirs before proceeding to examine the origin and dispersion of interlaced spandrels, analysis of a few examples, and some thoughts about their possible meaning.

Of all the destabilizing devices used in Syrian architecture, the joggled voussoir is perhaps the simplest and one of the oldest. Joggled voussoirs, generally used in lintels and more rarely in arches, are stone voussoirs that have been cut in a variety of zigzag or curvilinear planes and then precisely fitted together without mortar. According to Creswell, the joggled voussoir was sporadically known all over the late Roman world, although most of the known examples are from Syria, where the form is used in such important buildings as the monumental entrance to Sergiopolis (Rusafa) and the Church of the Nativity at Bethlehem.[26] The device was also used in some Umayyad palaces and several centuries later in the late eleventh-century gates of Cairo. These gates were built by masons from Edessa, once again suggesting northern Syria as the locus of stereotomic innovation.

Joggled voussoirs became fairly popular in the region of Aleppo from around the middle of the twelfth century, as exemplified by the Qasṭal al-Shu'aybiyya of 1150, one of the most astonishing examples of this device (fig. 81).[27] Both the extra wide lintel and the flat relieving arch above it are massive joggled voussoirs, whose joints are cut into intricate angular and curvilinear patterns. As with *muqarnas* or pendant vaults, the desired effect seems to be twofold: to emphasize the technical and geometric wizardry of the architecture;

and to employ this technical knowledge to mystify the static coherence of the architectural element. A similar effect is achieved a half-century later by the portal of the Ayyubid palace at Ṣahyūn (see fig. 78). Its monochrome lintel with joggled voussoir is just one passage of a large and complex composition of interlocking stones whose outlines and carved ornament closely resemble interlaced masonry.

Nearly all later examples employ bichrome masonry, which tends to emphasize the decorative and fragmented aspect of the device over the unity of the architectural form. One of the most spectacular examples is at the portal of the Ayyubid palace in the Aleppo citadel, datable to about 1210 (fig. 82). Not just the lintel but the entire door frame is composed of bichrome interlocking ashlars, which are overlaid with a net of carved geometric ornament that conforms precisely to the cut edges of the blocks. Despite its apparent simplicity, this technique is actually quite complex, since each stone block had to fulfill a structural and aesthetic function, combining mysterious support with decorative appeal. A few examples from the second half of the thirteenth century, both in Syria and Egypt, continue to use joggled voussoirs with overlaid geometric ornament. But nearly all later Mamluk examples substitute bichrome or polychrome inlay work for actual interlocking masonry. In other words, Mamluk architecture captures the expressive aspect of the technique while neglecting its equally fascinating structural features.

Although most interlaced spandrels are polychrome, the earliest specimens may have been monochrome, as evidenced by the spandrel above the *miḥrāb* of the *mashhad* al-Ḥusayn in Aleppo, built in the late twelfth century. Unable to rely on coloristic effects to produce the knotted and suspended impression seen in later interlaces, the artisan had to produce these effects by the precise cutting and subtle detailing of the stone surfaces (fig. 83). Each block in this masonry interlace was cut as a complex geometric form whose hidden portion was a regular rectangle, while its visible portion was cut into a predetermined number of shapes that would compose part of the interlaced or plaited design. Most stone interlaces were designed and constructed in this manner, although some of the coloristic effects in later examples were achieved through inlay work.

The *mashhad* al-Ḥusayn in fact contains other interesting examples of interlaced stonework, with the spandrel above the main *iwan* especially noteworthy as the earliest and one of the largest examples of polychrome interlaces (fig. 84). The voussoir of the *iwan* is laid out in regular courses, but the spandrel above it consists of two huge knots that interconnect in a circle at its exact middle. Despite its polychromy, very little inlay was used; the interlace is fully bonded with the masonry. Just like *muqarnas* vaulting, it performs both structural and decorative functions.[28]

82 Aleppo, Ayyubid Palace at the Citadel, c. 1210. Portal.

83 Aleppo, *mashhad* al-Ḥusayn, c. 1195. *Miḥrāb*.

84 Aleppo, *mashhad* al-Ḥusayn, c. 1195. Main *iwan*.

Several other polychrome interlaced spandrels are known in Aleppo, where they are mainly used in *miḥrābs*.[29] These differ from the interlace at *mashhad* al-Ḥusayn chiefly in their voussoirs, which are so interlaced as to resemble foliate arches. Such interlaces became quite common in the succeeding decades all over Syria and in parts of Anatolia, where they were sometimes used in portals. Of these, the portal at the mosque of Alaeddin in Konya, built in A.H. 617/A.D. 1220, is the most magnificent, for it combines a lintel with joggled voussoirs, a tympanum with a geometric interlace, and a spandrel with a splendid bichrome interlace (fig. 85). Closely resembling its predecessors in Aleppo, this spandrel differs from them in its larger size and its external location. The slippage of some of the stone blocks verifies my previous contention that this is structural stereotomy, not just inlay work, which would certainly have fallen off when disengaged from the sourrounding masonry. Rather, the disengagement of some of the blocks and their obvious depth when seen from the soffit demonstrate that they are integral structural components of the arch and the spandrel. This stereotomic tour de force is further emphasized by the four elbowed consoles that seem to provide precarious support for the arch above them, until we notice that they are directly carved out of the impost block.

Conclusion

The five architectural features discussed in this chapter—foliate arches, pendant vaults, stone *muqarnas*, joggled voussoirs, and interlaced spandrels—constitute a family of stereotomic devices whose main purpose was to introduce a destabilizing element and wondrous effect into an otherwise planar architecture. Some of these effects had previously been known in the brick and stucco architecture of Iran and Mesopotamia, while others are entirely original creations of northern Syrian masons of the twelfth century. By the first half of the thirteenth century, these effects became commonplace in Syria, Palestine, Anatolia, and somewhat later in Egypt. By the second half of the fourteenth century, they began to lose their centrality and vigor, as polychromy and surface ornamentation triumphed over solidity and architectonics. The massive stone blocks forming foliate arches, pendant and *muqarnas* vaults, and even interlaces became increasingly smaller, thinner, and more intricate, as they blended into coloristic tableaux that covered entire facades.

What was behind these special effects? Was it architectural showmanship or aristocratic prerogatives? Or did these devices embody some religious significance? I have already explored these questions in relation to *muqarnas* domes, and much the same argument obtains here as well. The first query is the easiest to resolve, for there is little question that these were showy effects, intended to demonstrate complete mastery over the stone in two and three dimensions. They were made by master masons who were evidently competing with each other for commissions and the production of ever more spec-

85 Konya, mosque of Alaeddin Kayqūbād. Main portal, 1220.

tacular effects. Because these masons were much in demand in Syria and elsewhere, they must have succeeded in promoting their craft and in creating an international market for their products.

But the success of Syrian stonework also rested on the demand for its products by the petty dynasts of the twelfth and thirteenth centuries, who were themselves equally engaged in a game of one-upmanship. This competitive spirit is evident in their architectural patronage, which inevitably centered on *madrasas*, hospitals, shrines, and palaces, and in their patronage of illuminated scientific and literary manuscripts, the first to be produced in Islam. Similarly, the stereotomic devices discussed in this chapter were seen as emblems of quality and distinction, leading patrons from western Anatolia to Egypt to import them into their architectural foundations. The extension of such devices as polychrome interlaces and *muqarnas* vaulting from the interior of buildings to their facades in itself suggests that they were specially valued for their wondrous effect and emblematic quality.

Like *muqarnas* domes and vaults, these stereotomic devices seem to have been used equally in palatial and religious settings. Although the remaining examples in religious institutions far outnumber those in palaces, this imbalance may reflect accidents of survival and should not be used to argue for their strictly religious associations. Furthermore, the spectacular stereotomic effects used in the several palaces from northern Syria[30] should in itself suggest the palatial significance of these forms. Their appeal for medieval Islamic dynasts was most likely related to their sumptuous materials, their wondrous effects, and perhaps their foundation in contemporary geometric knowledge, which seems to have been widely appreciated in this period. This is the same applied and assimilated geometry that we have already located at the creation of proportioned writing, the arabesque, the *muqarnas*, and also the geometric plans of monuments.

The prevalence of these devices in religious and quasi-religious monuments might argue for a measure of intentionality and specifically religious significance, but it is difficult to confirm these speculations in the absence of any relevant contemporary texts. Nevertheless, it is notable that the use of these devices is generally restricted to the most significant parts of the monument: the portal, the *miḥrāb*, or the main *iwan*. Moreover, a few bear Islamic formulas and Qur'ānic excerpts that seem to underline their religious significance. The most noteworthy example is the portal vault of the *madrasa* al-Qillījiyya in Damascus, which bears the *shahāda* on its pendant keystone.

Also contributing to the possible religious, or at least sectarian, significance of these forms is their extreme rarity in Egypt before the end of the Fatimids. Just as with proportioned writing and *muqarnas* vaulting, these stereotomic devices did not enter Egypt until the Ayyubid period, and some not until the early Mamluk period. This lag can be partly explained by Egypt's isolation during the late Fatimid period, but it may also result from the Fatimids' opposition to the institutions and symbols of the Sunni revival. The first *madrasas* and Sunni shrines in Cairo were also the first monuments to contain these forms, which, once accepted, were elaborated and combined in the most inventive manner.

7

The Mediation of Symbolic Forms

Three broadly cultural themes have been developed in this book; I hope their regular recurrence has imparted some coherence to the myriad architectural forms and ornamental patterns discussed. The first, and perhaps most important, is the Sunni revival, the theological and political movement that sought to reaffirm traditionalist Islam and reject rationalist thought while declaring allegiance to the Abbasid caliphate and opposing all its enemies, in particular the Fatimids. Whereas the links between this movement and the rise of the specifically Sunni institutions, in particular the *madrasa*, have long been noted, this book for the first time investigates the impact of the theological tenets of the Sunni revival on the contemporaneous transformations in calligraphic, ornamental, and architectural forms. I have therefore argued that two central tenets of the new theology—the uncreated and exoteric nature of the Qur'ān and the occasionalistic view of the universe—bore directly on the transformation of some of the most important features of Islamic art, including Qur'ānic calligaphy, public inscriptions, vegetal and geometric ornament, and *muqarnas* vaulting. Specifically, I have proposed that the Ash'arī view concerning the eternity of the Qur'ān and the exoteric (*ẓāhirī*) nature of the word of God directly contributed to the application of more easily legible cursive scripts to the Qur'ān and the proliferation of these scripts in public inscriptions. I have also argued that the widespread acceptance of occasionalism among the theologians of the eleventh century would have contributed to the creation and proliferation of arabesque ornament, particularly in its most distilled and potent form, the *muqarnas* dome.

Political factors also underlie the development and spread of these newly created forms, for this was a time of heightened tension between the Abbasid caliphate and its various supporters and the Ismā'ili Fatimids. This political alignment had two major consequences. Positively, the petty dynasties of the twelfth and first half of the thirteenth centuries sought the legitimating powers of the Abbasids, thus reciprocally enhancing the Abbasid temporal and spiritual authority. This symbiotic relationship between a center possessing the means of legitimation but lacking power and a periphery lacking legitimacy but wielding real power had existed for several centuries, but it seems to have acquired a symbolic level of representation in the eleventh century. Forms created or at least systematized or monumentalized in Baghdad, including proportioned scripts and the *muqarnas* dome, were quickly appropriated by the rising Sunni dynasties of Syria, the Jazīra, and North Africa, becoming in the process emblems of allegiance to the symbolic center of the Sunni community. Negatively, this political alignment seems to have created an invisible barrier against the Fatimid Egyptian state, to the extent that calligraphic and architectural forms associated with resurgent Sunnism or with the Abbasid caliphate did not enter Cairo until after the end of the Fatimid period.

This differential development of artistic forms across an ideological divide simultaneously counters both the essentialist and positivist arguments that have dominated the study of Islamic art until recently. Thus, it is no longer plausible to either offer essentialist explanations for the transformations of calligraphic and architectural forms in medieval Islam as direct emanations from a central, all-encompassing dogma or system of representation, or positivist explanations for them as "natural developments" from early or pre-Islamic art. Rather, their difference from what had preceded them and their selective adoption in various parts of the Islamic world strengthen the case for their specific associations and sectarian or ideological, rather than pan-Islamic, message. Necipoğlu writes:

> It was not visual similarity, but difference, that communicated contested religiopolitical ideologies within the extensive Muslim domains whose internal boundaries were marked by constantly shifting abstract sign systems capable of conveying semiotic messages to insiders who were familiar with culturally determined codes of recognition. Despite their apparent unity, these visual signs hardly constituted a homogenous "Islamic" style with fixed horizons; discontinuities and ruptures resulted in a lively spectrum of competing paradigms.[1]

This book focuses on one, and perhaps the most significant, of these "internal boundaries," demonstrating the quest for legitimation by the emergent Sunni dynasties and their urge toward self-definition by establishing differences from the Ismā'ili state.

Was the late Abbasid caliphate therefore engaged in the production of symbolic forms that encapsulated its view of the dogma, and does that in itself explain the wide acceptance of these forms in much of the Sunni Islamic world? Or were these simply beautiful forms and wondrous devices whose long history and wide dissemination rested on their appeal to the sensibilities of aristocratic patrons?[2] Without in any way dismissing the persisting aesthetic and technological significance of these forms, I would still insist on their symbolic dimension within specific historical and hermeneutical contexts. Thus, while it is true that some of the calligraphic and ornamental forms discussed here were known from the early tenth century, often in nonofficial, even vernacular contexts, I have argued that they were in fact systematized and monumentalized in the late tenth and eleventh centuries under Abbasid patronage. Iconically charged by means of their association with Ash'arism and the Abbasid state and through their geometric regularization, these forms became the veritable symbols of the Sunni revival and the resurgent caliphate and as a result were adopted and further developed by Sunni dynasties in different parts of the Islamic world.[3]

Decentered during the tenth and eleventh centuries, the deeply fragmented Islamic world of the twelfth century was groping for legitimate political authority and a spiritual center. Real unity, which was impossible to achieve and for the most part undesirable, was replaced by ceremonial allegiance, and caliphal symbols were introduced in order to mitigate the gap between reality and myth. The widespread dissemination of these symbolic forms within a remarkably short time operated, therefore, within a system of reciprocating ceremonial gestures and material artifacts, a medieval adaptation of the patron-client relation that characterizes the early caliphate.

But this system suffered from two basic weaknesses that conspired to shorten the iconographic life of artistic forms and weaken their symbolic charge. First, despite the expanded ambitions of some caliphs (e.g., al-Muqtadir in the early tenth century, al-Qādir in the early eleventh century, or al-Nāṣir in the late twelfth century), the authority of the late Abbasid caliphate was restricted in both spiritual and secular domains. The Epistle of al-Qādir was unquestionably a courageous act that enjoyed considerable resonance, but it was by no means a papal edict ratified by an ecumenical council and approved by local congregations. No one was obliged to follow its precepts, and its ultimate success was perhaps due more to the willingness of various Muslim dynasts to embrace it and its symbolic forms than to the enduring political and religious strength of the Abbasid caliphate. In other words, the reverberations of these edicts often outweighed their central message.

The second weakness is the absence in medieval Islam of a permanent institution or ecclesiastical body to engage in a sustained interpretation of artistic forms or important monuments. Monuments as great as the Dome of the Rock or the Taj Mahal, for example, seem to lose their original purpose and significance with the diminishing resonance, or abrupt change, of the political and religious forces that led to their creation. This is perhaps equally true of the new calligraphic and ornamental forms discussed in this book, whose once-vibrant meaning and symbolism declined after the religious controversies and dynastic struggles in which they were created no longer resonated with later generations. Thus, increasingly ubiquitous forms and elaborate techniques came to convey only a generalized Islamic meaning.

The second recurring theme in this book is geometry, particularly its application to proportioned scripts, *muqarnas*, *girih* mode, and stereotomy. Geometric patterns, to be sure, were known in the earliest Islamic monuments, for example, the Dome of the Rock and the Great Mosque of Damascus, but these were fairly simple, late antique patterns used discretely within overwhelmingly floral, even pastoral, contexts. By the eleventh century, quite likely inspired by geometric treatises such as al-Buzjānī's and disseminated by drawings on paper or design scrolls, geometric patterns developed "dynamic radial grid systems whose rotational symmetries were far more complex than their late antique and early Islamic counterparts, which were based on simpler rectilinear grids with diagonal coordinates."[4] The increasing sophistication of geometric patterns went hand in hand with their expanded ornamental role, leaving friezes and cartouches to cover entire walls, vaults, and domes.

Geometric ornament has been seen to have a spiritual dimension, as a reflection of the order of the universe and a concretization of its atomistic composition and occasionalistic structure. Geometric ornament and stereotomic design also possessed an allegorical dimension that links the splendor of human efforts with the wonders of God's creations. Finally, geometry could fulfill a didactic function by focusing the minds of worshippers on central issues of dogma and "clearing error from one's mind like soap."[5] The contemporary developments in calligraphy and the *girih* mode were certainly neither fortuitous nor mandated by an Islamic spirit. Rather, they were both based on similar geometric systems that were themselves motivated by an appeal to Sunni unity, exoteric messages, and clear signs.

The third theme concerns patronage, or more specifically, idealization of certain patrons who became models for later generations. These included Abbasid caliphs, such as al-Muqtadir and al-Qādir, the outstanding vizier Niẓām al-Mulk, and local dynasts, such as Yūsuf b. Tāshufīn and Nūr al-Dīn. Abbasid caliphs issued edicts and promulgated epistles, attempting to regain some of their secular and spiritual authority as the safeguard of Sunni Islam. But their elaborate statements and vehement exhortations would have come to naught were it not for Niẓām al-Mulk, who fashioned them into policy and integrated them within the political and administrative apparatus of the Great Seljuqs. The Sunni revival, particularly its institutional, rhetorical, and symbolic dimensions, began with him and suffered a major setback with his death.

For the central Islamic world, however, there is little question that Nūr al-Dīn represented the model of ideal rulership, a status based on his *jihād*, his struggle in the path of Sunnism, and his creation of an institutional basis for the Sunni revival. His impact was not restricted to matters of ideology and institutions, but was equally felt in formal and artistic matters as well, specifically the adoption of cursive writing for his public inscriptions and *muqarnas* vaulting for his two most important monuments. In addition, he was instrumental, through his patronage of several wooden *minbars* and *miḥrābs*, in the promotion of vegetal and geometric arabesque and its exportation to both Anatolia and Egypt. His architectural and artistic commissions, like his own person, became models for subsequent periods and touchstones for the patronage of later dynasts.

Four main forces, theology, politics, technology, and patronage, therefore contributed to the formation of new forms and formal structures in Islamic calligraphy and ornament and their dispersion through much of the Islamic world. Neither pan-Islamic nor specific to one dynasty, race, or geographic region, these calligraphic and ornamental forms cannot be ascribed to an Islamic essence nor to the genius of one particualr racial or linguistic group, whether Turkish, Persian, or Arab. They were, rather, produced within specific religio-political, social, and technological contexts that shaped medieval Islamic culture but were not part of a timeless Islamic essence. Spreading differentially to some but to not all Islamic regions, these forms encapsulated and concretized the religious tenets and political forces of the Sunni revival, serving as mediatory symbols between a mythical unified Islamic nation and the actual state of political fragmentation. Their ultimate success and subsequent ubiquity in most of the Islamic world in fact reflects the widespread victory of the forces of ecumenical Sunnism, rather than supports an essentialist interpretation of Islamic art.

This book argues that medieval Islamic ornament and calligraphy did not develop smoothly and uniformly from their classical phase in the ninth and tenth centuries but underwent significant transformations, which can be variously attributed to theological, dynastic, and scientific factors. Engendered in a period of intense political and sectarian conflict, and one in which high science was being transmitted to artisans, these new forms and formal systems embodied a theological perspective, acknowledged a political progeny, and assimilated a geometric system that had eluded earlier artisans and calligraphers. By problemitizing instead of glossing over the innovations, ruptures, and discontinuities that characterized the Islamic world of the eleventh and twelfth centuries, this book strives for a better understanding of the mechanisms of change and the production of meaning in Islamic art and architecture. Conflict, challenge, and controversy, long abhorred by Islamist scholars and dismissed by positivist writers, were at the very foundation of change in medieval Islamic architecture.

Notes

Introduction

1 The recent conference on Creswell, "K.A.C. Creswell and his Legacy," published as a special issue of *Muqarnas* 8 (1991), explores facets of his intellectual background, methodology, and involvement with positivism. See in particular Robert Hillenbrand, "Creswell and Contemporary Central European Scholarship," 23–35; and J. Michael Rogers, "Architectural History as Literature: Creswell's Reading and Methods," 45–54. Rogers' views on interpretation were perhaps first expressed in his article "The 11th Century—A Turning Point in the Architecture of the Mashriq?" in *Islamic Civilization 950–1150*, ed. D. S. Richards (Oxford: Cassirer, 1973), esp. 223–24; and more recently in J. M. Rogers, "Notes on a Recent Study of the Topkapi Scroll: a Review Article," *BSOAS* 60/3 (1997): 433–39. As for Michael Meinecke, his overall disinclination to take up the question of meaning is perhaps best expressed in his last publication before his untimely death, *Die mamlukische Architektur in Aegypten und Syrien*, 2 vols. (Gluckstadt: Verlag J. J. Augustin, 1992), which remains almost completely devoid of any interpretation. Most recently, see the provocative study by Doris Behrens-Abouseif, *Beauty in Arabic Culture* (Princeton, N.J.: Markus Weiner Publishers, 1999), in which she consolidates the positivistic argument against any linkage between art and religion in Islam.

2 Louis Massigon was perhaps the first Orientalist to pay close attention to Islamic art and aesthetics, and his concise writings on the subject stand at the foundation of investigations by other scholars, especially Richard Ettinghausen. See Massigon, "Les methodes de réalisations artistiques des peuples de l'Islam," *Syria* 2 (1921): 47–53, 147–60; and idem, "The Origin of the Transformation of Persian Iconography by Islamic Theology," in *SPA* 3, 1928–36. Among art historians, see in particular Ernst Diez, "Simultaneity in Islamic Art," *AI* 4 (1937): 185–89; and Mehmet Aga Oglu, "Remarks on the Character of Islamic Art," *AB* 39 (1954): 175–202. Richard Ettinghausen wrote several general articles on the nature of Islamic art, beginning with "The Character of Islamic Art," in *The Arab Heritage*, edited by N. A. Faris (Princeton: Princeton University Press, 1946), 251–68. His remaining studies on the subject have been republished in Myriam Rosen-Ayalon, ed., *Richard Ettinghausen, Islamic Art and Archaeology, Collected Papers* (Berlin: Gebr. Mann Verlag, 1984). These are: "Al-Ghazzālī on Beauty," 16–21; "Decorative Art and Painting," 22–50; "Interaction and Integration in Islamic Art," 51–88; "Originality and Conformity in Islamic Art," 89–157; and, posthumously, "The Taming of the Horror Vacui in Islamic Art," 1305–9.

3 These were themes Richard Ettinghausen long favored, as exemplified by his articles: "Interaction and Integration" and "Originality and Conformity." While Ettinghausen remains always aware of the impact of historical conditions on artistic change, his oppositions have a static nature and are cast within a timeless framework.

4 Aga-Oglu, "Remarks," 196. The article was conceived as a response to Ettinghausen, "Character of Islamic Art." Interestingly, the author's main point, that Islamic art represents direct continuities with Byzantine, Sassanian, and Mesopotamian art, has been taken up quite recently by Terry Allen, *Five Essays on Islamic Art* (Sebastipol, Calif.: Solipsist Press, 1988), esp. 9–10.

5 For example, Smithsonian Institution, *7000 Years of Iranian Art* (Washington, D.C.: The Smithsonian Institution, 1964); and idem, *Art Treasures of Turkey* (Washington, D.C.: The Smithsonian Institution, 1966).

6 The most widely circulated publications of this genre are: Titus Burckhardt, "The Spirit of Islamic Art," *Islamic Quarterly* 1 (1954): 212–18; idem, "Perennial Values in Islamic Art," *Studies in Comparative Religions* 1 (1967): 132–41; idem, *Art of Islam, Language and Meaning* (London: World of Islam Festival Publications, 1976); Nasser Ardalan and Laleh Bakhtiar, *The Sufi Unity* (Chicago: Chicago University

Press, 1973); Issam el-Said and Ayse Parman, *Geometric Concepts in Islamic Art* (London: World of Islamic Festival Publishing, 1976); S. Husayn Nasr, *Islamic Art and Spirituality* (Albany: SUNY Press, 1987); Lois Lamyā' al-Fārūqī, *Islam and Art* (Islamabad, Pakistan, 1985); and Ismā'īl R. al-Fārūqī and Lamyā' al-Fārūqī, *The Cultural Atlas of Islam* (London and New York: MacMillan, 1986). In all fairness, Alexandro Papadopoulo, *Islam and Islamic Art* (New York: Abrams, 1976) stands apart from this group in his openness to the various philosophies and theologies that may have affected Islamic art. But he is also linked with them in his valorization of aesthetics over history.

7 Oleg Grabar, *The Mediation of Ornament* (Princeton: Princeton University Press, 1992), 151.

8 For example, L. al-Fārūqī in *Islam and Art*, 13, writes: "In almost every case, however, these non-Muslim scholars mastered the exterior knowledge of the Muslim artistic tradition but failed to penetrate beyond the outer veil to the heart of the Islamic aesthetic norms and standards. Because of their alien background and sometimes even apparent antagonism to the material, they were doomed to view Islamic artistic creation as misconceived and unsuccessful attempts to match the glories of Western art circles." Such unwarranted attacks are commonplace in the writings of fundamentalist writers. For a somewhat more favorable assessement of these writings, see most recently John Renard, *Seven Doors to Islam: Spirituality and the Religious Life of Muslims* (Berkeley, Los Angeles, and London: The University of California Press, 1996), esp. 128–32. Renard attempts to distinguish a "minimalist" and a "maximalist" group among these writers, positing that minimalists, such as al-Fārūqī, saw Islamic art primarily as symbolic attributes of *tawḥīd*, whereas maximalists, such as Burckhardt and Ardalan, viewed the same forms as nearly universal symbols that "correspond with ideal forms in the uncreated realm." This is indeed an important distinction, but the deeply-rooted essentialism and ahistoricism in both groups ultimately produces quite similar interpretations.

9 Al-Fārūqīs, *Atlas of Islam*, xiv, where the authors shamelessly state that "the materials presented were selected from an infinite variety of data" in order to establish maximium "proximity to the ideal, or the degree to which the data of history may be said to have instantiated the essence," which is none other than *tawḥīd*. Indeed, a similar attitude to the evidence and an unrelenting emphasis on *tawḥīd* can be found in as recent a publications as Wijdan Ali, *What is Islamic Art ?* (Amman: Al al-Bayt University, 1996). Intended as a primer on Islamic art, this book must perhaps present a unified and nonconflicting view of the art. Unfortunately, that is done at the expense of history.

10 Burckhardt, *Art of Islam*, xvi. Similarly vacuous statements are repeated throughout the book, e.g., 1, 63, 73, and 117.

11 See, for example, al-Fārūqīs in *Atlas of Islam*, p. xiii, and L. al-Fārūqī in *Islam and Art*, 25. Less stridently, Ali, *What is Islamic Art*, 10, gets over the dilemma of historical change by claiming that already by the Umayyad period, "Islamic art ... displayed a complete unity of configuration that would sustain itself over the centuries."

12 Perhaps the most incisive criticism of this kind of thought has come from Ernst H. Gombrich, *The Sense of Order, A Study in the Psychology of Decorative Art* (Ithaca, NY: Cornell University Press, 1979), p. 225. Referring in particular to the *Arts of Islam* exhibition, the centerpiece of the World of Islam Festival, Gombrich notes its unsubstantiated insistence on a "symbolic meaning" for arabesque decoration, adding that "it is clear ... that there is no concrete evidence for these interpretations." For a more detailed criticism, see Gülru Necipoğlu, *The Topkapi Scroll—Geometry and Ornament in Islamic Architecture* (Santa Monica, CA: The Getty Center for the History of Art and the Humanities, 1995), esp. 75–83.

13 Al-Fārūqī, *Atlas of Islam*, xiii-xiv.

14 One notable feature of much of this monographic interpretive work is its great reliance on the epigraphic evidence as a key for understanding the monument at hand. This problematic method, which perhaps saw its first systematization in Oleg Grabar's famous article, "The Dome of the Rock in Jerusalem," *AO* (1965): 33–62, will be further discussed in Chapter 2, which deals with writing.

15 Necipoğlu, *Topkapi Scroll*, 82 has also emphasized "the still popular conclusions of these methodologically unrigorous

publications." Curiously, at times there is even tacit approval of this theorization, as for example in *Images of Paradise in Islamic Art*, edited by Jonathan Bloom and Sheila Blair (Hanover NH: Dartmouth College, Hood Art Museum, 1991). Though edited and largely written by three well-known historians of Islamic art (the editors plus Walter Denny), this exhibition catalog adopts an ahistorical perspective that recalls the writings of Burckhardt and Nasr.

16 There are two important exceptions to this general trend. The first is Oleg Grabar, *The Formation of Islamic Art* (New Haven: Yale University Press, 1973), which, however, only deals with the Umayyad and early Abbasid period. The second is the controversial but perceptive and thought provoking work by Allen, *Five Essays*, of which the first two deal with questions of ornament and meaning. Formalist in approach and antiquarian in flavor, the book generally rejects any specifically Islamic meaning in Islamic art, preferring to view its later developments as directly continuing early and pre-Islamic art.

17 Grabar, *Mediation of Ornament* (as in n. 7) and Necipoğlu, *Topkapi Scroll*. It should be noted, however, that Grabar had already briefly explored some of the themes of *Mediation* in earlier publications, including *The Alhambra* (Cambridge: Harvard University Press, 1978); and especially, "The Iconography of Islamic Architecture," in *Content and Context of Visual Arts in the Islamic World*, Priscilla P. Soucek, ed. (University Park and London: Pennsylvania State University Press, 1988), 51–66.

18 The dynamics of this conflict define many of the themes discussed in Grabar's *Formation*, such as "the symbolic appropriation of the land" and "ideological warfare," wherein the overall development of early Islamic art was viewed in response to the opposing politics and theology of the Byzantines. It should, nevertheless, be noted that Grabar has recently modified his earlier polarized perspective, as in *The Shape of the Holy: Early Islamic Jerusalem* (Princeton, N.J.: Princeton University Press, 1996). See also my review of this book in *AO* 28 (1998): 115–16.

19 Jerrilyn Dodds, *Architecture and Ideology in Visigothic Spain* (University Park: The Pennsylvania State University Press, 1990).

20 Gombrich, *Sense of Order*, 225.

21 The term *girih* is given a technical definition in *Topkapi Scroll*, 9, as "the nodal points or vertices of the weblike geometric grid systems or construction lines used in generating variegated patterns for architectural plans and decorative revetments in two and three dimensions." Therefore, the *girih* mode refers to the patterns created by means of these principles.

22 R. S. Humphreys, "The Expressive Intent of the Mamluk Architecture of Cairo: A Preliminary Essay," *SI* 35 (1972): 69–119.

23 Yasser Tabbaa, "The Muqarnas Dome: Its Origin and Meaning," *Muqarnas* 3 (1985): 61–74.

24 Ardalan and Bakhtiar, *The Sufi Unity* (as in n. 6), for example, is still by far the most popular "history" book for architects interested in Islamic architecture.

Chapter 1. The Sunni Revival

1 From a speech of Maḥmud b. Naṣr the Mirdāsid to the people of Aleppo in A.H. 462/A.D. 1070, quoted in Kamāl al-Dīn Ibn al-ʿAdīm, *Zubdat al-Ḥalab fi Tārīkh Ḥalab*, ed. S. al-Dahhan (Damascus, 1951–68), 2, 17.

2 On the intense and lasting animosity between Fatimids and Seljuqs, see most recently Seta B. Dadoyan, *The Fatimid Armenians, Cultural and Political Interaction in the Near East* (Leiden, New York, Köln, 1997), 125f. According to Dadoyan, "The foreign policy of Badr [al-Jamālī] can be reduced to a single concern: to keep the Seljuk Turks out of Egypt."

3 Indeed, both sides described their war against the other side in terms of *jihād*. For the Fatimid side, see ibid., 125; for the Seljuqs, see C. E. Bosworth, "The Political and Dynastic History of the Iranian World (A.D. 1000–1217)," in J. A. Boyle, ed. *The Cambridge History of Iran*, vol. 5, *The Saljuq and Mongol Periods* (Cambridge University Press, 1968), 63–67.

4 On the intellectual climate during the early Abbasids, see for example, Tarif Khalidi, *Arabic Historical Thought in the Classical Period* (Cambridge University Press, 1994), esp. 93–130.

5 The early history of the Mu'tazilis is shrouded in mystery, partly because their texts have been systematically purged. See, meanwhile, Khalidi, *Arabic Historical Thought*, 104–5 and 151–59; and Francis E. Peters, *Allah's Commonwealth* (New York: Simon and Schuster, 1973), 180ff. Abdelhamid I. Sabra, "Science and Philosophy in Medieval Islamic Theology: The Evidence of the Fourteenth Century," *Zeitschrift für Geschichte der arabisch-islamischen Wissenschaften* 9 (1994): 1–42, gives a provocative reassessment of the role of rationalist discourse in later medieval theology; see esp. 5–9 for the Mu'tazilis.

6 Albert Hourani, *A History of Arab Peoples* (Cambridge, MA: Harvard University Press, 1991), 36. See also W. M. Watt, *The Formative Period of Islamic Thought* (Edinburgh: Edinburgh University Press, 1973), 175–80, and Peters, *Allah's Commonwealth*, 168–170.

7 See, for example, Sabra, "Science and Philosophy," 9, and Richard W. Bulliet, *The Patricians of Nishapur, A Study in Medieval Islamic Social History* (Cambridge, MA: Harvard University Press, 1972), 34–35. Although little discussed by contemporary writers, it seems clear that the Abbasid's adoption of Mu'tazilism was politically motivated. See, meanwhile, Sachicko Murata and William C. Chittick, *The Vision of Islam* (New York: Paragon House, 1994), 245: "For a large number of reasons, many of them political, the Mu'tazilites gained prominence with the early Abbasid caliphs in Bahdad." See also Watt, *Islamic Thought*, 179, where he proposes that the doctrine of createdness diminishes the power of the Qur'ān and enhances the power of the caliph.

8 Watt, *Islamic Thought*, 220–22.

9 On Mu'tazilī cosmology as utilized by the Ismā'īlī Fatimids, see most recently Irene A. Bierman, *Writing Signs: The Fatimid Public Text* (Berkeley, Los Angeles, London: The University of California Press, 1998), 62–70. See also Paul Walker, *The Wellsprings of Wisdom* (Salt Lake City: The University of Uhta Press, 1994).

10 See, for example, George Makdisi, *The Rise of Humanism in Classical Islam and the Christian West* (Edinburgh: Edinburgh University Press, 1990), 5.

11 Moojan Momen, *An Introduction to Shī'ī Islam, The History and Doctrine of Twelver Shī'ism* (New Haven and London: Yale University Press, 1985), 76.

12 See for example, Roy Mottahedeh, *Loyalty and Leadership in an Early Islamic Society* (Princeton University Press, 1980), 28, which speaks of the Buyids as "Shī'īs in only some vague sense."

13 Wilfrid Madelung, "Ismā'īliyya," *EI*^{2} 4, 200; Marshall G. S. Hodgson, "Bāṭiniyya," *EI*^{2} 1, 1098–1100; idem, *Venture of Islam* 2, 58–61.

14 Momen, *An Introduction to Shī'ī Islam*, 77.

15 There is some disagreement regarding the sectarian affiliation of the Buyids, which seems to have been quite ambiguous. See Mottahedeh, *Loyalty and Leadership*, 28; Momen, *Shī'ī Islam*, 75–76, cannot decide whether they were Zaydi or Twelver Shī'īs. Peters, *Allah's Commonwealth*, 589, concurs that "the quality of their Shī'ism is very difficult to determine."

16 George Makdisi, "Ash'arī and the Ash'arites in Islamic Religious History," *SI* 17 (1962): 37–80; 18 (1963): 19–39. For a critical evaluation of the legacy of Ash'arism, see Frithjof Schuon, *Islam and the Perennial Philosophy*, trans. J. Hobson (World of Islam Publishing Co. Ltd., 1976), 117.

17 But see Bulliet, *Patricians of Nishapur*, 28–46, for a brilliant discussion for this and other matters regarding the schism between these two prominent Sunni *madhhabs*. See also further explorations of this view in his *Islam: View from the Edge* (New York: Columbia University Press, 1994), 153–56.

18 Ibid., 43.

19 C.E. Bosworth, "The Rise of the Karrāmiyya in Khurasan," *MW* 50 (1960): 9–10; or idem, "Karrāmiyya," *EI*^{2} 4, 667–69.

20 On the Karrāmiyya and *madrasas* and *khanqahs*, see Bosworth, "Rise," 13, and Dominique Sourdel, "Reflexions sur la diffusion de la Madrasa en Orient du x^{ie} au xi^{ie} siècle," *REI* 44 (1976), 167–69.

21 The Qādirī Creed is cited verbatim in Ibn al-Jawẓī, *al-Muntaẓam fī tārīkh al-mulūk w'al-umam*, ed. Krenkow, 6 vols. (Hyderabad: Dā'irat al-M'ārif Press, 1938–40), 8, 109. It is also referred to by most contemporary and later historians, including 'Izz al-Dīn Ibn al-Athīr, *Al-Kāmil fī al-tārīkh*, 13 vols., ed. C. J. Tornberg (Beirut, 1965) 8, 205; and Ibn Khaldūn, *Kitāb al-'ibar*, 7 vols., ed. Naṣr al-Hūrīnī (Bulaq, 1867) 3, 442. According to Makdisi, *Rise of Humanism*, 45–47, it was publicly read numerous times from its formulation in 1021 until near the end of the century.

See also Yusuf Ibish, *The Political Doctrine of al-Bāqillānī* (Beirut: American University of Beirut, 1966). On the impact of al-Bāqillānī's political theology in western Islam, see Abdallah Laroui, *The History of the Maghrib: An Interpretive Essay*, trans. Ralph Manheim (Princeton, NJ: Princeton University Press, 1977), 160 and 175.

22 See in particular Henri Laoust, "La Pensée et l'action politique d'al-Māwardi," *REI* 36 (1968): 236–37; and George Makdisi, *Ibn 'Aqīl et la résurgence de l'Islam traditionaliste au XIe siècle, v siècle de l'Hégire* (Damascus: Institut français de Damas, 1963), 299–306.

23 Laroui, *History of the Maghreb*, 169–70.

24 Christopher Taylor, "Reevaluating the Shī'ī Role in the Development of Monumental Islamic Funerary Architecture," *Muqarnas* 9 (1992): 1–10.

25 Peters, *Allah's Commonwealth*, 589.

26 Momem, *Shī'ī Islam*, 82. See also Peters, *Allah's Commonwealth*, 589–90.

27 Ibn al-Jawzi, *Muntazam* , 7, 205–6.

28 The Egyptian tombstones with a specifically Sunni formula fill most of the second and third volumes of the *Répertoire*. The formula becomes somewhat diluted in the early tenth century and is eventually largely substituted by a Shī'ī version.

29 F. Sarre and E. Herzfeld, *Archäologische Reise im Euphrat- und Tigris-Gebiet*, 4 vols. (Berlin: Verlag von Dietrich Reimer, 1911–20), 2, 283–86, fig. 274. Two other tombstones, figs. 272 and 273, include the names of the four Companion Caliphs but do not mention the Qur'ān.

30 See, for example, S. M. Stern, "Cairo as the Center of the Ismā'ili Movement," in S. M. Stern, *Studies in Early Ismā'ilism* (Jerusalem: The Magnes Press, 1983), 234–53.

31 Bosworth, "Dynastic History," 71.

32 George Makdisi, *The Rise of Colleges: Institutions of Learning in Islam and the West* (Edinburgh: Edinburgh University Press, 1981), 300.

33 Bosworth, "Rise of the Karāmiyya," 13; Heinz Halm, *Die Ausbreitung der šāfi'itischen Rechtschule von den Anfängen bis zum 8/14 Jahrhundert* (Wiesbaden: Ludwig Reichert, 1974), 57; and Sourdel, "Reflexions," 167 (as in n. 20). All three authors quote Ibn Funduq, *Tārikh-i-Baihaq*, ed. A. Bahmanyar (Teheran, 1317/1899), 194–95 and 220–21.

34 See, however, Bulliet, *Islam*, 127, where he proposes an alternate definition of the Sunni revival as "the first stage in the dissemination of religious institutions and standardization of Sunni religious norms."

35 George Makdisi, "The Sunni Revival," in *Islamic Civilization, 950–1150*, ed. Donald S. Richards (Oxford: Cassirer, 1973), 157.

36 Bulliet, *Islam*, 148.

37 C. E. Bosworth, "The Political and Dynastic History of the Iranian World (A.D. 1000–1217)," in *The Cambridge History of Iran*, vol. 5, *The Saljuq and Mongol Periods*, ed. J. A. Boyle (Cambridge University Press, 1968), 71.

38 Population figures are lacking, but the strength of the Aleppine Shī'īs can be surmised from the many countermeasures that were instituted against them by the Seljuqs and especially by Nūr al-Dīn. Indeed, they remained opposed to strident Sunnism and defiant of various Turkish overlords well past the reign of Nūr al-Dīn.

39 Ibn al-'Adīm, *Zubdat* 2, 127–29 (as in n. 1).

40 This intellectual shift was certainly founded on the migration of scores of Iranian jurists who form the bulk of *madrasa* professors in Damascus and elsewhere throughout the twelfth century. See in particular Bulliet, *Islam*, 149–51.

41 For example, Zengi is not known to have built any *madrasas*, although he restored a number of Shī'ī shrines, including those of al-Muḥassin, Sidi Ghawth, and Qaranbiya, all in Aleppo. Furthermore, several anecdotes describing his visit to a Christian shrine in Edessa attest his interest in ancient shrines regardless of their sectarian affiliation. See J. B. Segal, *Edessa the Blessed City* (Oxford: Oxford University Press, 1970), 306–9.

42 On the relationship of Ibn Hubayra with Nūr al-Dīn, see Ibn Rajab, *Dhail 'alā ṭabaqāt al-Ḥanābila* (Cairo, 1952) 1, 279–90; Nikita Elisséeff, *Nūr al-Dīn un grand prince musulman de Syrie au temps des Croisades 511–569/1118–1174*, 3 vols. (Damascus: Institut français de Damas, 1967) 2, 603; 3, 750; S.A. 'Āshūr, *Buḥūth wa dirāsāt fī tārīkh al-'uṣūr al-wuṣṭā* (Beirut, 1977), 66–7; and Donald S. Richards, "'Imād al-Dīn al-Iṣfahānī: Administrator, Littératur and Historian," in *Crusaders and Muslims in Twelfth-Century Syria*, Maya Schatzmiller, ed. (Leiden: E.J. Brill, 1993), 135–37.

43 Great spectacles were staged in Baghdad to celebrate this joyous event. The city was decorated and domes of victory were erected in its quarters. See Elisséeff, *Nūr al-Dīn* 3, 669–70.

44 Saladin's Syrian campaigns have been chronicled in numerous publications. It is, however, curious that Nūr al-Dīn is almost never mentioned as the ruler of Egypt between 1171 and 1174, not even, for example, by Bosworth, *Islamic Dynasties*.

45 M.C. Lyons and D.E. Jackson, *Saladin: The Politics of the Holy War* (Cambridge, London, New York: Cambridge University Press, 1982), 72.

46 On Nūr al-Dīn's Sunni policy, see Elisséeff, *Nūr ad-Dīn* 3, 750–51.

47 These events are mentioned in Ibn al-'Adīm, *Zubdat* 2, 210 (as in n. 1).

48 On *jamā'ī* Sunnism, see Marshall G. S. Hodgson, *The Venture of Islam: Conscience and History in a World Civilization*, 3 vols., (Chicago and London: The University of Chicago Press, 1974), esp. 1, 384–89 and 2, 266–71.

49 Elisséeff, *Nūr ad-Dīn* 3, 750–51.

50 According to Henri Laoust, *Les Schismes de l'Islam* (Paris: Payot, 1983), 198–99, Ibn Hubayra took the position that "les madrasas, comme les mosquées, loin d'être reservées à une école determinée, devaient être ouvèrtes à tous les Musulmans."

51 Shihāb al-Dīn 'Abd al-Raḥmān Abu Shāma, *Kitāb al-rawḍatayn fī akhbār al-dawlatayn al-nūriyya wa'l-ṣalāḥiyya* , 2 vols, ed. M. H. Ahmad (Cairo: Wizārat al-Thaqāfa, 1956–62) 1, 32–33.

52 Ibn Jubayr, *Riḥlat Ibn Jubayr* (Beirut: Dar Sader, 1980), 24–25 and 73.

53 See Creswell, *EMA*, 1, 350–51, figs. 410–12 for technical and epigraphic analysis of these inscriptions.

54 The same formula exists in another building of Nūr al-Dīn, namely his mosque in Mosul, which was first built in 1170 and restored many times after that. The square Kufic inscription in the center of the miḥrāb belongs to a later phase, but it may have copied an earlier inscription of Nūr al-Dīn.

55 For example, Ibn al-Athīr, who compared him to the two 'Umars; and Ibn Qāḍi Shuhba, who wrote a biography of Nūr al-Dīn in 1475, under the patronage of Qaytbay.

56 Taha Wali, *Al-Masjid fi'l-Islam* (Beirut, 1990), 507.

57 Indeed, the *jamā'ī* policies of Nūr al-Dīn and Ibn Hubayra were continued and further systematized under the Abbasid caliph al-Nāṣir (1180–1225) and his propagandist 'Umar Suhrawardī, a Sufi and Shafi'ī theologian. According to Gülru Necipoğlu, *The Topkapi Scroll—Geometry and Ornament in Islamic Architecture* (Santa Monica, CA: The Getty Center for the History of Art and the Humanities, 1995), 108, the two "energetically supported the union of Sunnism and moderate Shī'ism by pointing out that Sufism, a mediating bridge between the two poles, could be sanctioned by the Caliphate."

Chapter 2. The Transformation of Qur'ānic Writing

1 Franz Rosenthal, "Abū Ḥayyān al-Tawḥīdī on Penmanship," *AI* 13–14 (1948): 9.

2 The rise of Islamic epigraphy went hand in hand with the creation of two related corpuses of historical inscriptions. The first and most important was the *Répertoire*, which published inscriptions within a skeletal format. The second was *MCIA*, which combined epigraphy with architectural documentation.

3 The first attempts at using epigraphy for the interpretation of objects and monuments were made somewhat tentatively within the format of *MCIA* by Max van Berchem and later by Ernst Herzfeld. But the method was further developed by Oleg Grabar in his seminal article, "The Dome of the Rock in Jerusalem," *AO* 3 (1959): 39–62. Even here, however, the author does not discuss the austerity and rigidness of Umayyad Kufic and its effective illegibility, although both factors may have further problematized his interpretation.

4 For example, even as recent a study as E.C. Dodd and S. Khairallah, *The Image of the Word, A Study of Quranic Verses in Islamic Architecture*, 2 vols. (Beirut: American University of Beirut, 1981) pays very little attention to calligraphic form. See also my review of this publication in *IJMES* 17/ii (May, 1985): 263–66.

5 This is true of even the most recent publications, including Anthony Welch, *Calligraphy in the Arts of the Muslim World* (Austin: University of Texas Press, 1979), 22–35; Priscilla Soucek, "The Arts of Calligraphy," in Basil Gray, ed., *The Arts of the Book in Central Asia* (Paris: UNESCO, 1979), 7–34; and David James, *Qur'āns of the Mamluks* (New York: Thames and

Hudson, 1988).

6 The trinity of Ibn Muqla, Ibn al-Bawwāb and Yāqūt al-Musta'ṣimī is repeatedly invoked by all writers on Islamic calligraphy, including Yasin Safadi, *Islamic Calligraphy* (Boulder: Shambhala Publications, 1978), 13–19, and all those mentioned in the preceding footnote. But the cultural and political context in which these calligraphers worked is very rarely explored. Glenn Lowry has raised a similar objection regarding this restrictive view of the development of Islamic calligraphy in his essay "Introduction to Islamic Calligraphy," in Shen Fu, Glenn Lowry, and Ann Yonemura, *From Concept to Context, Approaches to Asian and Islamic Calligraphy* (Washington DC: Smithsonian Institution, 1986), 104.

7 One of the few exceptions is Nabia Abbott, *The Rise of the North Arabic Script and Its Ḳur'ānic Development* (Chicago: University of Chicago Press, 1938), esp. 33–41. Although the book is rich in its references to political and religious factors, these are not considered as possible causes for changes and variations in calligraphy.

8 Estelle Whelan, "Writing the Word of God: Some Early Qur'ān Manuscripts and Their Milieux, Part I," AO 20 (1990): 113–47; and idem, "Early Islam, Emerging Patterns, 622–1050," in *Islamic Art and Patronage: Treasures from Kuwait*, ed. Esin Atil (New York: Rizzoli International Publications, 1990), 27–40. While critical of Abbott's indiscriminate use of textual sources, Whelan nevertheless reaffirms the usefulness of a more focused approach to these sources.

9 François Déroche in *Les Manuscrits du Coran, I: Aux Origines de la calligraphie coranique* (Paris: Bibliotheque National, 1983), 14.

10 Indeed, Grabar's recent work on calligraphy has already demonstrated what can be accomplished when one attempts a broadly cultural analysis of writing in the Islamic world: Oleg Grabar, *The Mediation of Ornament* (Princeton, NJ: Princeton University Press, 1992), 113–14.

11 This is easily demonstrated by a large number of early papyrus fragments that have been expertly examined by Abbott, *North Arabian Script*, 34–36.

12 The Arabic sources present two overlapping definitions of Kufic writing. The first, occurring in the earlier sources or describing early developments, refers to the mother script from which all subsequent Arabic scripts, whether angular or cursive, were developed. Qalqashandī, quoting an earlier source, says: "The Arabic script, which is now known as Kufic, is the source of all contemporary pens. ... The Kufic script has a number of pens which can be traced to two sources: concaveness and flatness." In *Subḥ al-A'shā fī Sinā'at al-Inshā'* (Cairo, 1964), vol. 3, 11. The second and much later definition of Kufic refers to only the angular script that dominated early Islamic calligraphy in Qur'āns and monuments. This is the standard contemporary usage of the term and the one employed in this chapter.

13 Nabia Abbott, "Arabic Palaeography: The Development of Early Islamic Scripts," *AI* 8 (1941): 68–9.

14 Ibid, 76.

15 Arthur Arberry, *The Koran Illuminated, A Handlist of the Korans in the Chester Beatty Library* (Dublin: Hodges, Figgis & Co. Ltd, 1967), xvii.

16 This method has been further refined by François Déroche in *Les Manuscrits du Coran, I.* Relying on these and other palaeographic features, the author has attempted further to subdivide the well-known categories of *Mā'il* (slanted script) and early Kufic into smaller and more precise groups or families of manuscripts. But keeping within the central Kufic groups (i.e., neither *mā'il* nor Eastern Kufic), one still notices a remarkable degree of consistency in the letter forms and the overall appearance of the scripts.

17 On the problem of legibility, see in particular Rchard Ettinghausen, "Arabic Epigraphy: Communication or Symbolic Affirmation," in *Near Eastern Numismatics, Iconography, Epigraphy and History: Studies in Honor of George C. Miles*, ed. Dickran Kouymijian (Beirut: American University of Beirut, 1974), 297–318; Erika Dodd, "The Image of the Word; Notes on the Religious Iconography of Islam," *Berytus* 18 (1969): 35–62; and Grabar, *Mediation of Ornament*, 60–68.

18 Whelan, "Writing the Word of God," 122: "Ibn Durustūyah included copyists of the Qur'ān among the *'ulamā'*, which is also confirmed by the manuscripts themselves." See Ibn Durustūyah, *Kitāb al-kuttāb*, Ibrahim al-Samarra'i, ed. (Beirut: Dar al-Jil, 1992), 20, where the author expressly exempts Qur'ānic calligraphers from the

rules of orthography he discusses.

19 The limited variation of these early Qur'āns has impeded their dating and classification, but it has also prevented their aesthetic evaluation. It is often impossible on the basis of script alone to evaluate the relative merits of these manuscripts, and most scholars have had to resort to their materials, vellum, tinting, use of gold, expensive bindings, and ornamentation. See Adolf Grohmann, "The Problem of Dating Early Qur'āns," *Der Islam* 33 (1958): 213–31.

20 Abbott, "Arabic Paleography," 76f.

21 Ibn al-Nadīm, *The Fihrist of al-Nadīm*, Bayard Dodge, ed. and trans. (New York: Columbia University Press, 1970), 13–15.

22 Cited in Abbott, "Arabic Palaeography," 67.

23 In *Rise of the North Arabic Script*, Abbott did in fact succeed in identifying one script, *al-musalsal*. But overall, her efforts in this regard were not very successful.

24 Ibid., 97.

25 Johannes Pedersen, *The Arabic Book* (Princeton: Princeton University Press, 1984), 45: "... it was not uncommon in the time of the early 'Abbāsids for an author to have his special *warrāq*."

26 For other specimens, see Georges Vajda, *La Paléographie arabe* (Paris, 1953) , pl. 4; and especially Evgenivs Tisserant, *Specimina Codicvm Orientalivm* (Rome, 1914): pls. 45a, 54, and 55.

27 See, for example, Edward Robertson, "Muhammad ibn 'Abd al-Rahman on Calligraphy," *Studia Semitica et Orientalia* (Glasgow, 1920), 57–83; and Nabia Abbott, "Arabic Paleography," 65–104 (as in n. 13) and idem, "The Contribution of Ibn Muḳlah to the North Arabic Script," *American Journal of Semitic Languages and Literatures* 56 (1939): 7–83.

28 The main proponent of this approach is François Déroche in *Les Manuscrits du Coran, I*, 14 (as in n. 9).

29 Qāḍī Ahmad, *Calligraphers and Painters: A Treatise by Qāḍī Ahmad, Son of Mīr Munshī (circa A.H. 1015/A.D. 1606)*, trans. T. Monorsky (Washington DC: Smithsonian Institution, 1959), 52–53; and Annemarie Schimmel, *Calligraphy and Islamic Culture* (New York: New York University Press, 1984), 3.

30 See, for example, Ibn al-Nadīm, *Fihrist*, 8–12; Qalqashandi, *Subḥ al-A'shā* (Cairo, 1962), vol. 3. 10–14; and al-Ṭībī, *Jāmi' maḥāsin kitābat al-kuttāb*, Salahuddin al-Munajjid, ed. (Beirut: Dar al-Kitab al-Jadid, 1962) . For the early history of Arabic writing, see Salahuddin al-Munajjid, *Dirāsāt fī tārīkh al-khaṭṭ al-'arabī mundhu bidāyatihi ilā nihāyat al-'aṣr al-umawiyy* (Beirut: Dar al-Kitab al-Jadid, 1972), 23; and Safadi, *Islamic Calligraphy*, 7–8 (as in n. 6).

31 On the distinction between scribe (*nassākh* or *warrāq*) and calligrapher (*khaṭṭāṭ*) see Pedersen, *The Arabic Book*, 43ff. and 83ff.

32 The patronage of calligraphers by princes can easily be demonstrated for later periods. For example, Thomas W. Lentz and Glenn D. Lowry, *Timur and the Princely Vision, Persian Art and Culture in the Fifteenth Century* (Los Angeles County Museum of Art and Arthur M. Sackler Gallery, 1989), 159 ff. It is far more difficult to establish such a connection for earlier periods.

33 See in particular Abbott, "Ibn Muklah," and Robertson, "Muḥammad ibn 'Abd al-Raḥmān" (as in n. 27).

34 Robertson, "Muhammad ibn 'Abd al-Raḥmān," 59–60, who cites Ibn Khallikān as his source.

35 The canon of proportions in the treatise of Ibn Muqla has been reproduced graphically by Ahmad Mustafa in his unpublished Master's thesis, "The Scientific Construction of Arabic Alphabets" (The University of London, 1979). Though unavailable for consultation, a color plate from this thesis has been reproduced in Priscilla Soucek, "The Arts of Calligraphy," in *The Arts of the Book in Central Asia*, Basil Gray, ed. (UNESCO: Serindia Publications, 1979), 21.

36 The method of Ibn Muqla is described in one early treatise and in a number of secondary sources. The anonymous treatise *Risāla fi'l-kitāba al-mansūba*, ed. M. Bahjat al-Athari, in *Majallat ma'had al-makhṭuṭāt*, 1 (1955), describes Ibn Muqla's method in detail and with diagrams. Of the secondary sources, see Abbot, *Rise of North Arabian Script*, 33–38 (as in n. 7); and Safadi, *Islamic Calligraphy*, 16–18.

37 Also known as *shish qalam*, these are *thuluth, naskh, muhaqqaq, riqā', tawqī'* and *rayḥān*. Of these pens, *thuluth* was to attain the greatest importance in view of its nearly exclusive use for monumental inscriptions and for *sūra* headings in the Qur'ān. *Naskh*, originally a minor and somewhat disdained script, became the preferred style for literary manuscripts and

small Qur'āns, especially during the Ottoman period. See Safadi, *Islamic Calligraphy*, 52–77 passim. for a discussion of the six scripts.

38 This point has been rarely discussed by palaeographers, although Ibn Muqla's lifetime involvement in politics would have left him little time to develop his talents in calligraphy. In L. A. Mayer's review "Nabia Abbott's *The Rise of the North Arabic Script*," *AO* 7/ii (1940): 172–73, the author describes Abbott's reconstruction of Ibn Muqla's script (see following note) as "exceedingly charmless," a deficiency that leads him to propose that "Ibn Mukla's reform must have lain in something very different from the building of the letters."

39 Abbott, *Rise of North Arabian Script*, 35, presents a tentative reconstruction of Ibn Muqla's method and script based on his treatise *Risālah fi'l-khaṭṭ al-mansūb*. Mustafa's illustrations (see n. 35) admirably present Ibn Muqla's geometric method but overly beautify the resulting letters.

40 Ibn Muqla has not before been linked to the development of the semi-Kufic script in Qur'āns, although Eric Shroeder has noted the possiblity of Ibn Muqla's indirect influence on Qur'ānic calligraphy of the tenth and eleventh centuries. See Eric Schroeder, "What Was the Badī' Script?" *AI* 4 (1937): 232–48. Unfortunately, Schroeder's attempts to determine the legacy of Ibn Muqla are diminished by the small number of Qur'ānic fragments he examined and by his insistence on identifying the so-called Badī' script of Ibn Muqla. In fact, Schroeder's conclusions were decisively refuted by M. Minovi, "The So-called Badī' Script," *Bulletin of the American Instutite of Art and Archaeology* 5 (1937): 146ff.

41 Both the British Library and the Chester Beatty Library (Add. Ms.) have Qur'ānic fragments claiming to be in the hand of Ibn Muqla.

42 Among the earliest must be CBL 3494, *Gharīb al-Ḥadīth of Ibn Qutayba*, dated A.H. 279/A.D. 892.

43 This is CBL 1434, a large fragment of a manuscript, portions of which also exist at the Ardabil Shrine and the University Library in Istanbul, whose section is dated A.H. 361/A.D. 972 and signed by 'Alī ibn Shādhān al-Rāzī (of Rayy). See David James, *Qur'āns and Bindings from the Chester Beatty Library* (London: World of Islam Festival Trust, 1980), 27.

44 This intriguing connection between the format of Qur'āns written in the *mā'il* script and that of secular manuscripts has not been explored. Although the Ḥijāzī manuscripts have been generally assumed to be earlier than Abbasid Qur'āns, their link with lesser manuscripts may suggest a lower level of patronage or provincial origin. This would cast further doubt on the already problematic chronological distinction between these two types of manuscripts.

45 Only one Kufic manuscript on vellum (CBL 1404) contains a verse count, but it is a later addition. See James, *Qur'ans and Bindings*, 23; and most recently, his *Qurans of the Mamluk*, 24 (as in n. 5), where he suggests that there is at least one Kufic Qur'ān on vellum where the verse count is given on the opening illuminated folios. This is an undated manuscript in the British Library (Add. 11,735). This manuscript, however, is very clearly semi-Kufic.

46 See Yasser Tabbaa, "The Transformation of Arabic Writing. Part I, Qur'ānic Calligraphy," *AO* 21 (1991), Table 2, for an attempt to tabulate the prevalence of verse counts in semi-Kufic Qur'āns.

47 According to Welch, *Calligraphy in the Arts of the Muslim World*, 29 (as in n. 5), "good writing was the indispensable tool for anyone aspiring to high governmental rank."

48 Brinkley Messick, *The Calligraphic State, Textual Domination and History in a Muslim Society* (Berkely, Los Angeles, and Oxford: University of California Press, 1993), in particular 3, and chapters 6 and 12.

49 See, for example, n. 1 above, which quotes the laudatory remarks of the tenth-century writer Abū Ḥayyān al-Tawḥīdī.

50 See in particular Arthur Jeffreys, ed., *Materials for the History of the Text of the Qur'ān* (Leiden: E.J. Brill, 1937), ix–x and 5–8. Jeffreys (p. 8) seems to have been fully aware of the political implications of 'Uthmān's act, proposing that it was "no mere matter of removing dialectal peculiarities in reading, but was a necessary stroke of policy to establish a standard text for the whole empire."

51 A. T. Welch, "Al-Ḳur'ān," *EI*[2] 5, 407.

52 Ibid.

53 Ibid., 408–9.

54 Ibid.; Jeffreys, *Materials*, 9–10; and

especially Henri Laoust, "La pensée et l'action politique d'al-Māwardi (364/450–974/1058)," *REI* 36 (1968): 64–66. Ibn Muqla's deep embroilment in the politics and statecraft of the time makes it more likely that he was less a calligrapher and more the innovator of a correct method.

55 R. Paret, "Ibn Shanabūdh," *EI*², 3, 935–36. Ibn al-Nadīm, who also mentions Ibn Shanabūdh's flogging at the order of Ibn Muqla, quotes his alleged recantation:

> I used to read expressions differing from the version of 'Uthmān ibn 'Affān, which was confirmed by consensus, its recital being agreed upon by the Companions of the Apostle of Allāh. Then it became clear to me that this was wrong, so that I am contrite because of it and from it torn away. Now before Allāh, may his Name be glorified for Him is acquittal, behold the version of 'Uthmān is the correct one, with which it is not proper to differ and other than which there is no way of reading."

Fihrist, vol. 1, 70–71 (as in n. 21).

56 On the *miḥna*, see Henri Laoust, *Les Schismes dans l'Islam* (Paris: Payot, 1983): 107–111; or idem, "Ahmad b. Hanbal," in *EI*², I, 272–77.

57 Ibn Khallīkān, *Wafiyyāt al-A'yān*, ed. Ihsan Abbas (Beirut: Dar Sader, 1970), 3, 342.

58 Ibn Kathīr, *Al-bidāya wa'l-nihāya*, 5th edition (Beirut, 1983), vol. 12, 14.

59 The most important study of this manuscript is D. S. Rice, *The Unique Ibn al-Bawwāb Manuscript* (Dublin: E. Walker, 1955). A facsimile edition of it was also made by Club du Livre Facsimile (Paris, 1972).

60 James, *Qur'āns of the Mamluks*, 17 (as in n. 5), has recently suggested that "the *naskh* of Ibn al-Bawwāb seems to be associated with areas east of Baghdad," an observation that is readily confirmed by several Iraqi and Persian manuscripts of the eleventh and twelfth centuries.

61 Rice, *Ibn al-Bawwāb*, 9–10.

62 This is Topkapi Serai, Sultan Ahmed Library A3.

63 al-Ṭībī, *Jāmi' maḥāsin kitābat al-kuttāb*, 6 (as in n. 30).

64 One excellent example of this simultaneity occurs in the Almoravid restoration of the Mosque al-Qarawiyyīn at Fez, 1135–40, where both *muqarnas* and cursive inscriptions are introduced for the first time. See Henri Terrasse, *La Mosquée al-Qaraouiyin a Fes* (Librarie Klincksieck, 1968), pls. 51–53.

65 Gülru Necipoğlu, The Topkapi Scroll—Geometry and Ornament in Islamic Architecture (Santa Monica, CA: The Getty Center for the History of Art and the Humanities, 1995), 107.

66 D. S. Rice, *The Unique Ibn al-Bawwāb Manuscript in the Chester Beatty Library* (Dublin: E. Walker, 1955), 13, arrived at this faulty conclusion primarily because the euology at the end of his Qur'ān manuscript refers to the "Pure Family of the Prophet," in accordance with Shī'ite usage.

67 Ibn Khallīkān, *Wafiyyāt al-A'yān*, 3, 343 (as in n. 57).

68 See Henri Laoust, "La Pensée et l'action politique d'al-Māwardi 364/450–974/1058," *REI* 36 (1968) : 50–55 passim, and George Makdisi, *Ibn 'Aqīl et la résurgence de l'Islam, traditionaliste au XI /V siècle de l'Hégire* (Damascus: Institut Français de Damas, 1963), 299–305.

69 Makdisi, *Ibn 'Aqīl*, 301, and Laoust, "Mawardi," 236–37.

70 Abū Bakr Muḥammad al-Bāqillānī, *Kitāb al-Tamhīd*, ed. R. J. McCarthy (Beirut, 1957).

71 Makdisi, *Ibn 'Aqīl*, 305 and Welch, "Al-Ḳur'ān," 409–10.

72 Specimens of this dispersed Qur'ān exist in numerous collections and have been published in a number of exhibitions. See Welch, *Calligraphy in the Arts of the Muslim World*, 15 (as in n. 5). Unfortunately, no study has attempted to reassemble all the available folios.

73 For example, ibid., 48; James, *Qur'āns and Bindings*, 27.

Chapter 3. The Public Text

1 Even when monumental inscriptions do end with the name of an artisan, this signature often refers to the architect or the building supervisor, not to the calligrapher. See L. A. Mayer, *Islamic Architects and their Works* (Geneva: Albert Kundig, 1956), 6.

2 See Irene A. Bierman, *Writing Signs: The Fatimid Public Text* (Berkeley: University of California Press, 1998), esp. 31–37 and 67–70,

for a thorough treatment of the "public" nature of monumental inscriptions.

3 On this problem, see Richard Ettinghausen, "Arabic Epigraphy: Communication or Symbolic Affirmation," in *Near Eastern Numismatics, Iconography, Epigraphy and History: Studies in Honor of George C. Miles*, ed. Dickran Kouymijian (Beirut: American University of Beirut, 1974), 297–318; Erika Dodd, "The Image of the Word; Notes on the Religious Iconography of Islam," *Berytus* 18 (1969): 35–62; Erika Cruikshank Dodd and Shereen Khairallah, *The Image of the Word, A Study of Quranic Verses in Islamic Architecture*, 2 vols. (Beirut: American University of Beirut, 1981); Irene Bierman, "The Art of the Public Text: Medieval Islamic Rule," *World Art: Themes of Unity in Diversity*, ed. Iriving Lavin (University Park and London: The Pennsylvania State University Press, 1989). Although Oleg Grabar's earlier studies, in particular "Dome of the Rock," have been primarily concerned with the informative and iconographic value of inscriptions, he has more recently paid considerable attention to the formal and symbolic aspects of writing in Islamic art. See his *The Mediation of Ornament* (Princeton, NJ: Princeton University Press), chapter 2.

4 "Arabic Epigraphy," 306.

5 *Image of the Word*, vol. 1, 25–26.

6 Bierman, "The Art of the Public Text," 284 and idem, *Writing Signs*, 62–99 passim.

7 One of the most interesting cases is that of Kamāl al-Dīn ibn al-'Adīm, the noted thirteenth-century historian of Aleppo, who was also a highly accomplished calligrapher. One example of his calligraphy remains in the *miḥrāb* at the *madrasa* al-Ḥallāwiyya in Aleppo.

8 Grabar, *Mediation of Ornament*, 113–14.

9 Some of the most notable works are: Max van Berchem, "Notes d'archéologie arabe. Monuments et inscriptions fatimites," *JA*, 8e sér., 17 (1891), 411–495, 18 (1891), 46–86; Sam Flury, *Die Ornamente der Hakim—und Ashar—Moschee* (Heidelberg, 1912); idem, *Islamische Schriftbänder Amida-Diarbekr XI. Jahrhundert. Anhang: Kairuan, Mayyāfāriqīn, Tirmidh* (Basel: Frobenius, 1920); partly translated as "Bandeaux ornementés a inscriptions arabes: Amida-Diarbekr, IX siècle," *Syria*, 1 (1920–21): I, 235–49, 318–28 and II, 54–62; idem,"La mosquée de Nayin," *Syria*, 11 (1930): 43–58; idem, "Le décor épigraphique des monuments fatimides du Caire," *Syria* 17 (1936): 365–76; Adolf Grohmann, "The Origin and Early Development of Floriated Kufic," *AO* 2 (1957): 183–213; Janine Sourdel-Thomine, "Le coufique alépin de l'époque seljoukide," *Mélanges Louis Massignon*, vol. 3 (Paris: Maisoneuve et Larose, 1957), 301–17; Ibrahim Jum'ah, *Dirāsa fī taṭawwur al-kitābāt al-kūfiyya 'alā al-aḥjār fī miṣr fi'l-qurūn al-khamsa al-'ūla lil-hijra* (Cairo: Dar al-Fikr al-'Arabi, 1969).

10 For example, Grohmann, "Origin and Early Development of Floriated Kufic," 207–8; Flury, *Islamische Schriftbänder*, 11; Jum'ah, *Dirāsa*, 230–31; and Yasser Tabbaa, "The Transformation of Arabic Writing. Part II, The Public Text," *AO* 24 (1994): 121–26. Cf. the conclusion reached by Sheila Blair in *Islamic Inscriptions* (New York: New York University Press, 1998), 57–59, where she proposes a more gradual development of the floriated Kufic, beginning a few decades before the Fatimids. See also my review of the three works—"Sheila S. Blair, *Islamic Inscriptions* (New York University Press, 1998); Irene A. Bierman, *Writing Signs: The Fatimid Public Text* (University of California Press, 1998); Eva Baer, *Islamic Ornament* (New York University Press, 1998)"—in *AO* 29 (1999):180–82. Overall, Blair's argument shades but does not reject the conclusions presented above.

11 Grohmann, "Origin and Early Development of Floriated Kufic," 209.

12 Janine Sourdel-Thomine, "Kitābāt," EI^2, vol. 5, 217. Lisa (Volov) Golombek was, however, the first to note the process of the internal transformation of Kufic characters; see "Plaited Kufic on Samanid Epigraphic Pottery," *AO* 6 (1966): 107–134.

13 Janine Sourdel-Thomine, "Khaṭṭ," EI^2, vol. 4, fig. 8.

14 Grohmann, in "Origin and Early Development of Floriated Kufic," states that "it is certainly from here [Egypt] that its development has advanced to Mesopotamia on one side and to North Africa on the other." Indeed, Max van Berchem, "Notes d'archéologie arabes," *JA* (juillet–août, 1891): 72, was the first to note the central role of the Fatimids in creating and disseminating the floriated Kufic: "Il se développe sur celles des Fatimides d'Égypte, des Abbasides, des derniers Omayades d'Espagne et des autres dynasties muslumanes jusqu'a l'introduction du caractère arrondi. On le trouve dans tous

les textes fatimites d'Égypte, dans un grand nombre d'inscriptions de la Syrie, du Caucase, de la Perse et de la Mésopotamie, de la Sicile, de l'Afrique du Nord de l'Espagne."

15 See Bierman, "The Art of the Public Text," 285–86, and *Writing Signs*, 60–99, for a more complex interpretation that takes into account Fatimid oculitic practices.

16 W. Madlung, "Ismāʿīliyya," *EI*², IV, 203–5.

17 Max van Berchem, "Notes d'archéologie arabe, I: Monuments et inscriptions fatimites," *JA* série 8, vol. 18 (1891): 73.

18 Some of these cenotaphs are illustrated in Sam Flury, "Le Décor épigraphique des monuments de Ghazna," *Syria* 6 (1925): 61–90.

19 Some of these are illustrated in *SPA*, 7, pls. 518 c, 519 e (dated 1141), and 520 (dated 1138).

20 Compare, for example, the inscription on the exterior of the *miḥrāb* dome of the Great Mosque of Isfahan, dated 1086–87—possibly the earliest cursive Seljuq inscription—with the slightly earlier Ghaznavid fragments.

21 Yasser Tabbaa, "The Transformation of Arabic Writing. Part I, Qur'ānic Calligraphy," *AO* 21 (1991): 135–36.

22 Ibid., figs. 19–21.

23 See page 58.

24 C. E. Bosworth, "The Imperial Policy of the Early Ghaznavids," *IC* 1 (1962): 50. Bosworth cites Jurbadhāqānī's description of this event: "When the news of the execution of the envoy from Egypt reached Baghdad, and the firmness of the Sultan's faith became known, the tongues of caluminators and the reproofs of censorious ones were silenced, and his name was always mentioned with praise and honour at the court of the commander of the Faithful."

25 Max van Berchem, *MCIA: Syrie du Sud, Jerusalem*, 2 vols. (Cairo: Institut Français d'Archéologie Orientale, 1922–27), vol. 1, 85ff and 254ff. "À l'est, le changement est un processus purement pratique et autonome, l'écriture cursive de la vie quotidienne supplante lentement, sans plan ou dessin, une écriture monumentale que personne ne pouvait plus lire."

26 Ibid., 7. The same idea is restated in "Notes d'archéologie arabe I," 73–75; and "Inscriptions arabes de Syrie, VI, Les inscriptions de Nūr al-Dīn et l'origine du charactère arrondi dans l'épigraphie syrienne," *MIE* 3 (1897): 34–39.

27 Ernst Herzfeld, "Damascus: Studies in Architecture—III," *AI* 11–12 (1946): 38; and *Inscriptions et monuments d'Alep* I, 210–11. See also Tabbaa, "Monuments with a Message: Propagation of Jihād under Nūr al-Dīn, 1146–1174," in *The Meeting of Two Worlds, Cultural Exchange between East and West during the Period of the Crusades*, ed. Vladimir Gross and Christine Vézar Bornstein (Kalamazoo, MI: Medieval Institute Publications, 1986), 223–40.

28 Sourdel-Thomine, "Kitābāt," *EI*², 5, 217.

29 See note 26. Many Iranian Seljuq monuments, six of which are listed in Tabbaa, "Public Text," note 47, include both floriated Kufic and cursive inscriptions.

30 Herzfeld, *Inscriptions et monuments d'Alep*, pl. LXXIX,a.

31 Tabbaa, "Propagation of Jihād," 224.

32 Tabbaa, "Qur'ānic Calligraphy," figs. 20–21 (as in n. 21).

33 Of these, the most important is a large floriated Kufic inscription carved on the entablature of the Qasṭal al-Shuʿaybiyya in Aleppo (A.H. 545/A.D. 1150). I have elsewhere (Tabbaa, "Propagation of Jihād under Nūr al-Dīn," 227–29) investigated this monument, proposing that it was rebuilt by Nūr al-Dīn as a commemorative structure intended to celebrate his triumphs against the Crusaders while evoking the earlier victories of ʿUmar ibn al-Khaṭṭāb, who had conquered Aleppo in A.H. 16/A.D. 637. The use of an archaizing script accords well with the deliberately archaizing architecture and the commemorative nature of the monument. For a complete inventory of these inscriptions, see Nikita Elisséeff, "La Titulature de Nūr al-Dīn d'après ses inscriptions," *BEO* 14 (1952–54): 155–96.

34 Claude Cahen, "Une chronique chiite du temps des croisades," *Comptes rendus, Academie des inscriptions et belles lettres* (1935), 263–64.

35 H. A. R. Gibb, "The Career of Nur al-Din," K. M. Setton, ed., *A History of the Crusades*, vol. 1, *The First Hundred Years*, ed. M. W. Baldwin (Madison, WI: University of Wisconsin Press, 1969), 515.

36 On Nūr al-Dīn's links with Ibn Hubayra, see Elisséeff, *Nūr al-Dīn*, vol. 3, 350–51; Herbert Mason, *Two Statesmen of Mediaeval Islam* (The Hague: Mouton & Co., 1972), 14 and 23; and Tabbaa, "The Architectural Patronage of Nūr al-Dīn,"

178–81.

37 Monumental inscriptions from the period of this energetic caliph are plentiful. One of his longest and finest inscriptions once existed in the Bāb al-Ṭilasm (Talisman Gate) in Baghdad, which was destroyed early in this century. Another fine inscription carved in wood frames the door to the so-called Bāb al-Ghaibah in Samarra, part of the Shi'i sanctuary dedicated to the two *imāms* 'Alī al-Hādī and Mūsā al-'Askarī. See anonymous author, *Bab ul Ghaibah at Samarra* (Baghdad, 1938).

38 This inscription was first discussed by Max van Berchem in F. Sarre and E. Herzfeld, *Archäologische Reise im Euphrat- und Tigris-Gebiet*, 4 vols. (Berlin: Verlag von Dietrich Reimer, 1911–20), 1, 17. On the basis of the *miḥrāb*'s early date and the assumption that it was made for the mosque of al-Nūri, Herzfeld (ibid., 2, 224–27) proposed that the mosque was begun more than twenty years before Nūr al-Dīn, a contention that is not supported by any textual evidence. The truth is that this *miḥrāb* was brought to the mosque of al-Nūrī in the first decades of this century. It may originally have been intended for the Umayyad mosque of Mosul, which is now destroyed. See Tabbaa "The Architectural Patronage of Nūr al-Dīn," 147–51, for the chronology of this mosque.

39 Elisséeff, *Nūr al-Dīn*," vol. 2, 657–62.

40 These and other fragments of the mosque of al-Nūri in Mosul are now preserved at the Iraqi Museum in Baghdad. See Tabbaa, "The Architectural Patronage of Nūr al-Dīn," 153–54; fig. 289.

41 These shrines are discussed in Sarre and Herzfeld, *Archäologische Reise*, 2, 249–70. Although built for alleged descendants of various Shi'i imams, these shrines do not represent the revival of political Shi'ism. Indeed, the official veneration of Shi'i shrines in the late twelfth century was even practiced by the contemporary Abbasid caliph al-Nāṣir, whose policy of rapprochement with the Shi'is was intended to strengthen his power base with the local population. See Mason, *Two Statesmen*, 99 and 116.

42 This development has not been studied in depth; meanwhile, see Georges Marçais, *L'Architecture musulmane d'Occident* (Paris: Arts et Métiers Graphiques, 1954), 250, and Henri Terrasse, *La Mosquée al-Qaraouiyin a Fès* (Paris: Librarie Klincksieck, 1968), 51 and 80. For the parallel development in Sicily, see 'Abd al-Mun'im Raslān, *Al-ḥaḍāra al-islāmiyya fī Ṣiqilliya wa junūb iṭāliya* (Jeddah: al-Kitāb al-Jāmi'ī, 1980), 80–82.

43 L. Golvin, "Kitābāt," *EI*², 221. Golvin adds that "it is in fact impossible, in the absence of precise documentary evidence, to propose an Andalusian influence, as it seems that cursive writing did not appear in Andalusia until much later." This is an important observation, for it underlines a switch in the prevailing cultural influences on al-Maghrib, from Andalusia to the central Islamic world.

44 See chapter 5 for a discussion of this dome.

45 This exquisite dome, the first in North Africa to use *muqarnas* in its squinches, has been studied by Marçais, *L'Architecture musulmane d'Occident*, 195–97 and figs. 125–26.

46 Terrasse, *La Mosquée al-Qaraouiyin*, chapters 2–7, discusses different facets of the Almoravid reconstruction.

47 See, for example, Tabbaa, "Qur'ānic Calligraphy," fig. 27 (as in n. 21).

48 Links between the Almoravids and the Abbasid caliphs have been alluded to by several writers, including Muhammad A. 'Anān, *Duwal al-Ṭawā'if mundhu qiyāmihā ḥattā al-fatḥ al-murābiṭī*, 3rd ed. (Cairo: al-Khanji, 1988), 314f, and more recently, Salāmah M. S. al-Hirfī, *Dawlat al-murābiṭīn fī 'ahd 'Alī b. Yūsuf b. Tāshufīn* (Beirut: Dar al-Nadwa al-Jadida, 1985), 168–75.

49 Abdallah Laroui, *The History of the Maghrib: An Interpretive Essay*, trans. Ralph Manheim (Princeton, NJ: Princeton University Press, 1977), 160. Laroui further notes that al-Bāqillānī was the teacher of Abū 'Imrān al-Fāsī (d. 1038), who was one of the foremost Māliki theologians and a propagandist for the Abbasid cause.

50 Al-Hirfī, *Dawlat al-murābiṭīn*, 170–72. The author mentions no fewer than seven exchanges of letters between the Almoravids and the Abbasids, between 1059 and 1118, during the reigns of Abū Bakr ibn 'Umar (1056–1073), Yūsuf ibn Tāshufīn (1061–1106), and 'Alī ibn Yūsuf (1105–1142). In the correspondence of A.H. 479/A.D. 1086, Yūsuf received the Abbasid caliph's approval of his newly assumed title *amīr al-muslimīn* along with a lengthy letter from Abū Ḥāmid al-Ghazzālī, in which the renowned theologian praises

Yūsuf as one of the great heros of Islam.

51 Max van Berchem, "Notes d'archéologie arabe, I: Monument et inscriptions fatimites," 69 (as in n. 9).

52 K. A. C. Creswell, *MAE*, 2, 35.

53 Caroline Williams, in "The Qur'anic Inscriptions of the *Tabut* al-Husayn in Cairo," *IA* 3 (1987): 3–14, has argued for a Fatimid dating of this commemorative cenotaph despite the fact that it contains both floriated Kufic and cursive inscriptions. But Williams's argument, which largely rests on the Shī'ī inscriptions on the cenotaph, is not completely foolproof, since the decline of political Shī'ism in the late twelfth century seems to have brought about a renewed tolerance of its pietistic aspects. In *Islamic Architecture in Cairo, an Introduction* (Leiden: E. J. Brill, 1992), 77, Doris Behrens-Abouseif has noted in passing that one of the window grills in the mosque of al-Ṣāliḥ Ṭalā'i' (1160) contains a cursive inscription. But the highly developed *thuluth* of this inscription makes it doubtful that it belongs to the Fatimid phase of the building, or even to the early Ayyubid period. It most likely belongs to a restoration of the late Ayyubid or early Mamluk period.

54 Creswell, *MAE*, 2, 64.

55 Imām Shāfi'ī lived the last fifteen years of his life in Cairo, where he died in 820. Although a small shrine had always existed at his burial, Saladin began building a new one with a magnificent wooden cenotaph (also bearing cursive inscriptions) and an associated *madrasa* the very same year that he declared the end of the Fatimids and his own sovereignty.

56 *Répertoire*, no. 3380. Even the *Répertoire*, which is not noted for its aesthetic judgment, described this inscription as "d'un trait lâche et peu soigné."

57 A similarly naive writing style is employed in another inscription bearing the name of Ṣalāḥ al-Dīn, a fragment preserved at the Islamic Museum in Cairo (Tabbaa, "Public Text," fig. 29).

58 A quick survey of the photographs in Creswell, *MAE*, vol. 2, suggests that this began during the reign of al-Malik al-Kāmil (1218–38).

59 See for example, Marius Canard, "Fāṭimids," EI^2, 2, 859; and W. Madelung, "Ismā'īliyya," EI^2, 4, 203–5, who provides a detailed presentation of Fatimid esoteric theology.

60 Obviously, the generally ruinous state of Abbasid mosques makes it difficult to be definite on this point. At the Great Mosque of Qayrawan, Abbasid inscriptions are to be found only in the *miḥrāb* and on some of the capitals. The mosque of Ibn Tulun is said to have contained the entire Qur'ān, but this was most likely just pious hyperbole. See Jonathan M. Bloom, "The Mosque of al-Ḥākim in Cairo," *Muqarnas* 1 (1983): 18.

61 See, for example, John Hoag, *Islamic Architecture* (New York: Abrams, 1977), figs. 169–71.

62 This need not mean that all Fatimid public texts aimed toward this dualistic expression. For example, the foundation inscriptions at both gates al-Naṣr and al-Futūḥ (1087) are somewhat more legible than those at the mosque of al-Ḥākim, possibly because they belong to secular structures.

63 Actually, this innovation is already predicted by the mosque of al-Ḥākim, some of whose exterior inscriptions are nearly at eye level. But as far as I can tell, this is a unique case.

64 Yasser Tabbaa, "The Muqarnas Dome: Its Origin and Meaning," *Muqarnas* 3 (1985): 61–74.

Chapter 4. The *Girih* Mode

1 Donald R. Hill, in *The Book of Knowledge of Ingenious Mechanical Devices, by Ibn al-Razzāz al-Jazarī* (Dordrecht, London, Boston: D. Reidel, 1974), 191. In his recent review article of Necipoğlu's *Topkapı Scroll*, entitled "Artisans and Mathematicians in Medieval Islam" (*JAOS* 119/iv [October–December, 1999]: 637–45), George Saliba questions the translation of the Arabic idiom "*tushaddu al-riḥāl*" as "saddles are strapped on," preferring the clearer but more mundane translation "it is well worth a journey." It is, however, permissible to translate an idiom with another idiom, provided that the translation conveys the idiomatic sense of the original. In my view, the expression "to view it saddles are strapped on" does just that.

2 Or, according to J. M. Rogers, in "Notes on a Recent Study of the Topkapi Scroll: A

Review Article," *BSOAS* 60/3 (1997): 433, "Many distinguished scholars have found it an embarrassment." There seems to be, on the other hand, no end to manuals of Islamic patterns that make fantastic and entirely ahistorical claims about their meaning.

3 Originally published in 1896 as *Stilfragen*, Riegl's book has recently been translated by Evelyn Kain as *Problems of Style* (Princeton, NJ: Princeton University Press, 1992). An entire chapter,"The Arabesque: An Introduction," is dedicated to Islamic vegetal ornament.

4 Ibid., 274f.

5 *Die Arabeske* (Wiesbaden, 1949), translated by Richard Ettinghausen as *The Arabesque: Meaning and Transformation of an Ornament* (Graz, Austria: Verlag für Sammler, 1976). See also Maurice Dimand, "Studies in Islamic Ornament, I: Some Aspects of Omaiyad and Early 'Abbāsid Ornament," *AI* 4 (1937): 293–337; and "Studies in Islamic Ornament, II: The Origin of the Second Style of Samarra Decoration." In *Archaeologia Orientalia in Memoriam Ernst Herzfeld*, ed. George Carpenter Miles (Locust Valley, N.Y.: J. J. Augustin, 1952), 62–68.

6 Thus Kühnel argues (p. 9) that the arabesque lacks "symbolic meaning" and is "devoid of meaningful purpose," while also maintaining (p. 5) that "the creative force was the concept that nature does not create out of itself but that it is the work of the divine creator which manifests itself in all happenings and phenomena."

7 Titus Burckhardt, *Art of Islam: Language and Meaning* (London: World of Islam Festival Trust, 1976), 57.

8 Creswell, *MAE* 1, 53–54.

9 Terry Allen, *Five Studies in Islamic Art* (Sebastopol, CA: Solipsist Press, 1988), 36.

10 See Gülru Necipoğlu, *The Topkapi Scroll—Geometry and Ornament in Islamic Architecture* (Santa Monica, CA: The Getty Center for the History of Art and the Humanities, 1995), esp. 185–96, where the author cites numerous instances of the interpenetration of art and culture in the medieval and postmedieval Islamic world.

11 Allen, *Five Studies*, 56.

12 Ibid., 57.

13 Oleg Grabar, *The Mediation of Ornament* (Princeton, NJ: Princeton University Press, 1992), 146–47.

14 Necipoğlu, *Topkapi Scroll*, 95. Cf. Rogers, "Topkapi Scroll," where he generally rejects the plausibility of this interpretation and the overall validity of any connection between theology and art.

15 Specifically, see Yasser Tabbaa, "The Muqarnas Dome: Its Origin and Meaning," *Muqarnas* 3 (1985): 61–74; "The Transformation of Arabic Writing. Part I, Qur'ānic Calligraphy," *AO* 21 (1991): 117–48; and "The Transformation of Arabic Writing. Part II, The Public Text," *AO* 24 (1994): 117–47.

16 Michael Rogers may have been the first to use the modern Persian artisanal term *girih* (or according to him *girīkh*) in his "The 11th Century—A Turning Point in the Architecture of the Mashriq?" in *Islamic Civilization 950–1150*, ed. D. S. Richards (Oxford: Cassirer, 1973), 224. The equivalent Arabic term *'uqda* is also sometimes used by craftsmen to designate certain aspects of geometric strapwork or vegetal interlaces. But the term *shabaka* (net) is more generally applied to geometric strapwork or latticework. See Hill, *Book of Knowledge of Mechanical Devices*, 9 (as in n. 1).

17 Necipoğlu, *Topkapi Scroll*, 100–101.

18 Ibid., 102, 217, and 103, 105, and 122.

19 See for example: Oleg Grabar and Derek Hill, *Islamic Architecture and its Decoration, A.D. 800–1500* (Chicago: University of Chicago Press, 1968): 73–76; Oleg Grabar, "The Visual Arts," in *The Cambridge History of Iran*, Vol. 4, *The Period from the Arab Invasions to the Saljuqs*, ed. R. N. Frye (Cambridge: Cambridge University Press, 1975), 342–44; and Rogers, "The 11th Century," 219–23.

20 Daniel Schlumberger et. al., *Lashkari Bazar: une résidence royale ghaznévide et ghoride*, 3 vols. (Paris: Klincksieck, 1963–78), vol. 3, pls. 130 and 149–50.

21 See Richard Ettinghausen, "The Bevelled Style in the Post-Samarra Period," in *Archaeologia Orientalia im Memoriam Ernst Herzfeld*, 72–83 (as in n. 5), where the author discusses the continuity of this style.

22 *SPA* 3, 2725.

23 The view of the Ghaznavid court as a distant mirror of that of the Abbasids has been expressed by C. E. Bosworth, *The Ghaznavids*, 2nd ed. (Beirut: Librarie du Liban, 1973), 133–34. It is clearly based on the visual similarity between Samarran and Ghaznavid palaces and on striking parallels in their ceremonials.

24 See Ernst Herzfeld, *Die Malereien von Samarra* (Berlin: D. Reimer, 1927); and

idem, "Damascus: Studies in Architecture —II," *AI* 10 (1943), 45, where Herzfeld identifies the animated scroll as a Hellenistic motif that had been introduced into Iran before the Sassanian period.

25 A supreme example is the ivory revetment plaque at the Museum für Islamische Kunst in Berlin, most recently discussed in Institut du Monde Arabe, *Trésors faitimides du Caire* (Paris: Institut du Monde Arabe, 1998), 138.

26 Creswell, *MAE*, 2, 50–51. See also Farīd Shāfi'ī, *Simple Calyx Ornament in Islamic Art (A Study in Arabesque)*, (Cairo: Cairo University Press, 1956), 203–5. This meticulous study generally lacks conclusions, but Shāfi'ī frequently refers to the survival or even revival of "Hellenistic-Byzantine ornamental types" in Fatimid Egypt well into the twelfth century.

27 See in particular Marius Canard, "Le Cérémonial fatimite et le cérémonial byzantin, essai de comparison," *Byzantion* 21 (1951): 355–420, and most recently, Paula Sanders, "From Court Ceremony to Urban Language: Ceremonial in Fatimid Cairo and Fusṭāṭ," in *The Islamic World from Classical to Modern Times: Essays in Honor of Bernard Lewis*, ed. C. E. Bosworth et al. (Princeton, N.J.: Darwin, 1989), 311–21.

28 Fatimid woodwork has not been studied recently. Meanwhile, see the still-valuable study by Carl J. Lamm, "Fatimid Woodwork, Its Style and Chronology," *BIE* 18 (1935–36): 59–91, and the perceptive remarks in Zaki M. Hassan, *Kunuz al-Fāṭimiyyīn* (Cairo: Dar al-Kutub al-Misriyya, 1937), 211–25.

29 For treatment of the woodwork, see L. H. Vincent and E. J. H. Mackay, *Hébron: Le Haram El-Khalīl, Sepulture des Patriarches* (Paris: Edition Ernest Leroux, 1923), 218–25. For a study of the inscriptions, see Max van Berchem, "La Chaire de la mosquée d'Hébron et la martyrion de la tête de Husain a Ascalon," in *Festschrift Eduard Sachau* (Berlin: Reimer, 1915), 298–31. It should be noted that the existing *minbar* is not all Fatimid: the heavy *muqarnas* cornices above the door and the backrest are certainly post-Fatimid, as is the door itself, whose fully-developed star patterns most likely belong to a Mamluk restoration.

30 For example, Hassan, *Kunuz*, 216; Vincent and Mackay, *Hébron*, 70; and Lamm, "Fatimid Woodwork," 76.

31 Lamm, "Fatimid Woodwork," 78 and pl. IX,d.

32 Illustrated respectively in *Trésors fatimides*, p. 150; and Pauty, "Qous," pl. 2/2. Similar harmony between a simple geometric grid and opulent vegetal designs can be seen in the splendid *minbar* at the Kutubiyya mosque (dated 1137–38), recently published in Jonathan M. Bloom et al., *The Minbar from the Kutubiyya Mosque* (New York: The Metropolitan Museum of Art, 1998).

33 Bloom, "The Muqarnas in Egypt," 27–28.

34 Necipoğlu, *Topkapi Scroll*, 107. See also the similar, though less comprehensive, conclusions reached by Tabbaa in "Muqarnas Dome."

35 Herzfeld has frequently reaffirmed the pivotal role played by Syria in the rationalization of arabesque ornament. Cf. however, Grabar, *Mediation*, p. 142, where he generally dismisses the Syrian contribution.

36 The Great Mosque at Harran remains inadequately published. Meanwhile, see Terry Allen, *A Classical Revival in Islamic Architecture* (Wiesbaden: Ludwig Recihert Verlag, 1986), which includes hitherto unpublished plans and drawings of the excavation by D. S. Rice.

37 Arabesque design on stone continues on a much-restricted scale in a handful of twelfth-century buildings, including the cartouches at the portal of the *madrasa* al-Muqaddamiyya (1168) and the portal of the *mashhad* al-Husayn (c.1200), both in Aleppo.

38 To this list should certainly be added the magnificent ebony *minbar* made for the mosque of Alaeddin in Konya, during the reigns of sultans Mas'ūd and Qillij Arslān. The *minbar* is signed by *al-ustādh* (the master) Makkī Mengubartī al-Akhlāṭī and dated to A.H. 550/A.D. 1155, making it "the first dated piece of Rum Seljuq art." Oktay Aslanapa, *Turkish Art and Architecture* (New York: Praeger, 1971), 107.

39 Although my photograph from around 1979 shows the door in nearly pristine condition, it has been irreparably damaged in the intervening time through various acts of negligence and vandalism.

40 Ibn abi Uṣaybi'ah, *'Uyūn al-anbā' fi ṭabaqāt al-aṭibbā'*, ed. Nizar Rida (Beirut: Maktabat al-Hayat), 669–70; and L. A. Mayer, *Islamic Woodcarvers and Their Works* (Geneva: Albert Kundig, 1953), 53.

41 Cf., for example, Allen's assertion (*Five Studies*, 36; as in n. 9) that "geometry was not necessarily part of a cultured man's education."

42 Mayer, *Islamic Woodcarvers*, 48.

43 Herzfeld, *Inscriptions et Monuments d'Alep*, 1, 123–34.

44 Max van Berchem in *MCIA - Jerusalem II*, 398–402, notes that the *minbar* may have been finished by the first date since it was immediately moved to the Great Mosque of Aleppo. See also Mayer, *Islamic Woodcarvers*, 63.

45 For a discussion of the meaning of this *minbar* in light of its inscriptions and the circumstances of its creation, see Tabbaa, "Propagation of Jihād," 232–35.

46 The project to build a replica of the original *minbar*, which burned in 1968, is headed by the Ministry of Awqaf in Jordan and a committee composed of professors from Jordan University and the architectural firm Mihrab. I was briefly retained as consultant to the project during the summer of 1997.

47 *Répertoire* no. 3331: "Made by 'Ubayd, the carpenter, known as Ibn Ma'ālī."

48 Caroline Williams in "Quranic Inscriptions in the Tabut al-Husayn in Cairo," *Islamic Art* 2 (1989): 3–14, has argued on the basis of the Shī'ī implications of its Qur'ānic inscriptions for a late Fatimid date for the casket of al-Husayn. But its cursive inscriptions and especially the signature of this Aleppine artisan strongly argue for an Ayyubid date, most likely during the reign of Saladin.

49 See, for example, Shāfi'ī, *Calyx Ornament*, 204 (as in n. 26), where the author comments on the advanced vegetal arabesques in Syrian woodwork, proposing that "all of them are of the pure Islamic conventional type" and that, unlike contemporary Egyptian examples, they are free of Hellenistic-Byzantine influences.

50 Herzfeld, "Damascus–II," 65. Actually, similarly complex patterns were done in stone a few decades later in Rum Seljuq architecture, such as the portal to the Sultan Khan near Aksaray, dated 1236.

51 See above, note 1. This door was first studied by F. Hauser, "Uber eine Palasture und Schlosse nach al-Jazari," *Der Islam* 11 (1921): 215–44. It has subsequently been more fully examined in Hill, *Mechanical Devices*, 191–95 and 267–68 (as in n.1).

52 This is my own translation from al-Hassan's *Jazari* edition, 474. It differs slightly from Hill's in *Mechanical Devices*, 193.

53 Cf. the completely different conclusions reached by Doris Behrens-Abouseif in her recent *Beauty in Arabic Culture* (Princeton: Markus Wiener Publishers, 1999), 117–23.

54 Allen, *Five Studies*, 72–75 (as in n. 9); and Necipoğlu, *Topkapi Scroll*, 99–100.

55 These are summarized in Necipoğlu, *Topkapi Scroll*, 130–33.

56 See Gombrich, *Sense of Order*, 17–19, for a definition of "Decorum," which is one of the key concepts in the book.

57 For excellent illustrations of numerous *miḥrābs*, *minbars*, minarets, and domes, see Alexandro Papadopoulo, *L'Islam et l'art musulman* (Paris: Mazenod, 1976), figs. 104ff.

Chapter 5. *Muqarnas* Vaulting and Ash'arī Occasionalism

1 Nikolaos Mesarites in Cyril Mango, *The Art of the Byzantine Empire, 312–1453* (Englewood Cliffs, NJ: Prentice Hall, Inc., 1972), 228–29.

2 Mohammad al-Asad, "The Muqarnas: A Geometric Analysis," in Gülru Necipoğlu, *The Topkapi Scroll—Geometry and Ornament in Islamic Architecture* (Santa Monica, CA: The Getty Center for the History of Art and the Humanities, 1995), 349.

3 E.g., Jonathan Bloom in "The Introduction of the Muqarnas into Egypt," *Muqarnas* 5 (1988), 21; and Yasser Tabbaa, "Muqarnas," *The Dictionary of Art*, ed. Jane Turner (New York: Macmillan, 1996), 321–25.

4 Oleg Grabar, *The Mediation of Ornament* (Princeton, NJ: Princeton University Press, 1992), 146.

5 Titus Burckhardt, *Art of Islam: Language and Meaning* (London: World of Islam Festival Trust, 1976), 73.

6 This indigenous name may have been *girih* (Persian: knot), as Necipoğlu (*Topkapi Scroll*, 9) suggested. But there is no Arabic equivalent for this term, and even its use in Persian seems to be fairly late.

7 F. Sarre and E. Herzfeld, *Archäologische Reise im Euphrat- und Tigris-Gebiet*, 4 vols. (Berlin: Verlag von Dietrich Reimer), vol. 3, 157; and Ernst Herzfeld, "Damascus: Studies in Architecture—II," *AO* 10 (1942): 11. In fact, Quatremère de Quincy had already proposed this etymology a century earlier.

8 Curiously, this questionable derivation still enjoys wide acceptance among scholars of

Islamic art, including Doris Behrens-Abouseif in her recent article "Muḳarnas," *EI*², vol. 7, 50; and even more recently, J. Michael Rogers, "Notes on a Recent Study of the Topkapi Scroll: A Review Article," *BSOAS* 60/iii (1997).

9 "Gelé or figé," as in J. Rosintal, *Pendentifs, trompes, et stalactites dans l'architecture orientale* (Paris: Paul Geuthner, 1928), 66; and "joined" in J. Rosintal and E. Schroeder, "Squinches, Pendentives, and Stalactites," *SPA*, vol. 3, 1255.

10 Georges Marçais, *L'Architecture musulmane d'Occident* (Paris: Art et Métiers Graphiques, 1954), 237.

11 Lucien Golvin, *Essai sur l'architecture religieuse muslumane, tome 1, Généralités* (Paris: Librarie Klincksieck, 1970), 157.

12 *Persian Dictionary*, vol. 11, 729.

13 Ibn Manzūr, *Lisān al-'arab* (Bulaq, 1930), 77–78, and al-Fīrūzābādī, Abu'l-Tāhir Muḥammad, *al-Qāmūs al-Muḥīṭ*, 6th ed. (Cairo, 1357/1938), 1414. Similar meanings are provided by other Arabic and Persian dictionaries, although their relative silence about a ubiquitous form and a frequently occurring term is surprising.

14 See al-Asad in Necipoğlu, *Topkapi Scroll*, 350 (as in n. 2), where he refers to the Persian lexicon of 'Ali Akbar Dihkhuda (1879–1955), *Lughat-nāmā*.

15 Wolfhart Heinrichs, "The Etymology of Muqarnas: Some Observations," in *Humanism, Culture, and Language in the Near East: Studies in Honor of Georg Krotkoff*, ed. Asma Afsaruddin and A. H. Mathias Zahniser (Munich: Eisenbrauns, 1997), 175–84. I thank Gülru Necipoğlu for alerting me to this publication and regret that I became aware of it only when the manuscript had already gone to press.

16 Ibid., 183 where Heinrichs describes this process as "a bold metaphorical transfer from a natural phenomenon to an artificial object."

17 Henri Pérés, *La Poésie andalouse en Arabe classique* (Paris: Adrien-Maisonneuve, 1953), 129. This early literary use of *qarnasa* also argues against the recent assertion by Doris Behrens-Abouseif, *Beauty in Arabic Culture* (Princeton: Markus Wiener Publishers, 1999), 121, that "the word *muqarnas* ... must also derive from craftsmen's jargon."

18 Ibn Jubayr, *Rihlat* (Beirut: Dar Sader, 1980): for example, 77 (*qarnasa* of wood); 83 (*qarnasiyya* carving on plaster); 327 (*qarnasiyya* craft on wood).

19 Heinrichs, "The Etymology of Muqarnas," 183.

20 E. H. Gombrich, *The Sense of Order: A Study in the Psychology of Decorative Art* (Ithaca, NY: Cornell University Press, 1979), 210. See also Jessica Rawson, *Chinese Ornament: The Lotus and the Dragon* (London: British Museum Publications Ltd, 1984), 24–32, for a fuller discussion of the role of traditional transmission in non-Western cultures.

21 George Kubler, *The Shape of Time: Remarks on the History of Things* (New Haven: Yale University Press, 1967), 68.

22 Charles Wilkinson, "The Museum's Excavation at Nīshāpūr," *Bulletin of the Metropolitan Museum of Art* 33/2 (Nov. 1938): 9.

23 See for example, Oleg Grabar, "The Visual Arts," *The Cambridge History of Iran, vol. 4: The Period from the Arab Invasion to the Saljuqs*, ed. Richard Frye (Cambridge: Cambridge University Press, 1975), 344.

24 Ibid. Grabar had in fact reached a similar conclusion a few years earlier in "The Visual Arts," *The Cambridge History of Iran, vol. 5: The Saljuq and Mongol Periods*, ed. J. A. Boyle (Cambridge: Cambridge University Press, 1968), 638. In later publications, Grabar has opted for a multicentered origin of the *muqarnas*: "The origins of the muqarnas lie in the almost simultaneous, but apparently unconnected, developments in northeastern Iran and Central North Africa": *The Alhambra* (Cambridge: Harvard University Press, 1978), 175.

25 See, for example, Ulrich Harb in *Ilkhandische Stalaktitengewölbe: Beiträge zur Entwurf- und Bautechnik* (Berlin, 1978), 16. Although this work is exemplary in its focused and exhaustive treatment of an excavated brick slab with an incised *muqarnas* net, it suffers in its introductory chapter from overemphasis of Iranian specimens.

26 Marçais, *L'Architecture musulmane*, fig. 57 (as in n. 10).

27 Lucien Golvin, *Rechèrches archéologiques a la Qal'ah des Banu Hammād* (Paris: Klincksieck, 1965), pl. XLV and fig. 41. The smallness of the sample makes it difficult to be definite about the nature of the fragment.

28 Creswell, *MAE*, 1, 253.

29 *Rihlat*, 66 and 77–78, where Ibn Jubayr further describes the wood and plaster *qarnasa* in these domes.

30 Ibid., 83. See also Bloom, "The Introduction of the Muqarnas into Egypt," 27, who was the first to notice the significance of this passage for the history of the *muqarnas*.

31 Bloom, "The Introduction of the Muqarnas into Egypt," 27.

32 This is indeed the conclusion reached by most Iraqi scholars, including Sharif Yusuf, *Tārīkh al-'imārah al-'irāqiyya fī mukhtalaf al-'uṣūr* (Baghdad, 1982), 384–91, and Khāliq K. al-A'ẓamī, *Al-Zakhārif al-jidāriyya fī athār Baghdād* (Baghdad, 1980), 35.

33 For this dome and others in Iraq, see 'Atā al-Ḥadīthī and Hanā' 'Abd al-Khāliq, *Al-Qibāb al-makhrūtiyya f'il-'Irāq* (Baghdad, 1974). The book is mainly useful as an inventory and for some factual details. Its illustrations are extremely poor in quality.

34 Cited by Ernst Herzfeld, "Damascus: Studies in Architecture —I," *AI* 9 (1942): 19. See also Ḥadīthī, *Al-Qibāb*, 21–22, for a more accurate reading of the inscriptions.

35 Ḥadīthī, *Al-Qibāb*, 26.

36 The Twelver Shi'ism adopted by the 'Uqaylids is not a serious obstacle to this suggestion, for they were in fact loyal supporters of the Abbasids, whom they considered the true leaders of all Arabs and from whom they derived their cultural influences. See Khāshi' al-M'ādhidi, *Dawlat banī 'Aqīl fi'l-Mawsil* (Baghdad, 1968), 75–79 and 105–7.

37 Since 1985 in "Muqarnas Dome," when I first proposed Baghdad as the most likely place of origin for the *muqarnas* dome, several other writers have concurred, including Doris Behrens-Abouseif, "Muḳarnas," EI^2 7, 701–6; Necipoğlu, *Topkapi Scroll*, 108; and Terry Allen, *Five Studies in Islamic Art* (Sebastopol, CA: Solipsist Press, 1988), 85.

38 Gaston Deverdun, *Inscriptions arabes de Marrakech* (Rabat, 1956), 27–30, was the first to decipher the preserved part of the dedicatory inscription and to argue for the date of 1117. The same argument is repeated in Jacques Meunié, Henri Terrasse and Gaston Deverdun, *Nouvelles recherches archéologiques à Marrakech* (Paris: Arts et Métiers Graphiques, 1957), 40–42.

39 Gaston Deverdun, *Marrakech* (Rabat: Edition Techniques Nord-Africaines, 1959), 42, states that "Islamic art has never surpassed the splendor of this extraordinary cupola."

40 A seven-pointed star is extremely unusual in Islamic geometric ornament, where even numbers are far more common. See meanwhile the interesting but inconclusive comments made by Meunié, *Nouvelle recherches*, 35–37, where the author acknowledges the uniqueness of this carved dome and its decoration.

41 See chapter 3 for a short discussion and references on the links between the Almoravids and the Abbasid caliphate.

42 See chapter 3. Boris Maslow, "La Qoubba Barudiyyin a Marrakus," *Al Andalus Cronica arqueologica* 13 (1948): 180–95, and Richard Parker, *A Practical Guide to Islamic Monuments in Morocco* (Charlottesville, Virginia: The Baraka Press, 1981), 59.

43 Georges Marçais, *L'Architecture musulmane*, 200 (as in n. 10), has long doubted this identification, maintaining that "its luxurious decoration ... allows us to propose that that was not its original function." Its present location, 25 meters south of the mosque to which it allegedly belonged, is also problematic and has never been adequately explained.

44 See in particular, Henri Terrasse, "La Mosquée d'al-Qarawiyyin a Fez et l'art des Almoravides," *AO* 2 (1957): 135–47; and idem, *La Mosquée al-Qarawiyyin à Fez* (Paris: Librarie C. Klincksieck, 1968).

45 Baghdad was the unparalleled center of Islamic medicine and hospital construction until the twelfth centuty, when Damascus began to replace it.

46 In fact, two domes in Damascus and a third in Aleppo approximate the internal articulation of *muqarnas* domes but are actually much simpler. These are the mausoleum of Ibn al-Muqaddam (c. 1200) in Damascus, the mihrab dome of the *madrasa* al-Sharafiyya (completed 1246) in Aleppo, and the Turba al-Najibiyya (1374), adjacent to the mausoleum of Nūr al-Dīn. None of these domes has the exterior faceted appearance of Baghdadi domes; the one at al-Najibiyya is a recent restoration.

47 See chapter 3.

48 This identification has been the subject of several articles as well as one book by Naji Ma'rūf, entitled *Al-Madāris al-Sharābiyyya bi-Baghdād, wa-Wāsiṭ wa-Makka* (Baghdad, 1976). Despite the length and erudition of this study, the identification remains problematic in several respects, not the least of which is that the location of the portal on the Tigris side and its form with a bent entrance and a vestibule are more in

keeping with a palace entrance.

49 The passage is quoted in Mango, *Art of the Byzantine Empire*, 228–29 (as in n. 1).

50 Ibid.

51 Translated in Mirjam Gelfer-Jorgensen, *Medieval Islamic Symbolism and the Paintings in the Cefalu Cathedral* (Leiden: E. J. Brill, 1986), 160–61.

52 For example, Burckhardt, *Art of Islam*, 73 (as in n. 5): "The honeycomb of *muqarnas*, linking the cupola to its quadrangular base is therefore an echo of the motion of heaven in the terrestrial order. ... the honeycomb of the *muqarnas* expresses a coagulation of cosmic motion, its crystallization in the pure present."

53 Allen, *Five Essays*, 57 (as in n.37).

54 Grabar, *Mediation of Ornament*, 148–49 (as in n. 4).

55 Necipoğlu, *Topkapi Scroll*, 120–23 and elsewhere (as in n. 2).

56 Ibid., 121.

57 Ibid., 123.

58 See most recently Jonathan Bloom, "The Qubbat al-Khaḍrā' and the Iconography of Height in Early Islamic Architecture," *Pre-modern Islamic Palaces*, Gülru Necipoğlu, ed. in *AO* 23 (1993): 135–42. See also an earlier version of this argument in Bloom, *Minaret: Symbol of Islam* (Oxford: Oxford University Press, 1989), 67–73. Although Bloom's interpretation of the Qubbat al-Khaḍrā' as a dome of heaven is open to question, the article nevertheless contains several important conclusions about secular domical tradition.

59 Ibn Jubayr as quoted in Bloom, "Introduction of the Muqarnas into Egypt," 27 (as in n. 3).

60 On these matters, see the different interpretation provided by Oleg Grabar, "From Dome of Heaven to Pleasure Dome," *JSAH* 49 (March 1990): 15–21.

61 Yasser Tabbaa, "Toward an Interpretation of the Use of Water in Courtyards and Courtyard Gardens," *Journal of Garden History* 7/iii (1987): 202–5.

62 There is a considerable literature on these mechanical devices. For bibliography, see Donald R. Hill, *Kitāb al-Ḥiyal, the Book of Ingenious Devices of Banu Mūsā b. Shākir* (Dordrecht: D. Reidel, 1979), and Ahmad Yahya al-Hassan and Donald R. Hill, *Islamic Technology: An Illustrated History* (Cambridge: Cambridge University Press, 1986).

63 Grabar, "From Dome of Heaven," 20 and passim.

64 See page 124.

65 On this development, see in particular Oleg Grabar, "The Earliest Islamic Commemorative Structures, Notes and Documents," *AO* 6 (1966): 7–46. See also Christel Kessler, *The Carved Masonry Domes of Mediaeval Cairo* (Cairo: The American University in Cairo Press, 1976).

66 See the recent critical overview of literature on funerary architecture by Chistopher S. Taylor, "Reevaluating the Shi'i Role in the Development of Monumental Islamic Funerary Architecture," *Muqarnas* 9 (1992): 1–10.

67 Ibn al-Jawzi, *Al-Muntaẓam fī tārīkh al-mulūk w'al-umam*, 6 vols. ed. C. Krenkow (Hyderabad: Dā'irat al-Ma'ārif Press, 1938–40), 7, 205–6; Francis Peters, *Allah's Commonwealth* (New York: Simon and Schuster, 1973), 589.

68 For a somewhat later manifestation of this rivalry, see Yasser Tabbaa, *Constructions of Power and Piety in Medieval Aleppo* (University Park, PA: Pennsylvania State Press, 1997), esp. chapters 6 and 8.

69 This form, in turn, provided a model for the Great Mosque of Tunis (al-Zaytouna), which was rebuilt in c. 860 with two domes that emphasize both ends of its axial nave. See Lucien Golvin, *Essai sur l'architecture religieuse musulmane, tome 3* (Paris: Editions Klincksieck, 1974), 136–37 and 150–51.

70 See in particular Jerrilyn D. Dodds, *Architecture and Ideology in Early Medieval Spain* (University Park, PA: The Pennsylvania State Press, 1990), 94–106; and idem, "The Great Mosque of Cordoba," in *Al-Andalus, The Art of Islamic Spain*, ed. Jerrilynn D. Dodds (New York: The Metropolitan Museum of Art, 1992), 11–25.

71 This is the case in the two spectacular *muqarnas* domes in Mosul—Imam Yaḥyā and Imam 'Awn al-Dīn—whose pyramidal covering allowed windows at the base only. The same is true at the Alhambra Palace.

72 Majid Fakhry, *A History of Islamic Philosophy*, 2nd ed. (New York: Columbia University Press, 1983), 33.

73 Necipoğlu, *Topkapi Scroll*, 97 (as in n. 2).

74 This interpretation was first proposed in *The Alhambra*, 144–48 and 180–81, and later reiterated in "Iconography of Islamic Architecture, " 57–59; "From the Dome of Heaven," 16–17; and *Mediation of Ornament*, 148–51.

75 A prime example of this effect can be seen at the Sa'adian Tombs in Marrakesh.

Chapter 6. Stone Muqarnas and Other Special Devices

1 Ernst Herzfeld in "Damascus: Studies in Architecture—III," *AI* 11–12 (1946), 17.

2 See ibid., 16–19, for the first attempt to outline the problems involved in the transmission of eastern brick motifs to Syrian architecture.

3 On the Eastern origin and later development of lobate moldings and arches, see Lucien Golvin, *Essai sur l'architecture religieuse musulmane, tome 1, Généralités* (Paris: Librarie Klincksieck, 1970), 94–101. See also Creswell, *EMA*, 2, 89–90.

4 Creswell, ibid., figs. 44, 59 and, pl. 19b.

5 Ibid., 362–63, fig. 258, and pl. 116.

6 Golvin, *Essai sur l'architecture religiuse musulmane*, 1, 94–95.

7 See in particular Christian Ewert, *Spanisch-islamisches System sich kreuzender Bögen I. Die senkrechten ebenen Systeme sich kreuzender Bögen als Stützkonstruktionen der vier Rippenkuppeln in der ehemaligen Hauptmoschee von Cordoba* (Berlin: Madrider Forschungen, 1968); Jerrilyn D. Dodds, *Architecture and Ideology in Early Medieval Spain* (University Park, PA: The Pennsylvania State Press, 1990), 94–106; idem, "The Great Mosque of Cordoba," in *Al-Andalus, The Art of Islamic Spain*, ed. Jerrilynn D. Dodds (New York: The Metropolitan Museum of Art, 1992), 11–25; and Marianne Barrucand and Achim Bednorz, *Moorish Architecture in Andalusia* (Cologne: Taschen, 1992), 73–93.

8 See the discussion of the *muqarnas* in North Africa in chapter 5.

9 The first dating by Creswell was challenged by John Warren in "The Date of the Baghdad Gate at Raqqa," *AARP* 13 (1978): 22–23, who proposed a tenth-century date. Robert Hillenbrand, "Eastern Islamic Influences in Syria: Raqqa and Qal'at Ja'bar in the later 12th Century," in *The Art of Syria and the Jazira, 1100–1250* (Oxford University Press, 1985), 32–36, has, however, convincingly argued that the gate should be dated to the second half of the twelfth century, possibly to the period of Nūr al-Dīn.

10 Tabbaa, "The Architectural Patronage of Nūr al-Dīn," 140–43; and Hillenbrand, "Eastern Islamic Influences," 35–37.

11 See in particular Terry Allen, *A Revival of Classical Antiquity in Syria* (Wiesbaden: Ludwig Reichert Verlag, 1986); and Yasser Tabbaa, "Survivals and Archaisms in the Architecture of Northern Syria, ca. 1080–ca. 1150," in *Essays in Honor of Oleg Grabar*, *Muqarnas* 10 (1993), 33–34.

12 Oktay Aslanapa, *Turkish Art and Architecture* (New York: Praeger, 1971), 97–98: "The cusped arches of the main door in two different colours of stone bear the imprint of Zengid architecture."

13 Ibid., 128–29.

14 Ernst Herzfeld, "Damascus: Studies in Architecture —I," *AI* 9 (1942): 46–49.

15 Curiously, this astonishing effect, which is magnificently elaborated in Tudor Gothic architecture, does not turn up again in Islamic stone architecture, although it is relatively common in stucco *muqarnas* of the Western Islamic world.

16 Herzfeld, "Damascus III," 4.

17 Also examined by Maurice Éochard, "Notes d'archéologie musulmane. I, Stéréotomie de deux portails du XIIe siècle," *BEO* 7–8 (1937–38): 98–108; repeated in idem, *Filiation de monuments grècs, byzantin et islamiques, une question de géométrie* (Paris: Librarie orientaliste Paul Geuthner, 1977), 86–87.

18 Illustrations in Écochard, "Stéréotomie de deux portails," demonstrate that individual stone blocks were carved into several constituent elements of the vault. This feature has been previously mentioned by Herzfeld, "Damascus III," 17, where he notes that "numerous elements of each zone are sculptured out of one block, the size and shape of which is determined by considerations of stability."

19 One notable exception is the portal vault of the *khānqāh* al-Dawādāriyya in Jerusalem, 695/1295, whose twin *muqarnas* vaults and pendant keystone closely resembles the Damascene series of pendant vaults. See Michael Burgoyne, *Mamluk Jerusalem: An Architectural Study* (London: World of Islam Festival Trust, 1987), 15–61; and Michael Meinecke, *Die Mamlukische Architektur in Ägypten und Syrien*, 2 vols. (Glückstadt: Verlag J.J. Augustin, 1992), 55a. Interestingly, the founder, Amīr 'Alam al-Dīn Sanjar al-Saliḥī al-Najmī, was one of the Mamluks of the last Ayyubid sultan, and his long career of military and administrative service included an extended period in Damascus.

20 "Damascus III," 2–15.

21 Écochard, "Stéréotomie de deux portails," 98–108; repeated in idem, *Filiation*, 86–87.

See also Mamoun Sakkal, "An Introduction to Muqarnas Domes' Geometry," *Structural Topology* 14 (1988): 21–34. Sakkal's important analysis seems to rest on two independent parameters: the regular division of the surface of domes; and the generation of a finite number of "muqarnas families" that would completely fill the divided dome. Its main weakness is that, unlike Écochard and al-Asad, it stems from abstracted geometric ideas rather than from the analysis of extant specimens or original drawings. Also, despite the author's fascination with the stone architecture of Aleppo, his work applies best to Persian and North African domes.

22 Gülru Necipoğlu, *The Topkapi Scroll: Geometry and Ornament in Islamic Architecture* (Santa Monica, CA: The Getty Center for the History of Art and the Humanities, 1995), 348–62. Al-Asad's conclusions largely confirm the conclusions previously reached by Ulrich Harb, *Ilkhandische Stalakitengewölbe: Beiträge zur Entwurf und Bautechnik* (Berlin, 1978), for Ilkhanid *muqarnas* vaults.

23 See Yasser Tabbaa, *Constructions of Power and Piety in Medieval Aleppo* (University Park, PA: Pennsylvania State University Press, 1997), 109–110. Cf. Creswell, *MAE*, 2, 146–47, who lists al-Shādbakhtiyya as the earliest *muqarnas* portal.

24 Cf. Creswell, ibid., 146–47, who also concludes that "the stalactite portal is a feature which appears to have come down through Syria from the north." Perhaps the one instance of a stone *muqarnas* vault that closely imitates the stucco vaults of the *bīmāristān* al-Nūrī of Damascus and other stucco vaults in North Africa is La Zisa outside Palermo, which, unlike Syrian *muqarnas* vaults, was not assembled from previously cut stone blocks but was rather carved directly on an already standing vault. See Écochard, *Filiation*, 76, fig. 11.

25 For example, the portal vault of the *madrasa* of Sultan Hassan (1356) in Cairo.

26 Creswell, EMA, I/2, 538–40.

27 Other examples of the joggled voussoir can be seen at Qasṭal al-Shu'aybiyya in Aleppo (1150) and in the late eleventh-century gates of Cairo, which are known to have been built by Syrian craftsmen. See Creswell, *MAE*, 1, 170ff, for a discussion of some early examples of this motif in Cairo.

28 Some have attempted to decipher words and formulas, such as Allāh, Muḥammad, and the Shahāda, in these curvilinear forms. But none of these attempts are convincing, and it is very unlikely that these interlaces were intended as calligraphic messages. Square Kufic would have been a much more effective medium for such messages.

29 These are the *miḥrāb*s at the *madrasas* al-Shādbakhtiyya, al-Sulṭāniyya, and al-Firdaws. See Tabbaa, *Constructions of Power and Piety*, figs. 171, 172, and 200.

30 These include the palaces at the citadels of Aleppo, Sahyūn, and Najm as well as the Maṭbakh al-'Ajami in Aleppo, all discussed in ibid., chapter 4.

Chapter 7. The Mediation of Symbolic Forms

1 Gülru Necipoğlu, *The Topkapi Scroll—Geometry and Ornament in Islamic Architecture* (Santa Monica, CA: The Getty Center for the History of Art and the Humanities, 1995), 220.

2 For example, Oleg Grabar, *The Mediation of Ornament* (Princeton, NJ: Princeton University Press, 1992), 154, concludes that geometric ornament is "an abstraction that seems to be devoid of cultural specificity. It is only meant to be beautiful."

3 Cf. the similar conclusions reached by Necipoğlu, *Topkapi Scroll*, 97f.

4 Ibid., p. 103.

5 Ibid.

Abbreviations

Journals, Encyclopedias, and Collective Works

AARP	*Art and Archaeology Research Papers*
AAS	*Annales archéologiques de Syrie*
AB	*Art Bulletin*
AI	*Ars Islamica*
AO	*Ars Orientalis*
BEO	*Bulletin d'études orientales*
BIE	*Bulletin de l'Institut d'Egypte*
BIFAO	*Bulletin de l'Institut français d'archéologie orientale*
BSOAS	*Bulletin of the School of Oriental and African Studies*
DM	*Damaszener Mitteilungen*
EMA	K.A.C. Creswell. *Early Muslim Architecture*, 2 vols. (Oxford, 1932, 1940); vol. 1 rev. (Oxford, 1969)
EI²	*The Encyclopaedia of Islam*, 2nd ed., 12 vols. (Leiden: E.J. Brill, 1954–)
IA	*Islamic Art*
IC	*Islamic Culture*
IJMES	*International Journal of Middle East Studies*
JA	*Journal asiatique*
JSAH	*Journal of the Society of Architectural Historians*
MAE	K.A.C. Creswell. *The Muslim Architecture of Egypt*, 2 vols. Oxford: Clarendon Press, 1959.
MCIA	*Matériaux pour un Corpus Inscriptionum Arabicarum*
MIE	*Mèmoires de l'Institut d'Egypte*
MIFAO	*Mèmoires de l'Institut français d'archéologie orientale du Caire*
MMAF	*Mèmoires de la Mission archéologique française au Caire*
MW	*The Muslim World*
REI	*Révue des études islamiques*
Répertoire	*Répertoire chronologique d'épigraphie arabes*, 16 vols. (Cairo, 1931–)
SI	*Studia Islamica*
SPA	*A Survey of Persian Art*, 16 volumes. Ed. Arthur Upham Pope and Phyllis Ackerman. London: Oxford University Press, 1938–39.

Bibliography

Abbot, Nabia. *The Rise of North Arabian Script and its K'ur'ānic Development*. Chicago: University of Chicago Press, 1938.

———. "Arabic Palaeography: The Development of Early Islamic Scripts," *AI* 8 (1941): 65–104.

———. "The Contribution of Ibn Muḳlah to the North Arabic Script," *American Journal of Semitic Languages and Literatures* 56 (1939): 7–83.

Abu Deeb, Kamal. *Al-jurjānī's Theory of Poetic Imagery*. Warminister: Aris and Phillips, 1979.

Abu Shāma, Shihāb al-Dīn 'Abd al-Raḥmān. *Kitāb al-rawḍatayn fī akhbār al-dawlatayn al-nūriyya wa'l-ṣalāḥiyya* (The book of the two gardens in the history of the Nūrī and Ṣalāḥī nations). 2 vols. Ed. M. H. Ahmad. Cairo: Wizārat al-Thaqāfa, 1956–62.

———. *Al-Dhayl 'alā al-rawḍatayn* (Addendum to the two gardens). Ed. M. al-Kawthari. Cairo: Dar al-Kutub al-Malikiyya, 1947.

Aga-Oglu, Mehmet. "Remarks on the Character of Islamic Art," *AB* 36/3 (1954): 175–202.

Ali, Wijdan. *What Is Islamic Art?* Amman: Al al-Bayt University, 1996.

Allen, Terry. *A Revival of Classical Antiquity in Syria*. Wiesbaden: Ludwig Reichert Verlag, 1986.

———. *Five Studies in Islamic Art*. Sebastopol, CA: Solipsist Press, 1988.

———. "Some Pre-Mamluk Portions of the Courtyard Façades of the Great Mosque of Aleppo," *BEO* 35 (1983): 6–12.

'Anān, Muhammad A. *Duwal al-ṭawā'if mundhu qiyāmihā ḥattā al-fatḥ al-murābiṭī* (The Taifa kingdoms from their emergence until the Almoravid conquest), 3rd ed. Cairo: al-Khanji, 1988.

Anon. *Bab ul Ghaibah at Samarra*. Baghdad: Ministry of Antiquties, 1938.

Anon. *Risāla fi'l-kitāba al-mansūba* (A treatise on proportioned writing). Ed. M. Bahjat al-Athari, in *Majallat ma'had al-makhṭuṭāt* 1 (1955).

Arberry, Arthur. *The Koran Illuminated: A Handlist of the Korans in the Chester Beatty Library*. Dublin: Hodges, Figgis & Co. Ltd, 1967.

Ardalan, Nader and Laleh Bakhtiar. *The Sense of Unity: The Sufi Tradition in Persian Architecture*. Chicago: University of Chicago Press, 1973.

al-Ash'arī, Abu'l-Ḥasan 'Alī b. Ismā'īl. *Maqālāt al-Islāmiyyīn wa Ikhtilāf al-Muṣallīn* (Doctrines of the Muslims and difference among those who pray). Ed. Helmut Ritter. Wiesbaden: Franz Steiner Verlag, 1963.

———. *The Theology of al-Ash'arī: The Arabic Texts of al-Ash'arī's Kitāb al-Luma'* (Book of the radiances) *and Risālat Istiḥsān al-khawḍ fī 'ilm al-kalām* (A treatise on the virtues of plunging into the science of scholastic theology). Trans. Richard J. McCarthy. Beirut: Imprimerie catholique, 1953.

Ashūr, S.A. *Buḥūth wa dirāsāt fī tārīkh al-'uṣūr al-wusṭā* (Researches and studies in the history of the middle ages). Beirut, 1977.

Aslanapa, Oktay. *Turkish Art and Architecture*. New York: Praeger, 1971.
Atil, Esin. *Art of the Arab World*. Washington, D.C.: Smithsonian Institution, 1975.
A'ẓamī, Khāliq K. *Al-Zakhārif al-jidāriyya fī athār Baghdad* (Wall ornaments in the antiquities of Baghdad). Baghdad, 1980.
Baer, Eva. *Islamic Ornament*. New York: New York University Press, 1998.
al-Bāqillānī, Abū Bakr Muḥammad b. al-Tayyib, *Kitāb al-tamhīd* (Book of preparation), ed. Richard J. McCarthy. Beirut: al-Maktaba al-Sharqiyya, 1957.
Barrucand, Marianne, and Achim Bednorz. *Moorish Architecture in Andalusia*. Cologne: Taschen, 1992.
Behrens-Abouseif, Doris. *Islamic Architecture in Cairo, an Introduction*. Leiden: E. J. Brill, 1992.
———. "Mukarnas," *EI*^{2}. 7: 501–6.
———. *Beauty in Arabic Culture*. Princeton, NJ: Markus Wiener Publishers, 1999.
Berchem, Max van. "Notes d'archéologie arabe. Monuments et inscriptions fatimites." *JA* 8e sér., 17 (1891): 411–95; 18 (1892): 46–86.
———. *MCIA, Première partie, Egypte, MMAF* 19 (1894, 1903).
———. "Inscriptions arabes de Syrie, VI, Les inscriptions de Nūr al-Dīn et l'origine du charactère arrondi dans l'épigraphie syrienne." *MIE* 3 (1897): 34–39.
———. "La Chaire de la mosquée d'Hébron et la martyrion de la tête de Husain à Ascalon." In *Festschrift Eduard Sachau*, 298–31. Berlin: Reimer, 1915.
———. *MCIA, Syrie du Sud, Jerusalem*, 2 vols. Cairo: Institut Français d'Archéologie Orientale, 1922–27.
———. *Opera Minora*. 2 vols. Geneva: Editions Slatkine, 1978.
Bierman, Irene A. "The Art of the Public Text: Medieval Islamic Rule." In *World Art: Themes of Unity in Diversity*, 283–90, ed. Iriving Lavin. University Park and London: Pennsylvania State University Press, 1989.
———. *Writing Signs: The Fatimid Public Text*. Berkeley, Los Angeles, and London: University of California Press, 1998.
Blair, Sheila S. *Islamic Inscriptions*. New York: New York University Press, 1998.
Bloom, Jonathan M. "The Mosque of al-Ḥakim in Cairo," *Muqarnas* 1 (1983): 15–36.
———. *Minaret: Symbol of Islam*. Oxford: Oxford University Press, 1989.
———. "The Introduction of Muqarnas into Egypt," *Muqarnas* 4 (1986): 7–20.
———. "The Qubbat al-Khaḍrā' and the Iconography of Height in Early Islamic Architecture." In *Pre-Modern Islamic Palaces*, ed. Gülru Necipoğlu. *AO* 23 (1993): 135-42.
Bloom, Jonathan M. et al. *The Minbar from the Kutubiyya Mosque*. New York: The Metropolitan Museum of Art, 1998.
Bloom, Jonathan M., and Sheila S. Blair. *Images of Paradise in Islamic Art*. Hanover, NH: Dartmouth College, Hood Art Museum, 1991.
Bosworth, C. E. "The Rise of the Karrāmiyya in Khurasan." *MW* 50 (1960): 5–14 .
———. "The Imperial Policy of the Early Ghaznavids." *IC* 1 (1962): 49–82.
———. *The Islamic Dynasties: A Chronlogical and Genealogical*

Handbook. Edinburgh: Edinburgh University Press, 1967.

———. "The Political and Dynastic History of the Iranian World A.D. 1000–1217." In *The Cambridge History of Iran*, vol. 5, *The Saljuq and Mongol Periods*, ed. J. A. Boyle. Cambridge: Cambridge University Press, 1968.

———. *The Ghaznavids*. 2nd ed. Beirut: Librarie du Liban, 1973.

Bulliet, Richard W. *The Patricians of Nishapur: A Study in Medieval Islamic Social History*. Cambridge, MA: Harvard University Press, 1972.

———. *Islam: The View from the Edge*. New York: Columbia University Press, 1994.

Burckhardt, Titus. "The Spirit of Islamic Art," *Islamic Quarterly* 1 (1954): 212–18.

———. "Perennial Values in Islamic Art," *Studies in Comparative Religions* 1 (1967): 132–41.

———. *Art of Islam: Language and Meaning*. London: World of Islam Festival Trust, 1976.

Burgoyne, Michael. *Mamluk Jerusalem: An Architectural Study*. London: World of Islam Festival Trust, 1987.

Cahen, Claude."Une Chronique chiite du temps des croisades." *Comptes Rendus, Academie des Inscriptions et Belles Lettres* (1935): 263–64.

Canard, Marius. "Le Cérémonial fatimite et le cérémonial byzantin, essai de comparison." *Byzantion* 21 (1951): 355–420.

———. "Fāṭimids." EI^2 2, 859.

Creswell, K.A.C. "The Origin of the Cruciform Plan of Cairene Madrasas." *BIFAO* 21 (1922): 1–54.

———. *Early Muslim Architecture*. 2 vols. Oxford: Clarendon Press, 1932–40.

———. *The Muslim Architecture of Egypt*. 2 vols. Oxford: Clarendon Press, 1959.

———. *Early Muslim Architecture*. I: *Umayyads A.D. 622–750*. 2 parts. Oxford: Clarendon Press, 1969. (Revision of vol. 1 of *Early Muslim Architecture*, 1932–40.)

Dadoyan, B. *The Fatimid Armenians: Cultural and Political Interaction in the Near East*. Leiden, New York, Köln: E. J. Brill, 1997.

Déroche, François. *Les Manuscrits du Coran, I: Aux Origines de la calligraphie coranique*. Paris: Bibliothèque Nationale, 1983.

Deverdun, Gaston. *Inscriptions arabes de Marrakech*. Rabat, 1956.

———. *Marrakech*. Rabat: Edition Techniques Nord-Africaines, 1959

Diez, Ernst. "Simultaneity in Islamic Art," *AI* 4 (1937): 185–89.

Dimand, Maurice. "Studies in Islamic Ornament, I: Some Aspects of Omaiyad and Early 'Abbāsid Ornament," *AI* 4 (1937): 293–337.

———. "Studies in Islamic Ornament, II: The Origin of the Second Style of Samarra Decoration." In *Archaeologia Orientalia in Memoriam Ernst Herzfeld*, ed. George Carpenter Miles, 62–68. Locust Valley, N.Y.: J. J. Augustin, 1952.

Dodd, Erika. "The Image of the Word; Notes on the Religious Iconography of Islam," *Berytus* 18 (1969): 35–62.

Dodd, Erika, and Shereen Khairallah. *The Image of the Word, A Study of Quranic Verses in Islamic Architecture*. 2 vols. Beirut: American University of Beirut, 1981.

Dodds, Jerrilyn D. *Architecture and Ideology in Visigothic Spain*. University Park: Pennsylvania State University Press, 1990.

———. "The Great Mosque of Cordoba." In *Al-Andalus, The Art of Islamic Spain*, ed. Jerrilynn D.

Dodds, 11–26 . New York: The Metropolitan Museum of Art, 1992.
Écochard, Maurice. "Notes d'archéologie musulmane. I, Stéréotomie de deux portails du XIIe siècle," *BEO* 7–8 (1937–38): 98–112.
———. *Filiation de monuments grecs, byzantin et islamiques, une question de géométrie*. Paris: Librarie orientaliste Paul Geuthner, 1977.
Elisséeff, Nikita. "La Titulature de Nūr ad-Dīn d'après ses inscriptions," *BEO* 14 (1952–4): 115–96.
———. "Les Monuments de Nūr ad-Dīn: inventaire, notes archéologiques et bibliographiques." *BEO* 13 (1951): 5–49.
———. *Nūr al-Dīn un grand prince musulman de Syrie au temps des Croisades 511–569/1118–1174*. 3 vols. Damascus: Institut français de Damas, 1967.
Ettinghausen, Richard. "The Character of Islamic Art." In *The Arab Heritage*, ed. N. A. Faris, 251–68. Princeton: Princeton University Press, 1946.
———."Al-Ghazzālī on Beauty." In *Art and Thought: Issued in Honor of Dr. Ananda K. Coomaraswamy on the Occasion of His 70th Birthday*, ed. K. Bharatna Iyer, 160–65. London: Luzac, 1947. (Reprinted in *Richard Ettinghausen*. Ed. M. Rosen-Ayalon, 16–21.)
———. "The 'Beveled Style' in the Post-Samarra Period." In *Archaeologia Orientalia in Memoriam Ernst Herzfeld*, ed. George Carpenter Miles, 72–83. Locust Valley, N.Y.: J. J. Augustin, 1952.
———."Interaction and Integration in Islamic Art." In *Unity and Variety in Muslim Civilization*, ed. Gustave von Grunebaum, 107–31. Chicago, 1955. (Reprinted in *Richard Ettinghausen*, ed. M. Rosen-Ayalon, 51–88).
———. "Arabic Epigraphy: Communication or Symbolic Affirmation." In *Near Eastern Numismatics, Iconography, Epigraphy and History: Studies in Honor of George C. Miles*, ed. Dickran Kouymijian, 297–318. Beirut: American University of Beirut, 1974.
———. "Decorative Arts and Painting: Their Character and Scope." In *The Legacy of Islam*, eds. Joseph Schacht and C. E. Bosworth, 274–92. Oxford: Oxford University Press, 1974. (Reprinted in *Richard Ettinghausen*, ed. M. Rosen-Ayalon, 22–50.)
———. "Originality and Conformity in Islamic Art." In *Individualism and Conformity in Classical Islam*, eds. Amin Banani and Speros Vryonis, Jr., 95–103. Wiesbaden: Otto Harrassowitz, 1977. Reprinted in *Richard Ettinghausen*, ed. M. Rosen-Ayalon, 89–157.
———."The Taming of the Horror Vacui in Islamic Art," *Proceedings of the American Philosophical Society* 123/1 (February, 1979): 15–28. (Reprinted in *Richard Ettinghausen*, ed. M. Rosen-Ayalon, 1305–9.)
Ettinghausen, Richard, trans. *The Arabesque: Meaning and Transformation of an Ornament*. Graz, Austria: Verlag für Sammler, 1976. (Translation of Ernst Kühnel, *Die Arabesque*, Wiesbaden, 1949.
Ettinghausen, Richard, and Oleg Grabar. *The Art and Architecture of Islam, 650–1250*. London: Pelican, 1987.
Ewert, Christian. *Spanisch-islamisches System sich kreuzender Bögen I. Die senkrechten ebenen Systeme sich kreuzender Bögen als*

Stütz-konstruktionen der vier Rippenkuppeln in der ehemaligen Hauptmoschee von Cordoba. Berlin: Madrider Forschungen, 1968.

Fakhry, Majid. *A History of Islamic Philosophy*, 2d ed. New York: Columbia University Press, 1983.

al-Fārūqī , Ismā'īl R., and Lamyā' al-Fārūqī. *The Cultural Atlas of Islam*. London and New York: MacMillan, 1986.

al-Fārūqī, Lois Lamyā'. *Islam and Art*. Islamabad, Pakistan, 1985.

al-Fīrūzābādī, Abu'l-Tāhir Muḥammad. *al-Qāmūs al-Muḥīṭ* (The Encompassing Dictionary), 6th ed. Cairo, 1357/1938.

Flury, Sam. *Die Ornamente der Hakim—und Ashar—Moschee*. Heidelberg, 1912.

———. "Die Kanzel von Qus," *Sonntagsblatt der Basler Nachrichten* 14 (1912):

———. *Islamische Schriftbänder Amida-Diarbekr XI. Jahrhudert. Anhang: Kairuan, Mayyāfāriqīn, Tirmidh*. Basel: Frobenius, 1920.

———. "Le Décor épigraphique des monuments de Ghazna," *Syria* 6 (1925): 61–90.

———. "La Mosquée de Nayin," *Syria* 11 (1930): 43–58.

———. "Le Décor épigraphique des monuments fatimides du Caire," *Syria* 17 (1936): 365–76.

Gelfer-Jorgensen, Mirjam. *Medieval Islamic Symbolism and the Paintings in the Cefalu Cathedral*. Leiden: E. J. Brill, 1986.

Gibb, H. A. R. "The Career of Nur al-Din." In *A History of the Crusades*, ed. K. M. Setton. Vol. 1, *The First Hundred Years*, ed. M. W. Baldwin, 513–27. Madison, WI: University of Wisconsin Press, 1969.

Golombek, Lisa (Volov). "Plaited Kufic on Samanid Epigraphic Pottery." *AO* 6 (1966): 107–34.

Golvin, Lucien. "Kitābāt." *EI*² 5, 220–21.

———. *Essai sur l'architecture religieuse muslumane, tome 1, Généralités*. Paris: Librarie Klincksieck, 1970.

———. *Essai sur l'architecture religieuse musulmane, tome 3*. Paris: Editions Klincksieck, 1974.

Gombrich, Ernst H. *The Sense of Order: A Study in the Psychology of Decorative Art*. Ithaca, NY: Cornell University Press, 1979.

Grabar, Oleg. "The Umayyad Dome of the Rock in Jerusalem." *AO* 3 (1959): 65–85.

———. "The Earliest Commemorative Structures, Notes and Documents." *AO* 6 (1966): 7–46.

———. "The Visual Arts, 1050–1350." In *The Cambridge History of Iran*. Vol. 5, *The Saljuq and Mongol Periods*, ed. J. A. Boyle, 631–37. Cambridge: Cambridge University Press, 1968.

———. *The Formation of Islamic Art*. New Haven, CT: Yale University Press, 1973.

———. "The Visual Arts." In *The Cambridge History of Iran*. Vol. 4, *The Period from the Arab Invasions to the Saljuqs*, ed. R. N. Frye, 329–53. Cambridge: Cambridge University Press, 1975.

———. *The Alhambra*. Cambridge, MA: Harvard University Press, 1978.

———. "The Iconography of Islamic Architecture." In *Content and Context of Visual Arts in the Islamic World*, ed. Priscilla P. Soucek, 51–66. University Park and London: The Pennsylvania State University Press, 1988.

———. "From Dome of Heaven to Pleasure Dome." *JSAH* 49 (March 1990): 15–21.

———. *The Great Mosque of Isfahan*. New York and London: New York

University Press, 1990.
———. *The Mediation of Ornament*. Princeton, NJ: Princeton University Press, 1992.
Grabar, Oleg, and Derek Hill. *Islamic Architecture and its Decoration, A.D. 800–1500*. Chicago: University of Chicago Press, 1968.
Grohmann, Adolf. "The Origin and Early Development of Floriated Kufic," *AO* 2 (1957): 183–213.
———. "The Problem of Dating Early Qur'āns." *Der Islam* 33 (1958): 213–31.
Hadīthī 'Atā, and Hanā' 'Abd al-Khāliq. *Al-Qibāb al-makhrūtiyya f'il-'Irāq* (Conical domes in Iraq). Baghdad, 1974.

Hajjī Khalīfa. *Kashf al-ẓunūn 'an asāmī al-kutub wa'l-funūn* (Uncovering doubts about the names of books and disciplines). Istanbul: Ma'ārif Press, 1941–43.
Halm, Heinz. *Die Ausbreitung der šāfi'itischen Rechtschule von den Anfängen bis zum 8/14 Jahrhundert*. Wiesbaden: Ludwig Reichert, 1974.
Harb, Ulrich. *Ilkhandische Stalaktitengewölbe: Beiträge zur Entwurf und Bautechnik*. Berlin, 1978.
al-Hassan, Ahmad Yahya. *Al-Jāmi' bayn al-'ilm w'al-'amal al-nāfi' fī sinā'at al-ḥiyal* (A compendium of science and useful practice in the making of mechanical devices). Aleppo: Institute for the History of Arabic Science, 1979.
al-Hassan, Ahmad Yahya, and Donald R. Hill. *Islamic Technology: An Illustrated History*. Cambridge: Cambridge University Press, 1986.
Hassan, Zaki M. *Kunuz al-Fāṭimiyyīn* (Treasures of the Fatimids). Cairo: Dar al-Kutub al-Misriyya, 1937.
Hauser, F., and E. Wiedemann. "Uber eine Palasture und Schlosse nach al-Jazari." *Der Islam* 11 (1921): 215–44.
Heinrichs, Wolfhart. "The Etymology of Muqarnas: Some Observations." In *Humanism, Culture, and Language in the Near East: Studies in Honor of Georg Krotkoff*, ed. Asma Afsaruddin and A. H. Mathias Zahniser, 175–84. Munich: Eisenbrauns, 1997.
Herzfeld, Ernst. *Die Malereien von Samarra*. Berlin: D. Reimer, 1927.
———. "Damascus: Studies in Architecture —I," *AI* 9 (1942): 1–53.
———. "Damascus: Studies in Architecture —II," *AI* 10 (1943): 13–70.
———. "Damascus: Studies in Architecture—III," *AI* 11–12 (1946): 1–71.
———. "Damascus: Studies in Architecture—IV," *AI* 13–14 (1948): 120–23.
———. *MCIA. Troisième partie: Syrie du Nord. Inscriptions et monuments d'Alep*. 3 vols. *MIFAO* (1954–6), 76–8.
Hill, Donald R. *The Book of Knowledge of Ingenious Mechanical Devices, by Ibn al-Razzāz al-Jazarī*. Dordrecht, London, Boston: D. Reidel, 1974.
———. *Kitāb al-Ḥiyal: The Book of Ingenious Devices of Banu Mūsā b. Shākir*. Dordrecht, London, Boston: D. Reidel, 1979.
Hillenbrand, Robert. "Eastern Islamic Influences in Syria: Raqqa and Qal'at Ja'bar in the later 12th century." In *The Art of Syria and the Jazīra 1100–1250*, ed. Julian Raby, 21–48. Oxford: Oxford University Press, 1985.
———. "Creswell and Contemporary Central European Scholarship." In "K.A.C. Creswell and his Legacy," published as a special issue of

Muqarnas 8 (1991): 23–35.
al-Hirfī, Salāmah M. S. *Dawlat al-murābiṭīn fī 'ahd 'Alī b. Yūsuf b. Tāshufīn* (The kingdom of the Almoravids during the reign of 'Alī b. Yūsuf b. Tāshufīn). Beirut: Dar al-Nadwa al-Jadida, 1985.
Hoag, John. *IslamicArchitecture.* New York: Abrams, 1977.
Hodgson, Marshall G. S. *The Venture of Islam: Conscience and History in a World Civilization*, 3 vols. Chicago and London: The University of Chicago Press, 1974.
———. "Bāṭiniyya," *EI*² I, 1098–1100.
Hourani, Albert. *A History of Arab Peoples.* Cambridge, MA: Havard University Press, 1991.
Humphreys, R. Stephen. "The Expressive Intent of the Mamluk Architecture of Cairo: A Preliminary Essay," *SI* 35 (1972): 69–119.
Ibish, Yusuf. *The Political Doctrine of al-Bāqillānī.* Beirut: American University of Beirut, 1966.
Ibn 'Asākir, Abu'l-Qāsim 'Ali. *La Description de Damas d'Ibn 'Asakir*, ed. N. Elisséeff. Damascus: Institut Français d'Études Arabes, 1959.
Ibn abi Uṣaybi'a, Muwaffaq al-Din. *'Uyūn al-anbā' fi ṭabaqāt al-aṭibbā'* (Sources of information on the ranks of doctors), ed. Nizar Rida. Beirut: Maktabat al-Hayat.
Ibn al-'Adīm, Kamāl al-Dīn. *Zubdat al-Ḥalab fi Tārīkh Ḥalab* (The Cream in the history of Aleppo), 3 vols, ed. S. al-Dahhan. Damascus: Institut Français de Damas, 1951–68.
Ibn al-Athīr, 'Izz al-Dīn. *Al-Kāmil fī al-tārīkh* (The complete in history), 13 vols., ed. C. J. Tornberg. Beirut, 1965 (reprint, with new pagination, of the Leiden edition, 1851–76).
———. *Al-Tarīkh al-Bāhir fi al-Dawla al-Atābikiyya bi'l-Mawṣil* (The brilliant history of the Atābekid dynasty in Mosul), ed. A. A. Tulemat. Cairo, 1963.
Ibn Durustūyah. *Kitāb al-kuṭṭāb* (The book of scribes), ed. Ibrahim al-Samarra'i. Beirut: Dar al-Jil, 1992.
Ibn Funduq, *Tārikh-i-Baihaq* (History of Baihaq), ed. A. Bahmanyar. Teheran, 1317/1898.
Ibn al-Jawzi. *Al-Muntaẓam fī tārīkh al-mulūk w'al-umam* (The ordered in the history of kings and nations), 6 vols., ed. C. Krenkow. Hyderabad: Dā'irat al-Ma'ārif Press, 1938–40.
Ibn Jubayr. *Riḥlat Ibn Jubayr* (The journey of Ibn Jubayr). Beirut: Dar Sader, 1980.
———. *The Travels of Ibn Jubayr*, trans. R. J. C. Broadhurst. London: Jonathan Cape, 1952.
Ibn Khaldūn, 'Abd al-Rahmān. *Kitāb al-'ibar* (The Book of Lessons), 7 vols., ed. Naṣr al-Hūrīnī. Bulaq, 1867.
———. *The Muqaddima: An Introduction to History*, 3 vols., ed. and trans. Franz Rosenthal. Princeton: Princeton University Press, 1967.
Ibn Khallīkān. *Wafiyyāt al-A'yān* (Deaths of the patricians), 8 vols., ed. Ihsan Abbas. Dar Sader, Beirut, 1970.
Ibn Kathīr. *Al-bidāya wa'l-nihāya* (The beginning and the end),14 vols., 5th edition. Beirut: Maktabat al-Ma'ārif, 1983.
Ibn Manẓūr. *Lisān al-'arab* (The Arab tongue). Bulaq, 1930.
Ibn al-Nadīm. *The Fihrist of al-Nadīm*, ed. Bayard Dodge. New York: Columbia University Press, 1970.
Ibn Rajab. *Dhail 'alā tabaqāt al-Ḥanābila* (Addendum on the ranks of the Hanbalīs). Cairo, 1952.
Institut du Monde Arabe. *Trésors*

fatimides du Caire. Paris: Institut du Monde Arabe, 1998.
James, David. *Qur'āns and Bindings from the Chester Beatty Library*. London: World of Islam Festival Trust, 1980.
———. *Qur'āns of the Mamluks*. New York: Thames and Hudson, 1988.
Jefferys, Arthur, ed. *Materials for the History of the Text of the Qur'ān*. Leiden: E. J. Brill, 1937.
Jones, Dalu. "The Cappella Palatina in Palermo: Problems of Attribution." *AARP* 21 (1972): 41–57.
———. "The Elements of Decoration: Surface, Pattern and Light." In *Architecture of the Islamic World*, ed. Geroge Michell, 144–75. London: Thames and Hudson, 1978.
Jum'ah, Ibrahim. *Dirāsa fī taṭawwur al-kitābāt al-kūfiyya 'alā al-aḥjār fī miṣr fi'l-qurūn al-khamsa al-ūla lil-hijra* (A study in the development of Kufic writing on stone in Egypt during the first five Hijrī centuries). Cairo: Dar al-Fikr al-'Arabi, 1969.
Kain, Evelyn, trans. *Problems of Style* (trans. of Alois Riegl, *Stilfragen*, 1896). Princeton, NJ: Princeton University Press, 1992.
Kessler, Christel. *The Carved Masonry Domes of Mediaeval Cairo*. Cairo: The American University in Cairo Press, 1976.
Khalidi, Tarif. *Arabic Historical Thought in the Classical Period*. Cambridge: Cambridge University Press, 1994.
Kubler, George. *The Shape of Time: Remarks on the History of Things*. New Haven: Yale University Press, 1967.
Kühnel, Ernst. *Die Arabeske*. (See Ettinghausen; trans., 1976.)
Lamm, Carl J. "Fatimid Woodwork, Its Style and Chronology." *BIE* 18 (1935–36): 59–91.
Laoust, Henri. "Aḥmad b. Ḥanbal," *EI*[2] 1: 272–77.
———. "La Pensée et l'action politique d'al-Māwardi 364/450–974/1058." *REI* 36 (1968): 64–66.
———. *Les Schismes dans l'Islam*. Paris: Payot, 1983.
Laroui, Abdallah. *The History of the Maghrib: An Interpretive Essay*, trans. Ralph Manheim. Princeton, NJ: Princeton University Press, 1977.
Lentz, Thomas W., and Glenn D. Lowry. *Timur and the Princely Vision: Persian Art and Culture in the Fifteenth Century*. Washington DC: Los Angeles County Museum of Art and Arthur M. Sackler Gallery, 1989.
Lowry, Glenn. "Introduction to Islamic Calligraphy." In *From Concept to Context, Approaches to Asian and Islamic Calligraphy*, eds. Shen Fu, Glenn Lowry, and Ann Yonemura, 98–207. Washington, DC: Smithsonian Institution, 1986.
Lyons, M. C., and D. E. P. Jackson. *Saladin, The Politics of the Holy War*. Cambridge: Cambridge University Press, 1982.
Madelung, Wilfrid. "Ismā'īliyya," *EI*[2] 4, 198–206.
M'ādhidi, Khāshi'. *Dawlat banī 'Aqīl fi'l-Mawṣil*. Baghdad, 1968.
Magdalino, Paul. "Manuel Komnenos and the Great Palace," *Byzantine and Modern Greek Studies* 4 (1978): 101–14.
———. *The Empire of Manuel I Komnenos, 1143–1180*. Cambridge: Cambridge University Press, 1993.
Makdisi, George. "Ash'ari and the Ash'arites in Islamic Religious History." *SI* 17 (1962): 37–80; 18 (1963): 19–39.

———. *Ibn 'Aqīl et la résurgence de l'Islam, traditionaliste au XI / V siècle de l'Hègire*. Damascus: Institut Français de Damas, 1963.
———. "The Sunni Revival." In *Islamic Civilization, 950–1150*, ed. Donald S. Richards, 15–57. Oxford: Cassirer, 1973.
———. *The Rise of Colleges: Institutions of Learning in Islam and the West*. Edinburgh: Edinbrugh University Press, 1981.
———. *The Rise of Humanism in Classical Islam and the Christian West*. Edinburgh: Edinburgh University Press, 1990.
Mango, Cyril. *The Art of the Byzantine Empire, 312–1453*. Englewood Cliffs, NJ: Prentice Hall, Inc., 1972.
Marçais, Georges. *L'Architecture musulmane d'Occident*. Paris: Art et Métiers Graphiques, 1954.
Ma'rūf, Naji. *Al-Madāris al-Sharābiyyya bi-Baghdād, wa-Wāsiṭ wa-Makka* (The Sharābī *madrasas* in Baghdad, Wāsit, and Mecca). Baghdad, 1976.
Maslow, Boris. "La Qoubba Barudiyyin à Marrakuš," *Al Andalus* 13 (1948): 180–95.
Mason, Herbert. *Two Statesmen of Mediaeval Islam*. The Hague: Mouton & Co., 1972.
Massigon, Louis. "Les méthodes de réalisations artistiques des peuples de l'Islam." *Syria* 2 (1921): 47–53, 149–60.
———. "The Origin of the Transformation of Persian Iconography by Islamic Theology." *STA* 3 (1928–36).
Mayer, L. A. *Islamic Architects and Their Works*. Geneva: Albert Kundig, 1956.
———. *Islamic Woodcarvers and Their Works*. Geneva: Albert Kundig, 1953.
Meinecke, Michael. *Die mamlukische Architektur in Ägypten und Syrien*, 2 vols. Glückstadt: Verlag J. J. Augustin, 1992.
———. "Mamluk Architecture: Regional Architectural Traditions: Evolution and Interrelations." *DM* 2 (1985): 163–75.
Messick, Brinkley. *The Calligraphic State: Textual Domination and History in a Muslim Society*. Berkeley, Los Angeles, and Oxford: University of California Press, 1993.
Meunié, Jacques, Henri Terrasse, and Gaston Deverdun. *Nouvelles recherches archéologiques à Marrakech*. Paris: Art et Métiers Graphiques, 1957.
Minovi, M. "The So-called Badī' Script." *Bulletin of the American Instutite of Art and Archaeology* 5 (1939): 142–46.
Moaz, Khaled, and Solange Ory. *Inscriptions arabes de Damas: les steles funéraires*. Damascus: Institut Français, 1977.
Momen, Moojan. *An Introduction to Shi'i Islam: The History and Doctrine of Twelver Shi'ism*. New Haven and London: Yale University Press, 1985.
Mottahedeh, Roy. *Loyalty and Leadership in an Early Islamic Society*. Princeton: Princeton University Press, 1980.
Munajjid, Salahuddin. *Dirāsāt fī tārīkh al-khaṭṭ al-'arabī mundhu bidāyatihi ilā nihāyat al-'aṣr al-umawiy* (Studies in the history of Arabic calligraphy from its beginning until the end of the Umayyad period). Beirut: Dar al-Kitab al-Jadid, 1972.
Murata, Sachicko, and William C. Chittick. *The Vision of Islam*. New York: Paragon House, 1994.
Mustafa, Ahmad. "The Scientific

Construction of Arabic Alphabets." Master's thesis: The University of London, 1979.

Nasr, S. Husayn. *Islamic Art and Spirituality*. Albany: SUNY Press, 1987.

Necipoğlu, Gülru. *The Topkapi Scroll—Geometry and Ornament in Islamic Architecture*. Santa Monica, CA: The Getty Center for the History of Art and the Humanities, 1995.

Niẓām al-Mulk. *The Book of Government or Rules for Kings: The Siyāsat-nāma or Siyar al-Mulk of Niẓām al-Mulk*, trans. Hubert Drake. New Haven: Yale University Press, 1960.

Onians, John. *Bearers of Meaning: The Classical Orders in Antiquity, the Middle Ages, and the Renaissance*. Princeton: Princeton University Press, 1988.

Papadopoulo, Alexandro. *L'Islam et l'art musulman*. Paris: Mazenod, 1976.

Paret, R. "Ibn Shanabūdh," *EI*[2] 3: 935–36.

Parker, Richard. *A Practical Guide to Islamic Monuments in Morocco*. Charlottesville, Virginia: The Baraka Press, 1981.

Pauty, Edmond. "Le Minbar de Qous." In *Mélanges Maspero: III, Orient Islamique*, 41–48. Cairo: Institut Français d'Archéologie Orientale, 1940.

Pedersen, Johannes. *The Arabic Book*. Princeton: Princeton University Press, 1984.

Péres, Henri. *La Poésie andalouse en Arabe classique au XIe siècle, ses aspects généraux, ses principaux thèmes, et sa valeur documentaire*. Paris: Adrien-Maisoneuve, 1953.

Peters, Francis E. *Allah's Commonwealth*. New York: Simon and Schuster, 1973.

Qāḍī Ahmad. *Calligraphers and Painters: A Treatise by Qāḍī Ahmad, Son of Mīr Munshī (circa A.H. 1015/A.D. 1606)*, trans. T.Monorsky. Washington DC: Smithsonian Institution, 1959.

Qalqashandi, *Subḥ al-A'shā fī ṣinā'at al-inshā'* (The morning of the night-blind in the secretarial craft). Cairo, 1964.

Raslān, 'Abd al-Mun'im. *Al-Ḥaḍāra al-islāmiyya fī ṣiqilliya wa junūb īṭāliya* (Islamic culture in Sicily and southern Italy). Jeddah: al-Kitāb al-Jāmi'ī, 1980.

Rawson, Jessica. *Chinese Ornament: The Lotus and the Dragon*. London: British Museum Publications Ltd, 1984.

Redford, Scott. "Thirteenth-Century Rum Seljuq Palaces and Palace Imagery." In *Pre-Modern Islamic Palaces*, ed. Gülru Necipoğlu, 219–36. *AO* 23 (1993).

Renard, John. *Seven Doors to Islam: Spirtuality and the Religious Life of Muslims*. Berkeley, Los Angeles, and London: University of California Press, 1996.

Rice, D. S. *The Unique Ibn al-Bawwāb Manuscript in the Chester Beatty Library*. Dublin: E. Walker, 1955.

Richards, Donald S. "'Imād al-Dīn al-Iṣfahānī: Administrator, Littératur and Historian." In *Crusaders and Muslims in Twelfth-Century Syria*, ed. Maya Schatzmiller, 135–37. Leiden: E. J. Brill, 1993.

Riegl, Alois. *Stilfragen*. 1896. See Kain, trans.

Robertson, Edward. "Muḥammad ibn 'Abd al-Raḥmān on Calligraphy." In *Studia Semitica et Orientalia*. Glasgow, 1920.

Rogers, J. Michael. "The 11th Century—A Turning Point in the Architecture of the Mashriq?" In *Islamic Civilization 950–1150*, ed.

D. S. Richards, 211–50. Oxford: Cassirer, 1973.
———. "Architectural History as Literature: Creswell's Reading and Methods." In *K.A.C. Creswell and his Legacy*. Published as a special issue of *Muqarnas* 8 (1991): 45–54.
———. "Notes on a recent study of the Topkapi Scroll: a review article," *BSOAS* 60/iii (1997): 433–39.
Rosen-Ayalon, Myriam, ed. *Richard Ettinghausen, Islamic Art and Archaeology, Collected Papers*. Berlin: Gebr. Mann Verlag, 1984.
Rosenthal, Franz. "Abū Ḥayyān al-Tawḥīdī on Penmanship," *AI* 13–14 (1948): 1–30.
Rosintal, J. *Pendentifs, trompes, et stalactites dans l'architecture orientale*. Paris: Paul Geuthner, 1928.
Sabra, Abdelhamid I. "Science and Philosophy in Medieval Islamic Theology: The Evidence of the Fourteenth Century." *Zeitschrift für Geschichte der arabisch-islamischen Wissenschaften* 9 (1994): 1–42.
Safadi, Yasin. *Islamic Calligraphy*. Boulder: Shambhala Publications, 1978.
el-Said, Issam, and Ayse Parman. *Geometric Concepts in Islamic Art*. London: World of Islamic Festival Publishing, 1976.
Sakkal, Mamoun. "An Introduction to Muqarnas Domes' Geometry," *Structural Topology* 14 (1988): 21–34.
Saliba, George. "Artisans and Mathematicians in Medieval Islam," *Journal of the American Oriental Society* 119/iv (October/December 1999): 637–45.
Sanders, Paula. "From Court Ceremony to Urban Language: Ceremonial in Fatimid Cairo and Fusṭāṭ." In *The Islamic World from Classical to Modern Times: Essays in Honor of Bernard Lewis*, ed. C. E. Bosworth et. al., 311–21. Princeton, N.J.: Darwin, 1989.
Sarre, F., and E. Herzfeld. *Archäologische Reise im Euphrat- und Tigris-Gebiet*. 4 vols. Berlin: Verlag von Dietrich Reimer, 1911–20.
Sauvaget, Jean, Michel Écochard, and Janine Sourdel-Thomine. *Les Monuments ayyoubides de Damas*. 4 fascs. (continuous pagination). Paris, 1938–50.
Schimmel, Annemarie. *Calligraphy and Islamic Culture*. New York: New York University Press, 1984.
Schlumbeger, Daniel, et al. *Lashkari Bazar; une résidence royale ghaznévide et ghoride*, 3 vols. Paris: Klincksieck, 1963–78.
Schroeder, Eric. "What Was the Badīʿ Script?" *AI* 4 (1937): 232–48.
———. "Squinches, Pendentives, and Stalactites." *SPA* 3, 1252–57.
Schuon, Frithjof. *Islam and the Perennial Philosophy*, trans. J. P. Hobson. London: World of Islam Publishing Co. Ltd., 1976.
Segal, J. B. *Edessa the Blessed City*. Oxford: Oxford University Press, 1970.
Shāfiʿī, Farīd. *Simple Calyx Ornament in Islamic Art: A Study in Arabesque*. Cairo: Cairo University Press, 1956.
Sharif, Yusuf. *Tārīkh al-ʿimārah al-ʿirāqiyya fī mukhtalaf al-ʿuṣūr* (History of Iraqi Architecture During all Periods). Baghdad: Wizarat al-Thaqafa wa'l-Iʿlam, 1982.
Smithsonian Institution. *7000 Years of Iranian Art*. Washington DC: The Smithsonian Institution, 1964.
———. *Art Treasures of Turkey*. Washington DC: The Smithsonian

Institution, 1966.
Soucek, Priscilla. "The Arts of Calligraphy." In *The Arts of the Book in Central Asia*, ed. Basil Gray, 7–34. Paris: UNESCO, 1979.
Sourdel, Dominique. "Reflexions sur la diffusion de la Madrasa en Orient du xie au xiie siècle," *REI* 44 (1976): 165–84.
Sourdel-Thomine, Janine. "Khaṭṭ," *EI*² 4: 1113–22.
———. "Kitābāt," *EI*² 5: 214–19.
———. "Le Coufique alépin de l'époque seljoukide." In *Mélanges Louis Massignon*, vol. 3; 301–17. Paris: Maisonneuve et Larose, 1957.
———. "À Propos du Cénotaphe de Maḥmūd à Ghazna Afghanistan." In *Essays in Islamic Art and Architecture in Honor of Katherina Otto-Dorn*, ed. Abbas Daneshvari, 127–35. Malibu, CA: Undena Publications, 1981.
Stern, S. M. "Cairo as the Center of the Ismā'īlī Movement." *In S. M. Stern, Studies in Early Ismā'ilism*, 234–53. Jerusalem: The Magnes Press, 1983.
Stock, Brian. *The Implications of Literacy: Written Language and Models of Interpretations in the Eleventh and Twelfth Centuries*. Princeton, N.J.: Princeton University Press, 1983.
Tabbaa, Yasser. "The Architectural Patronage of Nūr al-Dīn Maḥmūd ibn Zangī, 1146–1174." Ph.D. diss., New York University, 1983.
———. "The Muqarnas Dome: Its Origin and Meaning." *Muqarnas* 3 (1985): 61–74.
———. "Monuments with a Message: Propagation of Jihād under Nūr al-Dīn." In *The Meeting of Two Worlds: Cultural Exchange between East and West during the Period of the Crusades*, ed. Vladimir Goss and Christine Vézar-Bornstein, 223–40. Kalamazoo, MI: Medieval Institute Publications, 1986.
———. "Toward an Interpretation of the Use of Water in Courtyards and Courtyard Gardens." *Journal of Garden History* 7/iii (1987): 197–220.
———. "Geometry and Memory in the Design of the Madrasat al-Firdows in Aleppo." In *Theories and Principles of Design in the Architecture of Islamic Societies*, ed. Margaret Ševčenko, 23–34. Cambridge, Mass.: The Aga Khan Program for Islamic Architecture, 1988.
———. "The Transformation of Arabic Writing. Part I, Qur'ānic Calligraphy." *AO* 21 (1991): 117–48.
———. "Typology and Hydraulics in the Medieval Islamic Garden." In *Garden and Landscape History: Issues, Approaches, Methods*, ed. John Dixon Hunt, 303–29. Washington DC: Dumbarton Oaks Publications, 1992.
———. "Circles of Power: Palace, Citadel, and City in Ayyubid Aleppo." In *Pre-Modern Islamic Palaces*, ed. Gülru Necipoğlu. *AO* 23 (1993): 181–200.
———. "Survivals and Archaisms in the Architecture of Northern Syria, ca. 1080–ca. 1150." In *Essays in Honor of Oleg Grabar*. *Muqarnas* 10 (1993): 29–41.
———. "The Transformation of Arabic Writing. Part II, The Public Text." *AO* 24 (1994): 117–47.
———. "Muqarnas." In *The Dictionary of Art*, ed. Jane Turner, vol. 8; 321–25. London: Macmillan, 1996.
———. *Constructions of Power and Piety in Medieval Aleppo*. Univer-

sity Park, PA: Pennsylvania State University Press, 1997.

———. "Canonicity and Control: The Sociopolitical Underpinnings of Ibn Muqla's Reform." *AO* 29 (1999): 91–100.

———. "Sheila S. Blair, *Islamic Inscriptions* (New York University Press, 1998); Irene A. Bierman. *Writing Signs: The Fatimid Public Text* (University of California Press, 1998); Eva Baer, *Islamic Ornament* (New York University Press, 1998)." *AO* 29 (1999): 180–82.

Taylor, Chistopher S. "Reevaluating the Shi'i Role in the Development of Monumental Islamic Funerary Architecture." *Muqarnas* 9 (1992): 1–10.

Terrasse, Henri. "La Mosquée d'al-Qarawiyyin à Fèz et l'art des Almoravides." *AO* 2 (1957): 135–47.

———. *La Mosquée al-Qaraouiyin à Fès*. Paris: Librarie Klincksieck, 1968.

al-Ṭībī, Muḥammad b. Ḥasan. *Jāmi' maḥāsin kitābat al-kuttāb* (Compendium of the qualities of the writing of scribes), ed. Salahuddin al-Munajjid. Beirut: Dar al-Kitab al-Jadid, 1962.

Tisserant, Evgenius. *Specimina Codicvm Orientalvm*. Rome: F. Pustet, 1914.

Vajda, Georges. *La Paléographie arabe*. Paris: Adrien-Maisoneuve,1953.

Vincent, L. H., and Mackay, E. J. H. *Hébron: Le Haram El-Khalīl, Sepulture des Patriarches*. Paris: Edition Ernest Leroux, 1923.

Wali, Taha. *Al-Masajid fi'l-Islam* (Mosques in Islam). Beirut, 1990.

Walker, Paul. *The Wellsprings of Wisdom*. Salt Lake City: University of Utah Press, 1994.

Warren, John. "The Date of the Baghdad Gate at Raqqa." *AARP* 13 (1978): 22–23.

Watt, W. M. *The Formative Period of Islamic Thought*. Edinburgh: Edinburgh University Press, 1973.

Welch, Anthony. *Calligraphy in the Arts of the Muslim World*. Austin: University of Texas Press, 1979.

Welch, A. T. "Al-Ḳur'ān," *EI*[2] 5, 400–29.

Whelan, Estelle. "Early Islam, Emerging Patterns, 622–1050." In *Islamic Art and Patronage: Treasures from Kuwait*, ed. Esin Atil, 27–40. New York: Rizzoli International Publications, 1990.

———. "Writing the Word of God: Some Early Qur'ān Manuscripts and Their Milieux, Part I." *AO* 20 (1990): 113–47.

Wiet, Gaston. "Les Inscriptions du mausolée de Shāfi'i." *BIE* 15 (1932–33): 167–85.

Wiet, G., J. Sauvaget, and E. Combe. *Répertoire chronologique d'épigraphie arabe*, 16 vols. Cairo: Institut Français d'Archéologie Orientale, 1931.

Wilkinson, Charles. "The Museum's Excavations at Nīshāpūr." *Bulletin of the Metropolitan Museum of Art* 33/2 (November 1938): 5–32.

Williams, Caroline. "The Cult of 'Alid Saints in the Fatimid Monuments of Cairo. Part I: The Mosque of al-Aqmar." *Muqarnas* 1 (1983): 37–52.

———. "The Cult of 'Alid Saints in the Fatimid Monuments of Cairo. Part II: The Mausolea." *Muqarnas* 3 (1985): 39–60.

———. "The Qur'anic Inscriptions of the *Tabut* al-Husayn in Cairo." *Islamic Art* 3 (1987): 3–14.

Index

Dates are all A.D. The Arabic article *al-* is ignored in alphabetizing. Except for the entries under "Great Mosque," institutions are listed by their proper names.